DROPOUT PREVENTION HANDBOOK

HOW TO ORDER THIS BOOK

BY PHONE: 800-233-9936 or 717-291-5609, 8AM–5PM Eastern Time

BY FAX: 717-295-4538

BY MAIL: Order Department
Technomic Publishing Company, Inc.
851 New Holland Avenue, Box 3535
Lancaster, PA 17604, U.S.A.

BY CREDIT CARD: American Express, VISA, MasterCard

DROPOUT PREVENTION HANDBOOK
APPRENTICESHIPS AND OTHER SOLUTIONS

William L. Callison, Ph.D.

Professor of Educational Administration
California State University at Fullerton

TECHNOMIC
PUBLISHING CO., INC.
LANCASTER · BASEL

Dropout Prevention Handbook
a **TECHNOMIC** publication

Published in the Western Hemisphere by
Technomic Publishing Company, Inc.
851 New Holland Avenue, Box 3535
Lancaster, Pennsylvania 17604 U.S.A.

Distributed in the Rest of the World by
Technomic Publishing AG
Missionsstrasse 44
CH-4055 Basel, Switzerland

Printed in the United States of America
10 9 8 7 6 5 4 3 2 1

Main entry under title:
    Dropout Prevention Handbook: Apprenticeships and Other Solutions

A Technomic Publishing Company book
Bibliography: p.
Includes index p. 403

Library of Congress Catalog Card No. 93-61488
ISBN No. 1-56676-063-1

To all those school staff who spend more than five hours each week working with at-risk students. They make a great contribution to the lives of students who, without their help, would spend much of their lives as marginal citizens, frequently in prison and often hungry and in pain.

3. CREATING A STUDENT
INFORMATION SYSTEM   35

4. PREDICTING DROPOUT AND
IDENTIFYING SUBSTANCE ABUSERS   51

5. IDENTIFYING AND PLACING STUDENTS
AT RISK   59

6. PLACING STUDENTS
IN INTERVENTIONS   65

America's educational system is both under attack and under study by nearly every segment of our society, including community, corporate and political leaders. These efforts are not judged to be harmful, because school reforms are certainly necessary to meet the new roles being asked of our educational system. These roles reflect the health and social services required by students and their families in order to create the best learning environment, for both the student and the adult community. School districts and communities must look closely at new research and reform efforts. State and local leadership must also look at the effective schooling research of the past that demonstrated how good schools devised their own missions, goals and objectives to meet their unique needs.

Dropout Prevention Handbook: Apprenticeships and Other Solutions provides a program planner with the rationale and practical guidelines to accomplish school reforms and operate successful programs targeted to students in at-risk situations. The approach presented in this text ranges from a basic primer on "what are dropout prevention programs" to "how to write a competitive proposal."

Dr. Callison's decades of experience are evident as he describes a very detailed sequence of steps useful in planning and implementing school improvement efforts directed to youth in at-risk situations. Included are many research-proven instructional strategies for at-risk youth. This nuts-and-bolts approach also includes ideas on how to evaluate program efforts.

Parental involvement in schooling is vital to the success of at-risk youth, and many excellent suggestions are offered throughout the text, along with ideas on how the school can link families with other community health and social services. These needed services are increasingly being integrated into schooling efforts, and should be seriously considered by program planners.

Dropout Prevention Handbook: Apprenticeships and Other Solutions captures the essence of a good comprehensive plan needed by every school district and community.

I feel that the school improvement guidelines offered in this text will address the needs of all school youth and their families. If a school and community build on these ideas, their educational objectives will be met to a degree never before achieved.

JAY SMINK
Executive Director
National Dropout Prevention Center
Clemson University

This book is for teachers and administrators working with students at risk of dropping out of school. It serves several purposes. It presents a comprehensive plan for developing a preventive and intervention program for dropouts and substance abusers, two-thirds of whom become dropouts. It provides three chapters on apprenticeships, a topic that has become important in the Clinton administration. It provides significant alternatives at each stage of program development, so a program can be built to suit the needs of the students of any school or district. Further, it invites teachers and administrators to compare the ways they educate all students, and the ways they provide for at-risk students. For school administrators and teachers who have no systematic way of dealing with at-risk students, this book offers a step-by-step plan for creating, describing and developing the features of a total district or school dropout prevention program.

We see apprenticeship development as part of an array of efforts which we call work-directed learning. These include programs such as experience-based career education programs (unpaid experience in naturally occurring jobs); career academies (a school-within-a-school where a team of teachers offers a career-related academic curriculum to students in grades ten through twelve or nine through twelve); cooperative education or co-op programs (school-supervised experience in paid jobs); two-plus-two or tech-prep programs (last two years of high school and two years of community college organized around a career theme). And, finally, they include apprenticeships, where candidates spend all their time on the job, and all their training and tasks are directly job related.

Work-directed learning captures the essence of the school-to-work transition programs. It also sums up what motivates professional people. It is a powerful model, since most people in our society find stimulus in learning new material and procedures. Clearly, it leads to improved performance.

Anticipating the practical needs of schools, this text covers in detail the following features:

(*1*) Student identification

(*2*) Program development

(*3*) Matching a program to particular students

(*4*) Computerized data handling

(*5*) In-service training of staff

(*6*) Program evaluation

It offers a conceptual base for the selection of a program and then provides you with a rich menu of services from which to choose. This plan can either be used as a template to put over your existing program to reveal gaps and weaknesses, or to create a program from scratch.

Paying special attention to the development of suitable programs for individual districts, the text recognizes that the catalogue of programs made available to students in one district will not, and should not, be identical to those in other districts. By providing this wide array of program offerings for elementary, intermediate and high school levels, and by providing the concepts and assumptions upon which a program is based, it is possible to tailor a program around such district realities as staff capabilities, budget constraints, board policy and community expectations and resources.

Current evidence, reflected in dropout rates of from 25–50 percent, suggests that schools are not meeting the needs of a high proportion of their students. Often-cited explanations for these dropout rates are institutional or unfriendly environments, low levels of academic expectation for certain categories of students and failure to provide counseling and special programs when students become discouraged or fall behind.

Because of the breadth and depth of schools' failure to meet the needs of students, many business communities insist that schools restructure. One way to restructure is to assess the needs of students who are not succeeding in the system, and then develop programs to reclaim them.

In many cases, these changes benefit all students. For example, if standards of learning have been inadequate, then clarify and raise the standards for all. This way faculty and administration build a preventive feature into a school's program while improving the program for all students.

We have placed the discussion of apprenticeships in a context of dropout prevention strategies. Chapters 1 through 6 present a general preparation for operating dropout prevention programs. Chapters 7 through 9 offer specific preparations for operating dropout prevention programs. Chapters 10 through 12 are directed to developing apprentice programs. Chapters 13 through 21 offer information about designing specialized support programs. At the close of the book, Chapters 22 and 23 guide staff in seeking outside support for program development.

In summary, this text presents concepts and principles to guide program selection by presenting a model of how these concepts can be implemented. Through a framework of principles, concepts and program examples, school administrators and faculty may operate from reasoned choices. It is the sort of practical guide principals and other practitioners will welcome.

Dr. Nancy Richards-Colocino is Director of Guidance Resources, Irvine Unified School District, Irvine, California. Nancy's contributions are part of Chapter 2, "Review of the Literature"; the description of interventions in Chapter 6; and part of Chapter 22, "Writing Proposals for Outside Funding."

We also are pleased to acknowledge the use of materials in Chapter 7, "Developing a Prevention and Recovery Plan for Students at Risk," and Chapter 18, "Evaluation of System Effectiveness," which were provided to us through the courtesy of Dr. Jan Novak and Dr. Barbara Dougherty at the University of Wisconsin. They have been published in their manual *Staying In . . . A Dropout Prevention Handbook K–12,* which is published by the University of Wisconsin.

Chapter 15, "Data-Based Change: The Homework Club," written by Cynthia J. Dixon and Arlene G. Reyes, is a practical, low-cost approach to improving student performance through a high-visibility homework club in the Hacienda La Puente Unified School District in southern California.

Many of the materials in Chapter 19, "Instructional Strategies for Students at Risk," were created by three of our students: Susan Allen, Mary Ellen Dougan and Peggy Marikian. Their thesis, "A Study of the Integral Role of a Change Agent in Facilitating Program Implementation," is an unpublished masters project from the Educational Administration program, California State University, Fullerton, California, 1987, describing strategies used under the leadership of Dr. Eileen Lilly in the Hacienda La Puente Unified School District.

The evaluations of technology programs in Chapter 21 have been prepared by Mr. Thomas Wilson, Director for Educational Services, Corona-Norco Unified School District. Mr. Wilson gives presentations on technology and its uses in schools at meetings throughout the U.S.

The policy recommendations were written in part by students in Governance, Educational Administration 561, at California State University, Fullerton, during the summer of 1990.

Child of Pain

I see you every day
young eyes
unlined faces
cornered smiles
walls of words
looks that demand
prove it
show me a better way.

Blindly following
asphalt sages
left to the electronic classroom
where you've learned well
to deaden those words of hurt,
mommy's too stoned to love me
daddy's busy at work.

Through cool and crowded
aloneness
games of escape you've learned
there's a force in you
like me
crying to be
set free.

Child of pain
child of craving
can you see

the blueprint to be free?
How far must you go
where winds of sadness
don't blow?

From *Young Alcoholics* © 1978
by Tom Alibrandi
CompCare Publishers, Minneapolis, MN
Used by permission.

Chapter 1

INTRODUCTION

Several factors are increasing national concern about dropouts from K–12 schools, including effects of the higher standards being put in place in many states, and a decrease in jobs available to nongraduates in the business world. Dropout and substance abuse together are the key factors in placing students at risk of not completing high school; two-thirds of abusers drop out. After we reengage the dropout/substance abuser in school, we need educational and work options that are appealing to them in order for them to complete school and/or job training.

This book is intended to offer a clear statement of the problems schools face in helping students at risk of dropping out of school, and to assist them in finding solutions that have worked in many school districts.

The Clinton administration is going to focus on apprenticeships, and will dramatically increase funding for students who are interested in preparing for jobs through this approach (Savage, 1992). If funding can be found, there may be as many as 300,000 apprenticeships created at a cost of $1 billion from 1993–1996. This is welcome news to those of us who have been working to help at-risk students for many years. As a nation, we are better prepared to work on the apprenticeship problem than it might at first appear. In the section of the book on apprenticeships, Chapters 10 through 12, we address this key issue.

AUTOMATING OR INFORMATING

Computer technology can be used two ways in the work environment. It can automate or de-skill work, reaching its greatest achieve-

1

ment in a factory operated by robots. Similar technologies can be used to support and inform a well-trained work force, allowing them to increase their productivity (Zuboff, 1988). Probably our industries will do both, flowing with management preferences for the amount of control workers have over their work. If our education and training capabilities improve, it will certainly facilitate worker empowerment, and help move management to choose informating over automating when there is a choice.

Secretary of Labor Robert Reich sees additional aspects of this issue. Technology is moving us away from high-volume, industrial mass production toward low-volume, high-value production. An increase in symbolic analysis skills is being rewarded in the marketplace. These include skills such as:

- abstraction, or the ability to find meaning in massive amounts of data
- system thinking, or the ability to see parts in relation to the whole
- experimental inquiry, which we can describe as the capacity to test and evaluate alternative problem solutions
- collaboration, which allows us to understand a variety of competing perspectives, and the ability to come to a working consensus about direction (Reich, 1991)

These conceptual skills will be resisted by some students, as well as their teachers. But in time they will be accepted, because it will become clear that students who have them are getting the best jobs. More difficult is the attitudinal change that is needed among students and teachers. We need workers and managers to collaborate and work as teams. Our schools typically teach students that there are two classes. There are the top college preparatory students who will be the thinkers and managers. And then there are all the others who will carry out the ideas of the managers. This is what is wrong with IBM and General Motors. Did any reader of this book ever imagine the time would come when IBM would begin to lose large amounts of money? IBM's problem is our problem in the schools. We need to teach students to work as teams in the classroom, just as the Japanese do. And when our students go into the work force, managers need to design companies that rely on workers thinking and solving problems.

You may ask, "How can high school graduates have the information to make complex decisions at their work stations?" We need to do what our competition is doing. Our workers need to become sufficiently computer literate to operate expert systems.

An expert system is a kind of artificial intelligence program that mimics human logic within a specific area of expertise, for example, the characteristics of at-risk students. Students self-report the needed data, which is then put through a scanner, thus eliminating the time-consuming process of gathering data from each student's cumulative folder. The data is then automatically entered into the software, thus saving the time needed for data entry. The expert system further makes possible another big time-saver, automatic scheduling of identified students into appropriate interventions. These recent developments save large amounts of time and expense, dramatically reducing the time required for a student study team or the equivalent to complete student placements.

We have learned quite a bit about introducing expert systems in the last few years in our own work. Most school staff are not ready to use a full-blown expert system. What is working is a partial system where the staff member has students self-report the data on a routine school form, not a purchased form, and then types the data into the computer. This is not as efficient as the scanned entry, but it is comfortable for staff. They don't have to learn to use the scanner. Later when they are comfortable, they can move to the scanned entry approach. We see this as a paradigm for movement into the world of expert systems, and the use of advanced technologies. We take two steps forward and one step back, as President Kennedy said.

HOW DOES SCHOOL DROPOUT HURT US?

Several factors are increasing national concern about dropout in the K-12 schools, including the effects of increasing world-wide economic competition, and a decrease in jobs available to nongraduates in the business world. A bipartisan commission of prominent American businessmen, educators and labor leaders said that "the United States productivity crisis can be solved only by radically restructuring both the country's educational system and its basic manufacturing philosophy along the lines of industrialized nations of Western Europe and Asia," according to Bob Baker, writing in the June 19, 1990, *Los Angeles Times.*

The commission, headed by former U.S. Labor Secretaries William E. Brock III and F. Ray Marshall, said the U.S. must quickly invest tens of billions of dollars in public schools and on-the-job training to emulate its overseas competitors, whose workers are far better educated, and handle a broader range of responsibilities, resulting in more productive companies and higher-quality goods and services. Brock and his colleagues conducted interviews with 2,000 people in 450 businesses in the U.S., Europe and Asia to gather their data. Brock said, "By silently accepting America's descent into a low-skill, low-wage economy, we are on the brink of sentencing our children and ourselves to a lower standard of living."

Kevin Phillips indicates that, in terms of changes in average family income, only families in the ninth and tenth deciles showed improvement from 1977–1988. All other families showed declines, with those at the bottom in the first decile showing the greatest decline, -14.8 percent (Phillips, 1990). At the very top, on the other hand, the top 1 percent showed a 49.8 percent improvement! Put another way, the U.S. has now surpassed France for the dubious distinction of the greatest gap of any industrial nation between the top 20 percent and the bottom 20 percent in family income. More to the point, in 1988 45.3 percent of New York City residents over the age of sixteen could not even be counted as labor force participants because of poverty, lack of skills, drug use, apathy or other problems. They did not even reach the bottom 20 percent because they had no income. What can we do to help these young people at the lowest level of our society?

The commission's recommendations for education called for a national program that would require all students to obtain certificates of academic achievement at age sixteen, a system of apprentice-like certification for older students who do not go on to a four-year college and a requirement that businesses spend an amount equal to 1 percent of their payroll on worker training. The best companies in the world reduce bureaucracy by giving autonomy to front line workers. Team production is a key element in increased productivity.

The implication for those of us in education is a need to accelerate our present movement toward competency assessment, with instruction focused on areas that research has shown to be critically weak. For example, the commission suggests that the U.S. establish a system to allow an orderly school-to-work transition for noncollege-bound students which would be implemented through a national system of industry-based standards to professionally certify young men and women.

On September 25, 1990, the U.S. House of Representatives passed the Carl D. Perkins Vocational and Applied Technology Education Amendments of 1990. There are four major changes in the new legislation.

(*1*) There is a shift away from traditional job skills toward learning academic and other kinds of thinking skills, and for linking thought with action.

(*2*) Resources will be increasingly focused on districts with the greatest need for reform and improvement.

(*3*) Districts rather than states will be largely responsible for designing programs.

(*4*) A distinction is made for the first time between secondary and postsecondary funding levels, which will allow funds to be targeted at either level (Wirt, 1991).

The biggest change is one of mission—from de-emphasizing preparation for full-time jobs to technical preparation for two-year postsecondary technical education. This change reflects what is happening in the job market. Most vocational students do not get full-time jobs upon graduation from high school; only 30 percent did in 1988 (Gray, 1991). They go on to two-year technical education to prepare for the more complex jobs in an increasingly high-tech society. For secondary schools the theme should be an emphasis upon learning to learn, accompanied by problem-solving skills that can be applied in many work situations.

There is an increase in our level of concern about students who are dropping out of school; a secondary consideration may be the business community's desire to save the costs of teaching new employees reading, writing and arithmetic. David T. Kearns, formerly chairman and chief executive officer of Xerox Corporation, writing for the op-ed section of the *Los Angeles Times* says "It's schools', not business's job, to offer basic education." He goes on to say, "American business will have to hire more than a million new service and production workers a year who can't read, write or count. Teaching them how, and absorbing the lost productivity while they are learning, will cost industry $25 billion a year, and nobody seems to know how long such remedial training will be necessary."

PURPOSES OF THIS BOOK

The first edition of this book, titled *Students-at-Risk: Strategies for Schools,* was written to give school districts information about how to establish programs to prevent dropout, and to recover dropped-out students back into the school system. There was one chapter that dealt with general information about substance abuse and, throughout the book, information about how to utilize technology to carry out many of the tasks connected to helping at-risk students. The second edition added a strong component of detailed information about how to plan and implement substance abuse prevention, including many interventions that have been evaluated carefully and shown to work.

This new edition is being published by Technomic Publishing Company, Inc. as the first in a series that will include volumes on substance abuse and gang prevention. At the back of this book, Technomic Publishing Company, Inc. has listed the address where readers can obtain the software we have developed over the last five years to identify students who are potential dropouts and substance abusers. Evaluation is a key factor in improving programs for students at risk, and our software, which uses student self-report forms, makes evaluation much easier and more economical than it had been in the past. A before-and-after comparison is available each year for each student, and the software has been published in a new, low-cost version that allows school staff to enter student data into a Macintosh or IBM-compatible computer. This makes it possible to have student identification results and suggested intervention approaches available as soon as students complete their self-report forms at each school site.

Here's how the book can help.

- The book is a comprehensive review of what public schools are doing about students at risk, and especially about dropouts.
- There are presentations of district- and site-level plans for the development of dropout prevention and recovery programs.
- We argue for work-directed learning as an instructional strategy that will connect to the real interests of dropout-prone students, who want to get a job as soon as possible.

- There is an argument for the use of technology, especially the Comprehensive Risk Assessment software, to assist school staff in working on problems related to dropout prevention strategies.

The book is intended to be used for information and reference, as any technical book is, but also for the preparation of proposals and reports. More specifically, the book suggests a sequence of steps to be taken in developing strategies for reducing dropout. These begin with the third chapter, which deals with creating a student information system, and continues through a sequence of chapters that many districts refer to as they add detail to their prevention planning.

The Comprehensive Risk Assessment system helps districts identify students likely to drop out, and, in the process, creates a very useful data base of problem students which can be used by school staff in setting priorities for the allocation of time and resources within a school. This process has been simplified in the past year by the introduction of the use of forms which allow self-report information from students to be manually entered into the software. This typically follows a referral from the teacher to the principal. Another innovation in the past year is the ability to automatically place students into interventions, based on their characteristics. For example, a student who expresses anger in a disruptive manner in the classroom, is scheduled into interventions that deal directly with those problems.

AT-RISK MODEL

Here are some points to remember in developing an at-risk model.

(*1*) Use a technology which identifies and places at-risk students into interventions, utilizing keyboard entry of student self-report data into Macintosh and IBM-compatible computers.

(2) Implement the technology so it is low in cost and very easy for the principal.

(3) Train administrators to identify at-risk students, place them in appropriate interventions and pre/post evaluate the interventions to see if they work.

(4) Give an annual award to top implementors with good publicity for the event.

Perhaps the most important step is four; if you don't give the principals an incentive, it won't happen. This goes over pretty well as long as you don't add any work for present staff, as step two indicates.

COMBINING EFFORTS TO REDUCE DROPOUT RATES AND SUBSTANCE ABUSE

Dropout and substance abuse together are the key factors preventing at-risk students from completing high school. There are many other situations which place students at risk, of course, such as pregnancy, child abuse and suicide. Many districts are now working to integrate their established efforts for dealing with students likely to drop out with new efforts in substance abuse prevention. As the research in Chapter 2 indicates, two-thirds of abusers drop out, so there is good reason to integrate these activities. It is important that the individuals responsible for substance abuse and dropout prevention both report to the same senior administrator, in order to assure sound coordination of the two efforts. There is a considerable overlap in the behaviors of the dropout and the abuser, such as poor attendance, low grades and poor self-image. Consequently, in a well-run system, both types of students will be placed in interventions that address these problems.

Once dropout-prone students are identified, there are four types of programs to serve them. We will describe them, then move on to provide a summary of strategies to use in substance abuse prevention. We close the chapter with several recommendations from the California Superintendent of Public Instruction's Middle Grade Task Force. Many districts like to place their initial thrust at the middle school level because problem behaviors are more visible at this age than they are in elementary school, and because substantial success can be achieved in these grades, whereas there is less payoff in later years.

Reducing Dropouts

Communities are placing pressure on school districts to deal with the rising number of dropouts which raises the issue of how they are counted. An article by Hammack in the *Teachers College Record* from Columbia University describes methods school districts use to compute their dropout rates (Hammack, 1986). Many districts do not find it advantageous to list a high dropout rate when they can compute a lower one using another method. Districts are often funded on the basis of the number of students attending. If another funding method were used (e.g., emphasizing student proficiency in basic skills), the reporting behaviors would change.

A survey of over 600 employers taken in 1983 indicated that 82 percent of all jobs screened out candidates with no high school diploma (Malizio and Whitney, 1984). Given the costs to business of teaching employees basic skills, we can predict that the percentage of dropouts screened out will increase in the years ahead. This factor is exacerbated by the increasingly technical demands placed on employees by complex technologies which business must use to compete effectively with advanced industrial nations. The problem is serious—even monumental—when one considers the complexity of improving schools where 50 percent or more of the students drop out.

Jonathan Peterson, writing in the *Los Angeles Times,* suggests another dimension to the problem. Not only do we need relevant training for students based on today's needs, but these needs are changing rapidly. "Every year, one out of eight jobs in the United States is newly created, and one out of nine is eliminated, as employers respond to the shifts in technology, consumer demand and competitive realities" (Peterson, 1987).

Not only do we have to keep updating our vocational opportunities for students, but we need to emphasize technology. Peterson, in the same article, quotes another researcher, William Johnston, of the Hudson Institute, as follows: "The haves and have nots in the year 2000 are going to be defined by their skills. . . . It's going to be the technologically able versus the technologically unable" (Peterson, 1987). These skills are needed just to survive. To do well, people will need to "be able to manage people, adapt to technological change, think analytically and communicate effectively" (Peterson, 1987). The use of technology in periods of conflict, such as the war with Iraq, underlines the need for students to acquire these survival skills.

Substance Abuse Pressures

Students report pressure from peers to use drugs and alcohol as early as fourth grade. These young people are at risk not only because of pressure from peers, but because substance abuse has been shown by research to be a symptom of socioeconomic deprivation, parental abuse or neglect, inadequate health care and cultural alienation (Goplerud, 1990). It is important for educators to understand that our best hope for success with young people with a tendency toward substance abuse is to intervene early. This requires us to identify potential abusers through indicators such as disruptive behavior, defiance of rules, hyperactivity, nervousness, talk about drugs, avoidance of contact with others, depression and irritability, to name some predictors. Characteristics such as frequent drunkenness, friends who use alcohol, marijuana and other drugs, drug sale offenses, pickups by police and sales of drugs have been used by some districts to identify abusers.

Attitudes that lead to abuse can be changed by peers with skill in communication and sensitivity. In Chapter 13 we describe the peer assistance leadership (PAL) program which is built around peer counseling and facilitation and the Peer Assistant software that is designed for students to help each other become aware of the consequences of dropping out and drug use.

THREE COMMON MISTAKES IN DEALING WITH AT-RISK STUDENTS

Many school districts attempt to deal with low-achieving students through flawed strategies that include retention in grade, tracking and assignment to special education classes. Recent research indicates that retention does not show consistent learning benefits when the records of retained students are compared with those of age-mates who are not held back (Shepard and Smith, 1989). Not only does retention not do what we hoped, it actually contributes to dropout, according to Natriello's research (Natriello et al., 1988).

Research by Goodlad and others indicates that tracking may, over time, actually increase the gap between top and bottom students rather than decrease it (Goodlad, 1984). This appears to result primarily from lowered teacher expectations in the lower tracks.

A macroanalysis of all tracking and ability grouping studies finds that high-track teachers are more enthusiastic and spend more time in preparing lessons than low-track teachers, who spend more time on behavior management and less on instruction (Gamoran, 1992).

Small Group Project.

Since successful change tends to be incremental, McPartland and Slavin (1990) suggest five steps to reduce tracking.

(*1*) Postpone between-class homogeneous grouping until as late in the grade span as possible; rather, utilize within-class groups for math or reading.

(*2*) Limit tracking in the later grades to those basic academic subjects where differences in students' prior preparation will hurt whole class instruction.

(*3*) Improve placement criteria and add resources where tracking is used.

(*4*) Try new incentives, such as pass-fail grading, which may encourage students to take challenging courses, rather than stay on a lower track.

(*5*) Retain separate classes for gifted, limited-English and special education students at each grade level, even as you reduce tracking.

The primary mistake in special education placement is to designate low-achieving students as learning disabled (LD) merely because of low achievement when there are no other LD characteristics. Whether this is done through poor placement procedures or to attract greater instructional resources, it is poor policy. Typically, the result creates a funding limitation, which in turn precludes students who really do need special education from obtaining it.

In our view, secondary schools and their students are seriously threatened by the increase of substance abuse and dropout. Perhaps new assumptions and important changes are in order.

THE NEED FOR NEW ASSUMPTIONS

First, we must move away from the notion that reducing the percentage of dropouts is the school's problem. It is the community's problem. In our national survey of state departments of education, to identify promising dropout prevention and recovery programs, we found that of the initial twelve high school programs put into our data base, eleven had work-experience components. The single exception had a component that offered students assistance in locating appropriate employment at the end of the program. We need to collaborate with business and industry.

Second, programs that require cooperation from business and community agencies, such as those to reduce substance abuse and dropout, need to be planned jointly from day one. As one of the creators of the successful dropout recovery program Upward Bound, we know from long experience that linking to agencies in the community can only work when there is true collaboration in the project design.

Third, we wait in vain for funding from the federal government to provide the primary resources to attack these problems. There will never be a return to massive federal intervention funding such as we had in the 1960s, not even in the Clinton administration. As one of the planners of the National Dropout Prevention Network, we are familiar with strategies that the various states are using or planning to use to address this issue. Every state we know about is using a plan that relies upon schools to find the needed resources at the local level to supplement state and federal funding.

Fourth, Wehlage and Rutter suggest that programs should be inventive and engage discouraged students, perhaps through approaches that include more than narrow vocational skills. Programs should emphasize personal and social development and be relatively small with twenty-five to one hundred students, two to six teachers (Wehlage and Rutter, 1986). This would apply to substance abusing students as well.

Fifth, no matter what kind of program we develop for preventing dropouts and substance abuse, we should identify students as early as possible. The model we use for dropout prediction was developed with Sappington (1979), one of our students. One can predict potential dropout as early as the third grade with an accuracy rate of 79 percent or better. Student characteristics used are all available in the student's cumulative file. They include absences, grades, reading scores, mobility, citizenship, juvenile delinquency, special education history, physical disability and grade retention. In order to save money, we have students self-report this information on a form, and a staff member then places the data in the Comprehensive Risk Assessment software, beginning in the third grade.

TYPES OF DROPOUT PROGRAMS

Dropout programs that are receiving the most attention involve students in a variety of settings for education and work experience. There are four types identified by Stern (1986).

(*1*) *Regular academic curriculum leading to local diploma* — An example is the Warren County High School program in Glasgow, Kentucky. Students meet with tutors during the latter part of class periods where they are experiencing problems, and they are given special counseling and help with academic assignments.

(*2*) *Remedial academic curriculum leading to diploma equivalent* — California now has a dozen school districts using the computer-based instruction program NOVANET to offer basic and other high school skills to students who have returned to learning centers after dropping out. They achieve the GED diploma through this approach.

(*3*) *Specialized vocational curriculum leading to job placement* — Connecticut, through its vocational-technical school system, provides bilingual vocational training programs which offer job-entry and trade-related skills taught bilingually; job-specific language using an English-as-a-second-language approach; preventive counseling and life coping skills; case management of trainees' problems such as child care and transportation; job development and placement.

(*4*) *Regular academic curriculum combined with a vocational one* — The Boston Compact consists of an agreement between employers and the school system to place students in jobs if the school system meets its quotas in terms of school attendance and reduction of dropout rates. Students who have satisfactory school attendance can qualify for summer jobs and, in some cases, move into apprentice programs upon graduation from high school.

Recommendations for At-Risk Students

We need to focus not only on substance abuse and dropout prediction much earlier in the student's school career, but look as well at the type and amount of contact students have with their teachers. In many school districts, elementary and middle/junior high schools have become large and, often, impersonal. This is especially troubling to students who don't do well in the typical school environment. The following set of recommendations are aimed at middle school at-risk students, but they certainly would benefit all at-risk students.

(*1*) Local school boards should mandate at least one extended time block daily in two or more of the core curriculum subjects during the middle grades to ensure that:

- Every middle grade student is known personally and well by one or more teachers.
- Individual monitoring of student progress takes place systematically so that teachers and counselors can quickly identify learning difficulties and take corrective measures.
- Cooperative learning strategies are implemented as a means of

building strong positive peer group relationships and reinforcing essential educational values and goals.

(2) Superintendents should give leadership in helping principals devise means for reducing the pressure of large, complex schools which leave many students with a sense of anonymity and isolation. Particular attention should be given to organizational and scheduling concepts which are student centered, and which maximize opportunities for strong personal bonds among smaller numbers of students and teachers throughout the full span of the middle grade years.

(3) Local school boards should authorize and fund peer, cross-age and/or adult tutorial and mentor programs in the middle grades as a proven response to the needs of many at-risk students.

(4) The state department of education and local district curriculum departments should assist teachers in devising instructional strategies that allow students with basic skills deficiencies to engage in learning experiences which develop higher-order thinking skills; these strategies should correspond with core curriculum goals, and should enable students to learn in regular classrooms. Learning experiences should be consistent with the maturity and interest levels of young adolescents.

(5) Principals should give leadership in creating cultural support systems for students—particularly those with limited English proficiency—whose self-identify is threatened through the loss and implicit devaluing of their native language. Teachers and counselors should understand the psychological trauma involved in the transition from one language to another, and the bearing which this phenomenon has on the negative attitudes and values of some categories of at-risk students.

(6) Teachers, counselors and principals should continuously model behavior which affirms their commitment to the basic mission of those who work in the middle grades: to enjoy young adolescents and to create conditions for academic success and educational commitment for every student (Middle Grade Task Force, 1987).

Chapter 2

REVIEW OF THE LITERATURE

Some of the major areas of concern reviewed in this chapter are dropout prediction, teacher efficacy, preventing the alienation of students, college bound versus dropout considerations and characteristics of dropouts. A special concluding section written by Nancy Richards-Colocino of Irvine Unified School District, Irvine, California, is a review of the substance abuse literature used as the research basis for the development of alcohol and other drug prevention and intervention programs in Irvine. Since two-thirds of substance abusers drop out, we include this information for the reader's convenience.

As we read the newspapers and view television, we notice an increase in coverage pertaining to school dropouts and alcohol and other drug abusers. Several factors are working together to focus our attention on these ever-present problems. The most important one is the role that business has begun to play.

David Kearns, formerly chairman of Xerox Corporation, says, "American business will have to hire more than a million new service and production workers a year who can't read, write or count. Teaching them how, and absorbing the lost productivity while they are learning, will cost industry $25 billion a year" (Wehlage, 1986). All across the country business leaders are expressing concern, and going to work to do something about the dropout problem.

Alcohol and other drug abuse is a closely related issue, in that two-thirds of the abusers drop out (Skager and Frith, 1989). These issues need to be considered together, because they involve many of the same students and strategies for amelioration. Preventive strategies for dropping out and abusing drugs are easily combined when viewing student problems from a risk factor perspective, for example. Educational research has consistently found that dropouts can be identified in elementary school, and that many dropouts also abuse alcohol and other drugs (Sappington, 1979; Maspero, 1989). Also, once a student receives drug and alcohol treatment and is reengaged in a school, she/he needs an education and/or job training program to keep him/her motivated. To make this possible, state administrators need to arrange for access to training and jobs, as well as influence state legislators to create legislation that encourages school districts to link to local businesses.

The second force at work is the recognition that there will be fewer jobs available for dropouts in the future, because of the increasingly complex technology used in manufacturing and service industries. A 1983 survey of 643 employers indicated that 82 percent of jobs available required a high school diploma (Malizio and Whitney, 1984).

These powerful economic factors have, in turn, caused state and federal agencies to put pressure on school districts to accept a uniform definition of *dropout*. This will in turn make it possible for sensible comparisons to be made between districts within states and nationally. The typical state strategy is to require districts to use reporting procedures for attendance that use a single definition of dropout. Since districts have to use a statewide definition for state reports, it is likely that they will give up their local definitions in time. States were in turn given impetus to move in this direction by an article in *Teachers College Record* by Hammack (1986) describing how six U.S. cities use quite different methods to compute their dropout rates.

Of special concern are minority populations, such as Latinos, where, according to the U.S. Census Bureau, 17.3 million in population in 1986 will grow to 51 million in 2050. The California Postsecondary Commission estimated that 34 percent of Latino students who entered high school in 1979–1980 eventually dropped out, as did 33 percent of black students.

DROPOUT PREDICTION

As one of the creators of the dropout recovery program Upward Bound in the mid-1960s, the author recalls that little or no federal emphasis was placed on activities to prevent dropouts at the elementary school level. An innovative program called Follow Through for grades one through three was created to continue work begun in Head Start, but the program was, unfortunately, not implemented widely. Being familiar with dropout efforts throughout the country, and interested in students at risk and job training, the senior author has found great interest in dropout prevention programs in the elementary schools. This is especially true if one shows the administrators how to predict which students will drop out, and suggests possible interventions, as this book and the Students-at-Risk, Inc. Comprehensive Risk Assessment software does.

The prediction model developed with Sappington (1979), a former student, is especially appealing in that it indicates students likely to drop out at grades four, six and nine with an accuracy of 79 percent or better. Categories include attendance, low grades, reading level, retention, mobility within and outside the district and adjustment factors.

The chief goal of compensatory programs such as Head Start is to prepare children to enter elementary school on an equitable basis with other children. Malizio and Whitney (1984) found that many of these programs have proven to be effective, and the earlier the intervention the better. Administrators need to identify children with deficiencies in the early grades, guide them to needed services and track their progress until they are no longer predicted to drop out.

A particularly encouraging finding is reported by Pogrow in his development of computer software to teach basic skills through a problem-solving approach. Teachers are trained to use higher-order questioning techniques during instruction where, for example, they would ask "When do people usually run rather than walk?" instead of "What is the definition of the word run?" Students in the experimental groups are scoring as well in basic skills using a problem-solving curriculum as are students in a basic skills curriculum alone. The student gets two areas of content for one, in effect. Pogrow's materials are titled *Higher Order Thinking Skills,* and are being tested in more than thirty schools around the country (Pogrow, 1989).

Ogbu (1983) has found that parents of minority children believe that white teachers teach white children more effectively than they do minority children (Hammack, 1986). The author's own research in a Vermont reading improvement program indicated that students' perceptions of their parents' views of school had a strong effect on student performance (Callison, 1973). First grade students who perceived their parents had a positive view of their school grew fourteen months in a nine-month program, controlling for ability and sex. Students with neutral parents grew nine months and students who saw their parents as having negative views of the school grew seven months. This research indicates that an administrator's efforts to work with parents, and to arrive at a teacher assignment parents feel comfortable with, may have an important bearing on student performance.

TEACHER EFFICACY

Recent research (Berman et al., 1977) indicates that teachers who believe in their ability to teach dropout-prone students do, in fact, succeed with them. They answer the following question positively: "If I really try hard, can I get through to even the most difficult or unmotivated students?" Alternatively, teachers with low efficacy fail to

Staff Development on Teacher Efficacy.

reach dropout-prone students and they respond to the following item positively: "When it comes right down to it, a teacher really can't do much because most of a student's motivation and performance depends on his or her home environment."

Ashton and Webb, writing in their book *Making a Difference,* have done educators a great service by identifying the characteristics of high- and low-efficacy teachers in some detail. High-efficacy teachers maintain academic standards, are challenged by the opportunities presented by low-achieving students, focus on academic work in class and establish friendly relations with the students. Low-efficacy teachers, on the other hand, are not confident they can succeed with low-achieving students. They hold low expectations for them, demand little from them academically, are distant from them personally and use an authoritarian style in dealing with them (Ashton and Webb, 1986).

Perhaps the first thing that administrators can do in response to these new findings is identify their low-efficacy teachers and, to the extent possible, not place low-achieving students in their classes. Chapter 19 provides specific suggestions for working with low-efficacy teachers.

PREVENTION OF ALIENATION

Students' attitudes toward school are also influenced by what goes on in school itself. Wehlage (1986) reports that "schools send out signals to at-risk youth that they are neither able nor worthy enough to continue to graduation." Three variables, if limited or lacking, become indicators of alienation from school for at-risk students: perceived teacher interest in students, effectiveness of the school's discipline system and fairness of the school's discipline system.

The best time to prevent student alienation is in the elementary grades. Researchers Novak and Dougherty (1980) suggest the following prevention strategies.

(*1*) Center on the students.

(*2*) Serve all students.

(*3*) Offer a comprehensive array of services.

(*4*) Coordinate resources and personnel, in school and out.

(*5*) Translate to various school settings and populations.

(*6*) Incorporate feedback and evaluation information to improve.

These effective strategies apply equally well to secondary as well as elementary schools.

COLLEGE-BOUND STUDENTS VERSUS DROPOUTS

The problem for dropout-prone students in secondary schools is often one of self-image and inadequate expectation. These and other personal and family issues are extremely difficult for schools to address. To state the case boldly, when the principal seeks to help dropouts, she/he is almost always countering the interests of the college-bound students, because resources are limited. On the positive side, dropout prevention does often improve attendance and bring in more funds. Wehlage (1986) has identified four dilemmas school administrators face which do present educators with opportunities for positive action.

Educator Accountability versus Autonomy

To be accountable, the administrator seeks to respond to the needs of all students in an evenhanded manner. One does have the autonomy, however, to make choices about the use of resources for the best interests of the total school. It is much more likely that the community will support a special effort for college-bound students than for those about to drop out. Hence, it takes effort to educate the community so they will agree to provide work-experience counselors and/or any of dozens of other strategies to help the potential dropout.

Subjective versus Objective Authority

Subjective strategies are particularistic and take into account the special aspects of a student's background. Successful dropout programs are often informal, small and accommodating to students who don't "fit." Objective authority is impersonal and attractive to those such as the college bound who fit the norms of the organization.

Extended Educational Role versus Specialized Role

The extended teacher role is aimed at the whole child. It fits the dropout-prone student's needs well, whereas the specialized or content-oriented teacher is especially attracted to the college-bound student.

Diverse versus Common Curriculum

The diverse curriculum provides a wide range of activities, skills and opportunities, and responds to the need of the student who frequently has difficulty with the common or college preparatory curriculum.

Minimizing Political Costs

All of these dilemmas lead to real difficulty for the administrator as she/he seeks to respond to the requirements of the student with special needs. One way to do so with minimal political cost is to put the dropout-prone students into specialized, individually focused programs, such as a school-within-a-school or an alternative school.

It is important that each student receive a rigorous educational experience that she/he can respond to. For many job-oriented students, this means arranging for a work-experience component. Creating challenging choices for students is the key. As Bronfenbrenner (1986) indicates, if adolescents do not have healthy challenges, they will find avenues for expression through drugs, promiscuity, smoking and social withdrawal.

CHARACTERISTICS OF DROPOUTS

Stern (1986) introduced the helpful concept of early and late onset of dropout characteristics, also utilized by Treadway (1985). Thus some students have done poor work since the early elementary years while others have no difficulty until they get pregnant as juniors in high school. An effective dropout prediction model can be of great assistance in identifying these dropout-prone students, and planning timely programs to meet their needs.

The Los Angeles Unified School District Dropout Prevention/ Recovery Committee (1985) reported the following data from a study of their student population, which may be helpful in planning appropriate programs in other districts.

(*1*) Dropouts are retained five times more often than are graduates. A student who is retained in either first or second grade, has a 20 percent chance of graduating.

(2) Involving students in a vocationally oriented program with an ex-

plicit basic skills component often increases student performance in basic skills.

(3) The academic ability of dropouts and those who graduate but do not attend college is comparable, with a mean IQ of about ninety.

(4) Dropouts feel teachers have little interest in them and do not care about them; they further believe the school's discipline system is ineffective and unfair.

In addition, Peng and Takai (1983) found that more than half of the dropouts in the "High School and Beyond" study felt, soon after dropping out, that leaving school was not a good decision.

One of the most controversial issues for administrators concerned with reducing the dropout rate in their schools is helping teachers develop an appropriate level of expectation for each student. Natriello and Dornbusch's research (1984) indicates that increased effort by students, including low-ability students, is related to higher levels of demand by teachers. However, they found that low-ability students may need special help to meet these higher teacher demands.

SUBSTANCE ABUSE

The literature connecting dropping out with substance abuse is substantial. In a study by Friedman (1985) of 526 high school students, the majority of drug users dropped out, while only one in four nondrug users did. In a major national summary, prepared by the Select Committee on Narcotics Abuse and Control of the Ninety-ninth Congress (U.S. Congress, 1986a), the major conclusion of the hearing was that a relationship does exist between drug abuse and dropping out, especially among minority students, although no causal relationship could be determined.

Although the differences in rates of substance use between ethnic and racial groups is small, white and native American youth report the highest use rates (Goodstadt and Mitchell, 1990). In fact, there is special legislation directed to the needs of native Americans in U.S. Senate Bill 1298 of the Ninety-ninth Congress (U.S. Congress, 1986b). It requires coordination of information and services between the Bureau of Indian Affairs and the Indian Health Service and many special services. A study of Hispanic students identified as potential dropouts found drug use widespread, especially cigarettes, marijuana and alcohol. Smith (1986), in testimony before the New York State Legislature, indicated there were three reasons for the 50–70 percent dropout rate of black and Hispanic students. They were personal and cultural dehumanization, academic humiliation and drug addiction.

The author's experience in Upward Bound is reaffirmed in the literature on substance abuse. Programs that try to reach students at the high school level have less chance of succeeding than those begun earlier. The Irvine Unified School District is a good example of a district that has been faithful to the philosophy of prevention and early intervention, and has developed a number of innovative prevention curricula (GOAL, STAR, PLUS and STAGES programs, I.U.S.D., 1987) and guidance assistance programs for K–12 at-risk students.

RESEARCH BASIS FOR IRVINE PREVENTION AND INTERVENTION PROGRAM

Irvine's comprehensive school-based prevention and intervention program focuses on understanding the risk factors for alcohol and other drug abuse, similar to the medical community's focus on risk factors for heart disease. The Irvine program, described in Chapters 11 and 12, serves students at various stages of risk with age-appropriate prevention and intervention activities.

Research on youth most at risk for alcohol and other drug abuse has consistently demonstrated the importance or risk and resiliency factors in the development of drug abuse problems (e.g., Block et al., 1988; Newcomb et al., 1986; Jessor and Jessor, 1977). If risk factors, such as antisocial behavior, association with drug using peers, family management practices and academic failure can be assessed along with resiliency factors, such as involvement in church activities and strong attachment to parents and school, appropriate programmatic interventions can follow. Resiliency factors are important even if they only represent the opposite end of the risk factor continuum, because resiliency factors buffer the effects of risk indicators (Hawkins and Catalano, 1989). A list of these important risk and protective factors is shown in Figure 2.1.

While research on resiliency factors is relatively new, research on risk indicators over the years has identified that many paths lead to

Negative Factors

Laws and norms favorable toward behavior
Availability of drugs and alcohol
Extreme economic deprivation
Neighborhood disorganization
Physiological factors
Early and persistent problem behaviors
    (i.e., aggression, conduct, hyperactivity)
Family history of alcoholism and parental drug use
Poor and inconsistent family management practices
Family conflict
Low bonding to family
Academic failure
Low degree of commitment to school
Peer rejection in elementary grades
Association with drug using peers
Alienation and rebelliousness
Attitudes favorable to drugs
Early onset of drug use

Protective Factors

Small family with low conflict
High IQ
First born
Strong attachment to parents
Commitment to schooling
Regular involvement in church activities
Belief in the generalized expectations, norms and values of society
Low affiliation, autonomy, exhibition, impulsivity and play
High achievement, cognitive structure and harm avoidance

Figure 2.1 Risk Factors in Alcohol and Drug Abuse.

drug abuse (Oetting and Beauvais, 1987) and having more risk factors increases the chances of drug abuse (Newcomb et al., 1986).

FACTORS INCREASING THE RISK OF DRUG USE

Antisocial, Problem Behaviors and Drug Use

Research reveals that there is a direct, high correlation between anti-social behaviors, delinquency and illicit drug use among adolescents (Jessor et al., 1980; Elliott et al., 1982). Early signs of delinquency and antisocial behaviors are predictable starting in kindergarten through acting out, defiance, impulsivity, negativity, temper tantrums or even shyness (Spivack, 1983). It is therefore critical that the initial screening for high-risk adolescents include a review of their records of maladaptive behaviors such as aggressiveness, passivity, hyperactivity and acting out, along with teachers' current assessments of the student's behavior.

The youth's attitudes and behavior related to drug use are very predictive of later abuse of alcohol and other drugs. Kandel (1978) found that values favorable to drug use preceded initiation. She also found that the earlier the age of onset of use, the greater the involvement with other, more dangerous drugs. Other studies identify smoking and drinking as gateway drugs leading to harder substances. Youth who report smoking cigarettes frequently (Robinson et al., 1987) and experiencing intoxication frequently (Kovach and Glickman, 1986) are clearly statistical candidates for drug abuse.

Peer Risk Factors

Association with drug using peers has been among the strongest predictors of adolescent drug use (Swaim et al., 1989). Drug experimentation, according to Hawkins et al. (1985), may be viewed as a peer-supported phenomenon reflecting the importance of peers during adolescence. Peer-related risk factors include peers as a source of drug information, the number of peers who use or are perceived to use and the perceived level of resistance to peer pressure (Newcomb et al., 1986; Kovach and Glickman, 1986).

The link between peer rejection and substance abuse is unclear. However, low acceptance by peers does put youth at risk for school problems and criminality (Parker and Asher, 1987), which are also risk factors for drug abuse (Hawkins and Catalano, 1989). Whether personality creates rejection and subsequent problems, or rejection limits the child's positive opportunities, also remains unclear.

Family Risk Factors

The family role in preventing drug use among adolescent youth has been well documented. The importance of family socialization includes the adult role as a model for the youth of the family. Kandel (1982) found that three factors help predict youth initiation into drugs – parent drug use, parent attitudes about drugs and parent and child interactions. Parental use seems to act as an impetus to experimentation according to most findings (Rachal et al., 1980; 1982). Parents are quietly molding the child's behavior.

Early in life, children's antisocial behavior begins (i.e., temper tantrums or aggressiveness) and often continues into adulthood. Patterson et al. (1989) have found that the path to chronic delinquency unfolds very predictably in an action-reaction sequence. Likewise, there is evidence in their findings that antisocial children frequently have harsh and inconsistent disciplinary parents; these parents have poor parenting skills and give little positive reinforcement. The most successful intervention for these children appears to be parent training interventions, where family management and communication practices are offered (Kazdin, 1987; Patterson et al., 1989).

The correlation between living in a single parent family and using drugs remains unclear. Although parental discord may lead to family breakup, conflict among family members is a better predictor of drug abuse (Simcha-Fagan et al., 1986) than broken homes themselves.

School Performance

Poor school performance, though not always leading to drug use, is a common antecedent of drug initiation (Jessor and Jessor, 1977; Kandel, 1978). Robins (1980) noted that drug users are noticeably underachievers. Spivak (1983) further concluded that academic failure in the late elementary grades does exacerbate the effects of early antisocial behavior. Hawkins, previously cited, found that such factors as how much students like school, time spent on homework and perception of the relevance of coursework are related also to levels of drug use, confirming a negative relationship between commitment to education and drug use, at least for adolescents in junior or senior high.

Physical and Emotional Health

Adolescence is an appropriate time to learn how to tolerate pain due to physical or emotional problems (Jones and Battjes, 1985). However, the research shows that some adolescents learn early to retreat into regressive patterns, some life threatening (e.g., anorexia), rather than experience stress or pain. Adolescents may become phobic and even self-medicated in an attempt to alleviate suffering.

Personality

Many at-risk children suffer from poor coping skills and low self-esteem. Kaplan et al. (1982) noted that persons who fail in interacting with peers become self-critical and lose self-esteem. Likewise, if behaviors associated with traditional society have failed, deviant behaviors are tried in an effort to improve one's self-image. These behaviors include drug use, which serves as a mechanism for improving self-esteem among new peers when the old self-image has not worked. Research cited earlier by Botvin suggests strongly that such students need training in social and communication skills—along with some cognitive strategies—to increase their self-worth, and to interact confidently in resisting peer pressures to use substances.

One common personality characteristic found in at-risk students is chronic anger. Swaim et al. (1989) compared the effect of five emotional distress variables, including anger, self-esteem, depression, blame-alienation and anxiety. Only anger was found to be directly related to drug abuse, and serves as a mediator of other emotional distresses.

Environmental

A number of environmental risk factors have also been identified. For example, economic deprivation can be a factor in drug abuse. However, Hawkins and Catalano (1989) conclude after reviewing the literature that only when poverty is extreme and occurs in conjunction with childhood behavior problems, is it a predictive factor.

Studies have shown that laws, norms and alcohol distribution policies can predict use levels, according to Hawkins and Catalano (1989). Drinking levels vary by community, depending on the legal drinking age, the acceptance of drinking by others and the number of outlets selling alcohol. Skager and Frith (1989) found that perceived availability of drugs was also a factor, that is, the more youth or adults an adolescent knows who can supply him or her, the more likely he or she is to use.

The effect that neighborhood disorganization has on drug abuse remains unclear, according to Hawkins and Catalano (1989). However, some risk factors, such as neighborhood disorganization, extreme poverty, psychological predisposing factors and a family history of alcoholism, though not necessarily modifiable, can be useful to target high-risk groups.

PROTECTIVE FACTORS AGAINST DRUG ABUSE

Protective factors serve to increase resiliency, or inhibit the development of drug abuse problems. These factors have been inconsistently defined. However, they are generally viewed as opposites of risk factors (Hawkins and Catalano, 1989). For example, the effect of religious attachment has been frequently studied as a protective factor. In a recent study by Newcomb et al. (1986), low religiosity correlated 0.13 with drug use, ranking seventh out of ten variables studied.

Block et al. (1988) studied a number of factors longitudinally, and found drug use at age fourteen was related to concurrent and preschool personality characteristics, an absence of ego resiliency, undercontrolled ego and, in boys, lower IQ. Conversely, being raised in small families with low conflict, having a high IQ and being a first born child buffers the effects of other risk factors as found by Werner and Smith (1982). Research concerning protective factors usually occurs in the context of research on risk factors, such as attachment versus estrangement from parents, school and peers. The results to date do not indicate that protective factors are separate and distinct from risk factors, but rather, have a buffering effect on them. Therefore, being socially bonded to school, family and/or society can reduce the effect of risk factors, like extreme poverty, which may not be directly modifiable, especially in the school setting.

NEED FOR SCHOOL-BASED ASSESSMENT

There is a clear need to identify and intervene early in the development of addictive behavior. Settings like schools and local agencies have the opportunity to be successful with early intervention by focusing on decreasing individual risks, such as the inability to resist peer pressure and lack of attachment to family and school.

Schools play a major role in the implementation of an effective prevention program in at least two distinct ways. The school provides a reference point with credibility for initiating and ensuring community interest, and, in its primary educative role, allows educators to provide the students with appropriate prevention materials (curriculum, videos, handouts) and activities (e.g., Red Ribbon Week). Likewise, support staffs who recognize the risk factors can intervene rapidly, and make effective referrals for services outside the school.

In its role as an institution of learning, the school has an excellent opportunity to infuse prevention materials into regular classroom courses (e.g., health and social studies). To emphasize wellness as a choice requires health courses that teach the need for building both healthy bodies and attitudes. Students are taught also the detrimental aspects of drug use. However, health courses and lectures alone do not produce significant results. Research studies by Botvin, previously cited, and Baumarind verify that cognitive (i.e., appeal to health) and the social skills training (i.e., assertion training) when combined form the most effective basis for a strong prevention program for students at risk. Baumarind adds that through health and social skills training, an effort can be made to persuade adolescents that the personal attributes they value are impaired by substance use.

Research indicates that teachers observe school adjustment problems in 23–31 percent of all kindergarten through third grade students. These early adjustment difficulties often predict future maladjustment, including emotional problems, antisocial tendencies and drug abuse (Cowen et al., 1966; Rubin and Balow, 1978). Assessment of risk factors can also help identify the one out of four children who come from families of substance abusers—a need that is often ignored, according to Battjes and Jones (1985). Educators who are trained in screening and assessment of specific risk factors in young children are in an excellent position to effectively intervene to decrease at-risk behaviors through prevention, early intervention and referral for treatment.

Most research on risk factors continues to be gleaned from anonymous surveys with large samples (Battjes and Jones, 1985). What is needed is a way to identify an *individual* student's level of use, along with associated risk factors, to determine his or her individual risk level baseline. If schools can identify at-risk students as early as possible in their chronological and drug experience age, fewer resources will be needed to decrease the identified risk factors, and the interventions will be more successful.

NEED FOR PARENT AND COMMUNITY INVOLVEMENT

A primary reason for parent and community involvement in prevention is found in the research on the effectiveness of school prevention curricula. The reasons youth use alcohol and other drugs are so varied that any school curriculum can only produce a small decrease in use rates (Moskowitz, 1989). For example, businessmen and parents need to recognize that advertising and promotion of alcohol by role models (e.g., sports and rock stars) creates the wrong impression within the minds of vulnerable youth. Consequently, the community as a whole, backed by local law enforcement, must work together to change the attitudes and behaviors of youth and of adult citizens as well.

Research shows that parents are in denial about the possibility of their children using drugs. Parents need to become better informed on the current information about drugs, their prevalence and signs of drug use. Finally, parents' greatest impact is in the creation of positive family functioning, relationships and attachments that appear to discourage the initial experimentation with gateway drugs (Jessor and Jessor, 1977).

SUMMARY

A review of the research literature shows that much is known about why some youth are prone to use alcohol and other drugs, separate from their need to experiment and rebel. Most significantly related to drug use and abuse are:

- antisocial and problem behaviors
- previous drug use experience
- predisposing personality characteristics, such as chronic anger and low ego control
- association with peers who use

- parental conflict
- economic deprivation
- low academic interest and achievement

Conversely, resilient youths may be exposed to risk factors but be protected by high self-esteem or attachment to family or religion. These positive attachments compete with risk factors to guide youth in their decisions not to use, as described by the social development theory. Thus, the research literature on risk factors has evolved into a more cohesive understanding than in the past.

The school setting has become the obvious arena for prevention and intervention. Educators are advised to develop comprehensive programs with consistent community involvement (Pentz, 1986).

Chapter 3

CREATING A STUDENT INFORMATION SYSTEM

In order to deal systematically with potential dropouts, each school should invest in some type of student information system that offers standard computer applications such as grade reporting, student scheduling, course history, period attendance and test scoring. Types of data include reasons for student referral, prereferral services, academic functioning in mathematics, reading and language arts, behavior in and out of the classroom, primary language, social agency background, previous special support at school, health background, period-by-period teacher evaluation and, if possible, current survey of faculty to identify causes of dropout. For students who have dropped out, the school needs a master file with leave-destination categories and leave-reasons categories.

ALTERNATIVES FOR DEALING WITH POTENTIAL DROPOUTS

There are a variety of strategies administrators can use to work with students who are unable to operate successfully in the standard school environment. The following model was developed by Wayne Joseph at Simons Junior High School in Pomona, California. Simons has approximately 1,000 students, and 75 percent of them are from minority backgrounds.

The first level of contact with a problem student is from the principal's office and includes contact with the home to discuss the student's situation. This provides the administrators with background that may be useful immediately and/or as the case develops. The second level in the model is referral to a key teacher who, in the experience of the administrators, may be able to work with this student.

Level three is referral to the adjustment teacher, a teacher who holds high expectations for students who have difficulty in the standard school environment, and who likes to work with them. The adjustment teacher has responsibility throughout the day for about one to ten of these students per period, as well as several independent study students from level six (c) on the matrix. Other teachers provide the students, referred for adjustment, with their assignments.

Levels four and five are suspensions that fit the situation. For example, fighting might draw a two-day suspension, while drug use would draw five days. Suspension is no panacea, and many students are then moved to level six, where they are referred to one of three alternatives. Open door is for students with rather severe behavior problems, while outreach is provided for students with less serious difficulties, such as poor attendance records. Independent study is often used for students who are a general nuisance in a standard classroom, or who may be involved in the use of drugs.

Level seven is referral to the student study team, a remedy of last resort, since it is expensive in terms of staff time. Perhaps fifty students a year out of 1,000 are referred at Simons. If fifty students attend school only half the days in a school year, however, this costs the district 50 × $1,500 or $75,000. Hence it is worth the extra staff time to keep these students in school. They tend to fall into three categories: those whom the administrators think will probably be placed in special education; those who are not motivated academically; and those the administrators feel can be best served by teacher input.

THE STUDENT STUDY TEAM

The student study team concept has been in use for several years in California schools, and has been supported by the State Department of Education. Each student is analyzed as a whole, rather than in terms of special needs, such as special education or bilingual education. Hence, the staff concerned with students who are predicted to drop out, participate in a student study team rather than treating the student as though many other staff have not already been working to help him or her. This is easy to discuss and hard to implement, as is any strategy that requires extensive cooperation and communication.

Implementation of a student study team (SST), or the equivalent, re-

SST at Work.

quires the creation of a group that may include the student, the parent, administration, district support personnel, classroom teachers and special program personnel. The principal or her/his designee typically appoints the members and chairs the team.

The team is a function of the regular academic program. It uses a systematic problem-solving approach to assist students who are not progressing at a satisfactory rate. The SST clarifies problems and concerns, develops strategies, organizes resources and provides a system for accountability (Radius and Lesniak, 1986).

Team members should include people with a variety of competencies and skills. Some members should have the authority to provide support for implementing decisions the SST makes. The SST will be more effective if the potential implementors of SST decisions are also members.

The SST is not a special education function and is not, therefore, subject to the various restrictions associated with special education. On the other hand, the SST certainly can and should help with mainstreaming strategies for special education students.

Some typical services of an SST include:

(*1*) Clarify the problem(s) a student has, including a definition that leads toward realistic solutions.

(*2*) Gather data on student performance.

(*3*) Analyze information on student performance and help classroom teachers involved design strategies to work with the student.

(*4*) Assist with the implementation of these strategies by providing curriculum materials, consultation, monitoring and moral support.

(*5*) Provide assurance that when a student is referred for special education the referral is well considered, based on clearly identified need, and that less restrictive alternatives have been attempted.

(*6*) Provide training to teachers who need preparation to implement some of the SST's strategies.

SST benefits include efficiency in bringing together all of the resources needed to help a student, elimination of numerous site meetings about the same student, involvement of the parent in problem solving rather than just discipline, an expression of the school's concern for the student and the creation of a team that raises the morale of members as well as helping the school to improve its service to students and the effectiveness of its instruction.

Frequently, two days of training helps prepare staff to implement the SST approach. The training includes current ideas about parent involvement, strategies for running group meetings effectively, procedures for assigning responsibilities among team members and specific approaches to providing teacher support in the implementation process. The district staff must be committed to the SST approach and, through annual evaluations, see that principals work to make SSTs effective.

Most districts have found that a minimum of lecture/discussion and a maximum of practice using real cases are the best way to train teams. Roles are clarified (see Figure 3.1) (Butler and Gilmartin, 1986), especially for the student, parent and referring teacher, none of whom may be familiar with the approach. Group memory is used to emphasize student strengths, as is problem identification prior to recommendations for helping strategies, and to keep the team focused and accountable (see Figure 3.2).

One person should play the role of parent specialist, and recruit parents as team members. Students, if at the junior or senior high

Facilitator/Chairperson	Recorder	Team Member
Before Meeting	Listen carefully for the key words and ideas to be recorded.	Respect and listen to other individuals.
Coordinate logistics before and after meeting.	Write the input on the student study team summary.	Do not cut other people off or put words in their mouths.
Notify team members of meeting, time, place and students scheduled.	Organize the information in the appropriate columns.	Question any statement you feel is not accurate.
Insure parent and student are prepared.	Don't change the meaning of what was said.	Help recorder remain neutral and make sure ideas are being recorded accurately.
Know available resources and how to access them.	Ask for clarification, get accurate information on the summary.	Use facilitative behaviors as needed.
Assume ultimate responsibility for group decisions.	Capture basic ideas.	Focus energy on content of the student summary.
	Make corrections nondefensively.	

(continued)

Figure 3.1 *Defined Roles for Team Members—Facilitator and Chairperson May or May Not Be the Same Person.*

Facilitator/Chairperson	Recorder	Team Member
During Meeting	Write legibly and quickly.	Help group stay on task.
Primary role is to facilitate, not to present information.	Shorten words, abbreviate.	Serve as timekeeper or observer as needed.
Stand in front of group.	Don't be afraid to misspell.	Come prepared with information on student.
Account for time; appoint timekeeper.	Use colors as a visual aid.	Avoid side conversations.
Help recorder take accurate notes.	Use circles and arrows to connect related information.	Look for similarities/discrepancies in the information.
Check for meaning/understanding.		Account for agreed upon actions.
Encourage input from all team members by asking "Any additions any questions?"		Do not make commitments for people who are not present at the meeting.
Keep group focused on task.		Copy SST summary on a small sheet.
Ask for specifics, not generalities.		
Be positive, compliment group.		
Be nonjudgemental, encourage others to be nonjudgemental.		
Diffuse emotionally charged statements.		
See that team prioritizes concerns and actions.		
Help team find win/win solutions for teacher, student, parents.		
Expect accountability for group decisions.		

Figure 3.1 (continued) Defined Roles for Team Members—Facilitator and Chairperson May or May Not Be the Same Person.

TEACHER _____ SCHOOL _____ TEAM _____

STUDENT _____ PRIMARY LANG. _____ GR. _____ BIRTH _____ PARENTS _____

M _____ F _____

Strengths	Known Information	Modifications	Concerns Prioritized	Questions	Strategies Brainstorm	Actions Prioritized	Persons Responsible Who	When
Academic Social Physical What student likes Incentives	School background Family composition Health Performance levels	Changes in program Reading specialist Tutoring Counseling Repeating grade	Academic Social/ emotional Physical Attendance	Questions that can't be answered at this time	Team brainstorms multiple creative strategies to address top concerns	Two to three actions chosen from strategies brainstormed	Any team member, including the parent and student	Specific dates
							Follow-up date: (3–6 weeks)	

Figure 3.2 Use of SST Summary Sheet—Typical Column Topics.

ATTENTION: On request, this form will be shown to the parent, guardian or pupil over 18 years old.

Student's Name: _____ Birthdate: _____ Sex: _____ Date: _____
School: _____ Teacher: _____ Grade: _____
Referral Initiator(s): _____

(Parent, Teacher, Principal, etc.)

REASON FOR STUDENT STUDY REQUEST: Briefly describe why student is being referred to student study team.

ACADEMIC FUNCTIONING: At approximately what grade level is pupil functioning?
Math _____ Reading _____ Language Arts _____

BEHAVIOR: Describe behavior in and out of classroom.

ATTENDANCE: Days Present _____ Days Absent _____ Total Days This Covers _____

Figure 3.3 Sample Student Referral Information Sheet (Source: Mt. Diablo Unified School District, Concord, CA).

BACKGROUND INFORMATION: What languages other than English are spoken in the home? _____

Has student ever repeated a grade? Yes _____ No _____ If yes, what grade? _____ Number of Siblings _____
List any school support service the student is receiving (reading specialist, speech and language therapist, etc.).
List any prior special education service.
List social agency involvement.

HEALTH DATA:
Vision
　　Date of test _____ Within normal limits _____ Not within normal limits _____
Hearing
　　Date of test _____ Within normal limits _____ Not within normal limits _____
List any significant health problems.

ADDITIONAL COMMENTS (special strengths, skills, aptitudes, etc.): Please use objective, specific terms. Reference should be made to cumulative folder factors such as number of transfers, group testing summary and dramatic change in academic performance (approximate date).

Figure 3.3 (continued) Sample Student Referral Information Sheet (Source: Mt. Diablo Unified School District, Concord, CA).

school level, should be involved and the team should have information about the student from the student referral information sheet (see Figure 3.3). The team is responsible for setting up their own procedures, such as when to meet and how to provide in-service for staff. Team members need to be taught skills in group facilitation, time management and conducting effective meetings, for the team to be effective.

Elements of the SST model include use of the SST summary sheets, parent and student participation and carefully defined roles for team members. The summary is placed on butcher paper in the team meeting room, and allows members to see their work as they progress. Parent involvement is critical and, unfortunately, hard to achieve with parents of students who are predicted to drop out.

Referral of students must be done with care, because too many referrals will overload the staff and cause the system to break down. The procedure for student referral should include: evaluation of the student by appropriate teachers; a parent conference; a weekly progress check; and a conference with a dean in order to ensure that the time of the SST is used for students with the greatest need for help.

Once the decision is made to refer a student, the teacher evaluations should be given to the SST chairperson, and contact should be made with the parents and the student (if secondary level) to set up a meeting. Other SST members are notified and the meeting is held. During the meeting the student's strengths are discussed as well as areas of concern. Actions recommended should be based on both concerns and strengths, and should be prioritized to facilitate immediate, practical implementation by teachers involved. Recommendations should be behavioral in format so teachers understand clearly what is being suggested. The parents should be asked to play an active part in the actions recommended, and a plan for monitoring the recommendations should be one result of the meeting. At the close of the meeting a follow-up meeting should be scheduled. The SST should create a plan for evaluating the effectiveness of the SST's operations.

One member of the SST should summarize the group's discussion and recommendations and enter the data into a computer in some kind of organized format. Form design software will allow computer access to the data base. We show screens from Informed Designer and Informed Manager, software from Shana Corporation (see Figures 3.4, 3.5 and 3.6), which automatically creates a data base as you design your

"HEALTHY KIDS ~ HEALTHY DUARTE"
INDIVIDUAL INTERVENTION PLAN
CONFIDENTIAL

Name	Birthday
Callison, William PRINT Last First	

Address	Telephone
	714 497-13

Parents Name

Language	Home Language

Spec Prog: Spec Ed	Spec Prog: GATE	Spec Prog: Other

School	Teacher	Grade

School Status: Enrolled	School Status: Moved	School Status: Re-entered

Interviewer	Date

Assessment Survey Questions: (Circle) 1 2 3 4 5 6 7 8 9 10 11 12 13 14

Assessment Survey Questions: (Check)

Substance Abuse: Low Risk: ____Pre ____Post   Medium Risk: ____Pre ____Post   High Risk: ____Pre ____Post
Dropout: Low Risk: ____Pre ____Post   Medium Risk: ____Pre ____Post   High Risk: ____Pre ____Post

Level 1 Interview (After topics are discussed, summarize student responses)

Recommendation:
____No Further Intervention ____Level II ____Level III

Study Team Recommendation:
____No Further Intervention ____Level II ____Level III

Figure 3.4 Screen One.

45

Level II Interventions

Date	Parent Conference	Date	Positive Activities Assigned to:
Date	Interest Analyzer	Date	1.
Date	SST (Site) Attach Plan	Date	2.
Date	SIT District	Date	3.
Date	Student-Parent-School Contract	Date	4.
Date	Academic Assistance (Tutor)	Date	DCP Parent Classes
			SCH. ___ ENG. ___ SP. ___
	Days and Time	Date	Operation School Bell
Date	Program/Class/School Change	Date	Psychological Testing
Date	Being Useful Project	Date	School Nurse
Date	Other	Date	Monrovia Health Clinic
Date	Community Council Services	Date	Outside Health Provider (Agency)

Quarterly Progress Report: (Include dates of Parent Teacher contacts)

Date	Progress Report I

Date	Progress Report II

Date	Progress Report III

Date	Progress Report IV

Figure 3.5 Screen Two.

46

END-OF-THE-YEAR RECOMMENDATION

COUNSELOR		DATE

Level III Interventions

Date	Parent Conference	Date	SARB
Date	Counseling-Group/Individual	Date	GAPP
	Days and Time	Date	Child Protective Services
	Counselor	Date	Juvenile Justice
		Date	Nutrition

LIFE SKILLS: (STAR & STAGES)

Date	Coping Skills	Date	Big Sisters/Brothers
Date	Stress Management	Date	ESL Classes
Date	Social Skills	Date	Family Counseling
Date	Decision Making	Date	AAA/AL-ANON-ALATEEN
Date	"Latch Key"	Date	Substance Abuse Treatment Program
			Agency
Date	Resistance Skills	Date	County Social Human Services
			Specify
Date	Self Esteem Fundamental	Date	County Mental Health
Date	Special Placement	Date	Outside Mental Health Provider
			Agency
Date	SB 65 Outreach Consultant	Date	Other
	Attendance _____Academic _____		
Date	Special Friend (Peer)		
	Name		
Date	Church		
	Minister		
Date	Community Service Council		

Figure 3.6 Screen Three, First Part.

47

Quarterly Progress Report: (Include dates of Parent Teacher contacts)

Date	Progress Report I

Date	Progress Report II

Date	Progress Report III

Date	Progress Report IV

END-OF-THE-YEAR RECOMMENDATION

Counselor

S.I.T. RECOMMENDATION	DATE

N.F.I.	LEVEL II	LEVEL III	DATE

Figure 3.6 (continued) Screen Three, Second Part.

forms. The form we show is for use in Healthy Start, a program which links schools and community agencies in order to prevent duplication of agency efforts in serving low-income students and their families. These forms are used in Duarte Unified School District, Duarte, California. Healthy Start runs on the Macintosh SE or the Macintosh II. We recommended that our Comprehensive Risk Assessment software, which is described in Chapter 5, be used to identify students who are at such high levels of risk that they need to be assisted by an SST or the equivalent.

POLICY RECOMMENDATION

In order to deal systematically with potential dropouts, each school should invest in some type of student information system that offers standard computer applications such as grade reporting, student scheduling, course history, period attendance and test scoring. Types of data include reasons for student referral, prereferral services, academic functioning in mathematics, reading and language arts, behavior in and out of the classroom, primary language, social agency background, previous special support at school, health background, period-by-period teacher evaluation and, if possible, a current survey of faculty to identify causes of dropout. For students who have dropped out, the school needs a master file with leave-destination categories and leave-reasons categories.

PREDICTING DROPOUT AND
IDENTIFYING SUBSTANCE ABUSERS

A model is described which will allow an administrator to predict when students will drop out if no special assistance is provided for them. These predictions are based on factors such as attendance, grade point average, reading scores, retention at grade level, mobility (moving from school to school) and adjustment factors. The latter factors include juvenile delinquency record, citizenship grades, special education history and physical disability. The student information system described in Chapter 3 should be configured so staff can easily compute dropout rate, holding power rate, continuous enrollment rate, mobility rate and attrition rate, all of which are defined in this chapter. All of these efforts should exist in a context of positive academic and personal counseling.

Substance abusers, especially drug users, may be identified through a number of variables including personal drug use, number of times the person has been high or drunk, whether the person has been suspended or expelled from school, the number of friends the individual has who use alcohol or drugs, the number of adults the person knows well that are frequent users of alcohol or drugs, how often the person feels angry, the person's perception of his/her family's feelings toward drug use, the extent one's family members know her/his whereabouts during free time and the number and frequency of his/her arrests. These abuse variables have been identified by Hawkins and Catalano (1989); Kovach and Glickman (1986); and Callison and his students Crabtree, Ehlers, Evans, Sakanari, Youngblood and Richards at California State University at Fullerton (Callison et al., 1990). The Fullerton study validated the variables listed above in a study carried out in the Pomona Unified School District, Pomona, California. The study included 400 eighth grade students in a multiracial junior high school. The items on our

Preparing to Identify Potential Dropouts.

Scantron forms for inputting these data are seen in Chapter 5 in Figure 5.1.

In our experience with Upward Bound in the mid-1960s, we recall little or no emphasis on activities to prevent dropout at the elementary school level. There is a great interest now, however, in focusing resources for dropout prevention in the elementary and junior high years. We like a prediction model developed by one of our students, Sappington, that indicates which students are likely to drop out at grades four, six and nine with an accuracy of 79 percent or better, depending on the grade level (Sappington, 1979). It is summarized in Table 4.1.

DEFINITION OF TERMS

Dropout

A student who leaves school or an educational program in the district before receiving a high school diploma or the equivalent, and who does

TABLE 4.1 Dropout prediction model.

ATTENDANCE	
GRADE	NUMBER OF ABSENCES PER YEAR
2–3	20 or more
4–5	25 or more
6–8	30 or more
9–11	35 or more
NUMBER OF D's AND F's	
GRADE	NUMBER PER YEAR
2–3	1 + D's
4–5	2 + D's
6–8	3 + D's/F's
9–11	4 + D's/F's
READING LEVEL	
GRADE	BELOW
2–3	40th percentile
4–5	35th percentile
6–8	30th percentile
9–11	25th percentile
RETENTION DURING SCHOOL HISTORY	
GRADE	NUMBER OF YEARS BEHIND
2–3	1 or more
4–5	1 or more
6–8	1 or more
9–11	1 or more
MOBILITY FROM SCHOOL/HOME	
GRADE	NUMBER OF MOVES*
2–3	1 or more
4–5	1 or more
6–8	2 or more
9–11	2 or more
ADJUSTMENT FACTORS	
Juvenile delinquency record	_____ (check if applicable)
Citizenship record	_____
Special education record	_____
Physical disabilities	_____

*School-to-school moves predict just as well as moves to a new home outside the district.

not enroll within forty-five school days in another school or educational program (Staff, 1986a). Exceptions to this include enrollment in programs which do not provide instruction leading to meeting the requirements for a high school diploma or the equivalent, death, confinement and illness without possibility of instruction.

Dropout Rate

The percentage of students who meet the definition of a dropout during an annual or cumulative time period.

- The annual dropout rate accounting period is established for a one-year period and includes the last day of school in one year to the last day of school the following year.
- The cumulative dropout rate accounting period is established for longer than a one-year time span. The accounting period might be, for example, the last day of eighth grade (incoming ninth graders) 1982, to the last day of school in 1986 (twelfth graders).
- The classification of a student who originally met the definition of a dropout shall be dropped if the student is reenrolled in a school or an educational program, has graduated or has met exemption criteria by the statewide day established for making an official student enrollment count.
- The official data accounting day will be enrollment count day, but revision to the official document may be made up to November 1.
- Verification of enrollment means transcript was sent, transcript was requested or other acceptable written verification has been recorded.
- To be classified a dropout the student must have been out of school for forty-five consecutive *school* days.
- A student leaving school before the end of a school year, when there are fewer than forty-five school days remaining in that year, is not to be counted as a dropout until after the forty-fifth day requirement is met in the following year. This student is then counted as a dropout for the year in which the forty-fifth day occurs.
- The dropout rate is established by dividing the official dropout

number by the total number of students who have entered during an accounting period.

Holding Power Rate

The reciprocal (inverse) of the dropout rate. Within a specific time period, the percentage of the total number of students who have entered, that stay to graduate and/or meet the reenrollment or exemption requirements (complete a specified educational level).

Continuous Enrollment Rate

The percentage of the total number of students who matriculated at the beginning of a designated period of time, and who maintained enrollment for the entire matriculation span (K–6, 7–8, 9–12).

Mobility Rate

The percentage of the total number of students entering in a cumulative time period or an annual time period, who leave prior to completion of that time period.

Attrition Rate

The reduction in class size, for whatever reason, over a given period of time. The rate is established by comparing the number of students graduating or completing an educational level, as compared to the number entering at the beginning of the time period specified.

ACADEMIC AND PERSONAL COUNSELING

All the technical efforts to predict which students will drop out, and when, will achieve nothing if they are not quickly communicated to caring staff members who will contact the student at risk and give him/her immediate help. One way to accomplish this would be the use of a network of computers which allow the counselors to access the student information system. Students should be given timely information about the relationship between the curricula they are taking and the options they will have once they have completed the courses. Special care should be given to prepare the students for a broad range of opportunities.

Counselors should have a good grasp of the curriculum options available and the steps a student should take to elect them. This may not be as difficult as communicating clearly the likely consequences of various choices. For students at risk who require considerable personal counseling and attention, counselors need to have appropriate training and information to offer both academic and personal assistance. Counselors should involve parents and/or guardians as much as possible in their conversations about the future, especially as they make the consequences of various choices clear.

A key part of an effective counseling effort, whether or not it is carried out by people called counselors, is to provide students with information about their competencies in key areas. It is a hollow effort if one is given fine advice about academic and job options, and no information is provided about whether one has the skills to pursue one of these options successfully.

NEGATIVE EFFECTS OF TRACKING

Although most educators know there are negative effects from tracking, teachers who work with students at risk see them daily. Goodlad says:

> Consistent with the findings of virtually every study that has considered the distribution of poor and minority students among track levels in schools, minority students were found in disproportionately large percentages in the low track classes of the multiracial schools in our sample . . . there appear to be in our data, then, clear evidences of tracking's differentiating students in regard to their access to knowledge and, further, doing so disproportionately for minority students, especially poor minority students. (Goodlad, 1984)

Tracking is an ugly business. What can an administrator do about it? The remarks of an anonymous teacher get right to the point.

> Of course, students with different skills are going to participate differently. If you are a student with below-grade-level reading, it's going to be harder for you to get the same experiences out of an experiment as someone well above grade level. You will need help in reading the sci-

ence book and help in writing your observations. The teacher will have to provide direct instruction in reading and writing in the context of the science unit. But that direct instruction will be in response to an immediate need of the student to complete an assignment that is inherently, intrinsically more interesting and engaging than marching through repetitive skill sheets. So we're not saying that skills instruction is unnecessary; we are saying that the curriculum should be organized sequentially around content and the skills instruction inserted into that curriculum. Thus, rather than exaggerating differences in ability levels, which creates seemingly insurmountable instructional management problems, we will be diminishing the impact of individual differences and reducing the complexity of the teacher's management task. It changes the whole classroom management situation; heterogeneous grouping becomes practical and possible. (Staff, 1986a)

POLICY RECOMMENDATION

Each district should consider an effort to decrease the dropout rate through initiating an academic and personal counseling program which focuses upon students at risk. Counselors or teachers serving in that role should be given training which prepares them to work with a variety of at-risk students in personal and academic areas. Special care should be given to prepare the at-risk student for a broad range of opportunities, including vocational training.

Chapter 5

IDENTIFYING AND PLACING STUDENTS AT RISK

In this chapter we describe a dropout and substance abuse prediction system which utilizes the Macintosh or IBM family of computers. The variables used for prediction have been mentioned in Chapter 4 and are familiar to the reader. We provide a list of the substance abuse prediction items as well as the dropout items. The reader then sees a printout from our Comprehensive Risk Assessment software, which can not only identify potential abusers and dropouts, but also schedule them into interventions. A sample student report screen is shown, as is the completion of interventions form.

COMPREHENSIVE RISK ASSESSMENT SOFTWARE

Software using an expert system called Comprehensive Risk Assessment (CRA) has been developed by Students-at-Risk, Inc. It is available for both Macintosh and IBM-compatible computers. An expert system is a kind of artificial intelligence program that mimics human logic within a specific area of expertise, in this case, the characteristics of at-risk students. Students self-report the needed data, which is then entered into the software. The expert system schedules identified students into appropriate interventions. These recent developments dramatically reduce the time required for a student study team or the equivalent to complete student placements.

It is important for potential users of the system to know that it is designed to supplement whatever approach a school is now using. Principals need to develop options that do not require additional resources. In our recent experience, this is the essential concept in working with

59

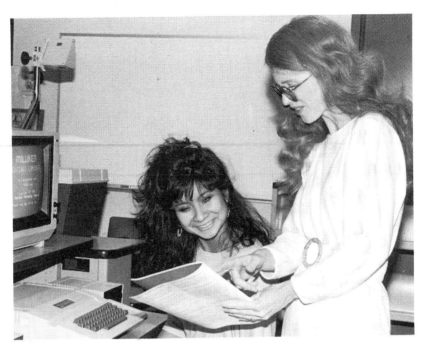

Planning Interventions.

school staff to initiate at-risk programming. With limited time available, teachers and other staff need to be guided to the most powerful interventions, and they must be the key players in developing them.

RESEARCH BASE FOR QUESTIONS

We have utilized research on risk factors for both substance abusers and dropouts to develop identification software. For substance abuse, we use the factors identified by J. David Hawkins (Hawkins et al., 1985) and validated by Richards-Colocino (1991). For dropouts we use variables identified by Sappington (1979). The Comprehensive Risk Assessment software we use is available for elementary and secondary levels in both English and Spanish. If you need them in additional languages, Students-at-Risk, Inc. can develop them for you upon request.

The questions, which appear in Figure 5.1, are on the CRA printed Scantron forms and also appear on the software screens in CRA.

Substance Abuse Questions (in the Comprehensive Risk Assessment software at the secondary level):

1. How frequently are you ANGRY?
   a) never
   b) sometimes
   c) frequently
   d) very frequently

2. How many of your FRIENDS or ASSOCIATES do you believe use alcohol or drugs?
   a) none
   b) 1 or 2
   c) 3 or 4
   d) 5 or more

3. How many ADULTS do you know well that are frequent users of alcohol or drugs?
   a) none
   b) 1 to 4
   c) 5 to 9
   d) more than 9

4. How many times have you been high or drunk?
   a) never
   b) once or twice
   c) 3 to 5 times
   d) 6 or more times

5. To what extent do you feel your family is AGAINST drugs?
   a) very much against
   b) quite a bit against
   c) a little against
   d) not against

6. When you are away from home, after school and evenings, how often do your parents know where you are?
   a) always
   b) usually
   c) seldom
   d) never

7. If a friend gave you marijuana and said that you're chicken if you don't try it, would you:
   a) not try it
   b) not sure what I would do
   c) try it

Dropout Questions:

8. How many times have you been ARRESTED?
   a) never
   b) 1 to 2
   c) 3 to 5
   d) more than 5

9. Have you ever been SUSPENDED or EXPELLED from school?
   a) yes
   b) no

10. How many D's and/or F's did you receive last semester? (6 maximum) _____

11. Have you ever been ARRESTED?
    a) yes
    b) no

12. Do you have a juvenile delinquency record?
    a) true
    b) false

13. Do you have a certifiable disability?
    a) true
    b) false

14. How many times last semester were you absent? _____

15. How many times have you moved or changed schools in the previous year? (maximum 6) _____

Figure 5.1 Risk Assessment Questionnaire.

The Comprehensive Risk Assessment software connects the identification of at-risk students with one or more of the interventions now available in your school. Student numbers are assigned for processing the student risk data. Only school staff who have direct responsibility for student advisement have lists of student names and ID numbers, so only they can identify students and connect them to their risk profiles.

INTERVENTION COMPLETION

Information about the extent to which staff are implementing interventions comes from the completion of interventions form from the

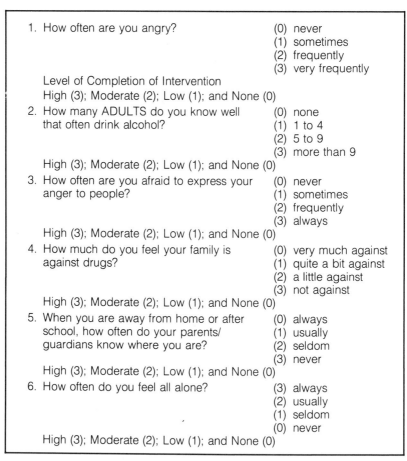

1. How often are you angry?
   (0) never
   (1) sometimes
   (2) frequently
   (3) very frequently

   Level of Completion of Intervention
   High (3); Moderate (2); Low (1); and None (0)

2. How many ADULTS do you know well that often drink alcohol?
   (0) none
   (1) 1 to 4
   (2) 5 to 9
   (3) more than 9

   High (3); Moderate (2); Low (1); and None (0)

3. How often are you afraid to express your anger to people?
   (0) never
   (1) sometimes
   (2) frequently
   (3) always

   High (3); Moderate (2); Low (1); and None (0)

4. How much do you feel your family is against drugs?
   (0) very much against
   (1) quite a bit against
   (2) a little against
   (3) not against

   High (3); Moderate (2); Low (1); and None (0)

5. When you are away from home or after school, how often do your parents/guardians know where you are?
   (0) always
   (1) usually
   (2) seldom
   (3) never

   High (3); Moderate (2); Low (1); and None (0)

6. How often do you feel all alone?
   (3) always
   (2) usually
   (1) seldom
   (0) never

   High (3); Moderate (2); Low (1); and None (0)

Figure 5.2 Completion of Interventions Form.

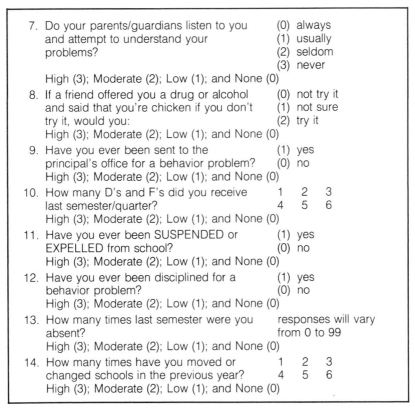

7. Do your parents/guardians listen to you and attempt to understand your problems?
   (0) always
   (1) usually
   (2) seldom
   (3) never
   High (3); Moderate (2); Low (1); and None (0)

8. If a friend offered you a drug or alcohol and said that you're chicken if you don't try it, would you:
   (0) not try it
   (1) not sure
   (2) try it
   High (3); Moderate (2); Low (1); and None (0)

9. Have you ever been sent to the principal's office for a behavior problem?
   (1) yes
   (0) no
   High (3); Moderate (2); Low (1); and None (0)

10. How many D's and F's did you receive last semester/quarter?
    1   2   3
    4   5   6
    High (3); Moderate (2); Low (1); and None (0)

11. Have you ever been SUSPENDED or EXPELLED from school?
    (1) yes
    (0) no
    High (3); Moderate (2); Low (1); and None (0)

12. Have you ever been disciplined for a behavior problem?
    (1) yes
    (0) no
    High (3); Moderate (2); Low (1); and None (0)

13. How many times last semester were you absent?
    responses will vary from 0 to 99
    High (3); Moderate (2); Low (1); and None (0)

14. How many times have you moved or changed schools in the previous year?
    1   2   3
    4   5   6
    High (3); Moderate (2); Low (1); and None (0)

Figure 5.2 (continued) Completion of Interventions Form.

Comprehensive Risk Assessment system (see Figure 5.2). A level of intervention completion for each CRA item is filled in by the school staff member responsible. When a pre/post test comparison of scores is made at the end of the testing period, the staff member can then check the level of intervention completion forms to see if any areas of no improvement resulted from staff not completing the interventions they agreed to implement.

Chapter 6

PLACING STUDENTS IN
INTERVENTIONS

This chapter presents a model for using the Comprehensive Risk Assessment system to place students into appropriate interventions. Each district needs a procedure for placing students into interventions. Since most districts have more at-risk students than existing staff can work with successfully, it is important to have a scientific, easily defensible means for prioritizing student needs. Districts can create their own approach or adapt the Comprehensive Risk Assessment (CRA) approach to their existing situation.

In the first district represented here each school takes a different approach to dropout prevention. There are no district approaches, and principals can pursue whatever strategies make sense to them and their staffs. To utilize the CRA approach, we began with a high school that has a dropout rate of about 20 percent. The dropout prevention effort the principal wanted to build the risk assessment system around was called Alternative to Suspension. Students could choose to work in a school for the physically handicapped rather than be suspended for a given period of time. Figure 6.1 is a sample student report and a description of the procedure for assignment of students into interventions for the secondary level.

(*1*) The first information to note is *032367* or some similar number. Each student will receive a number and will be identified by this number. (You will need access to the confidential key which links the number to the *name* of the student.) Note whether you are working with elementary or secondary students (secondary in this case), and whether you are working first with the substance abuse or the dropout prediction. Only areas of moderate or high risk are to receive interventions.

(2) Next, you will note that when you come to an area of moderate or high risk, *intervention is recommended.* Proceed to the next line to determine the area of risk.

(3) In this case, the subject of intervention is anger. Anger is the risk factor identified by the student and the area of concern, so you should arrange for interventions that are appropriate for an anger problem. See the section "The Questionnaire and Suggested Interventions," later in this chapter.

(4) An interview with the student is suggested. The level tells you what level of intervention may be beneficial. In this case, Level I is recommended. There are three levels of suggested interventions—Level I, Level II and Level III (see Figure 6.2).

Student # 032367   Version—Secondary

This student scored *0.19 on the substance abuse risk* assessment test which predicts a *medium* risk for substance abuse and scored *0.39 on the dropout risk* assessment which predicts a *high* risk for school dropout.

1. How often angry?—very frequently
   Use Level I, Level II and Level III interventions.
2. Friends who use alcohol or drugs?—5 or more
   Use Level I and Level II interventions.
3. Close adults who use alcohol or drugs frequently?—none
4. Times high or drunk?—once or twice
5. Family against drugs?—very much against
6. Parents know whereabouts?—always
7. Use if a friend dared you?—not sure what I would do
   Use Level I and Level II interventions.
8. Times arrested?—1 to 2
   Use Level I and Level II interventions.
9. Ever suspended or expelled?—yes
   Use Level I, Level II and Level III interventions.
10. Number of D's or F's?—3
11. Ever arrested?—yes
12. Juvenile delinquency record?—true
    Use Level I, Level II and Level III interventions.
13. Certified disability?—false
14. Times absent last semester?—10
15. Times moved or changed schools last year?—3
    Use Level I, Level II and Level III interventions.

Figure 6.1 Sample Comprehensive Risk Assessment Report.

1. The interventions suggested are in order of intensity, Level I requiring the least intensive intervention, and Level III the most intensive.

2. Teachers, counselors or administrators could provide most Level I or Level II responses as a part of their usual and expected interactions with students and parents. Level III interventions may include specialized programs and outside agencies.

3. In every instance that the student's response to the risk assessment questionnaire has triggered a suggested intervention, it is strongly recommended that you make at least a Level I response, which typically means a one-to-one interview with the student.

4. Level I interventions will suggest an individual meeting or interview with the student to gather more information. Suggestions for discussion will be offered. The Level I interview will help to ascertain whether Level II or Level III interventions will be most beneficial.

5. Level II interventions may suggest ongoing support by a teacher, counselor or mentor to monitor the student's situation. Ideas for skill building through particular programs may be noted, as well as possible referral to outside agencies for family counseling.

6. Level III interventions may be more immediate and acute. Specialized skills will be noted with interventions provided by school counselors or outside agencies, depending on the need and resources available at your site.

   In schools with counselors, Level III interventions might typically be provided by them. However, with special programs, training and support, interventions could also be provided by teachers. For example, many schools already have programs in place to provide drug and alcohol education as well as programs to foster self-esteem and communication skills.

   If a suggested Level III intervention does not seem to fall within any program you presently have, you may be able to use the intervention description to design your own intervention, or to refer the student/family to an outside agency.

   Educators are strongly urged to consult with others before undertaking Level III responses. Depending upon your school situation, you might consult with another teacher, with an appropriate administrator, with the school counselor and/or psychologist or with the student study team.

7. Since it is the student who decides how to respond to each question, it is also helpful for educators to use their knowledge and experience in interpreting the responses. For example, Question 1 asks: How often are you angry? The responses include: "never," "sometimes," "frequently" and "very frequently." What one student considers *frequently* may seem to peers and teachers to be *very frequently,* or, on the other hand, to be only *sometimes*. It all depends on the student's frame of reference. In deciding what level of intervention is necessary, it is helpful to look at what you know of—and can learn about—the student, in addition to the student's responses to the questionnaire.

Figure 6.2 Explanation of the Levels of Intervention.

GUIDELINES FOR COMPLETING
THE INTERVENTION COMPLETION QUESTIONNAIRE

Areas requiring interventions are the only questions to be completed. The list of required interventions is on the student pretest questionnaire. There are four degrees of implementation: high, moderate, low and none.

To receive a rating of *high,* the student/family must have:

- participated in the appropriate levels of intervention; that is, if Levels I, II and III are required, all three were received
- completed *all* the intervention activities; for example, in the suggested interventions under Level I, all the suggestions would have been implemented

To receive a rating of *moderate,* the student/family must have:

- participated in the appropriate levels of intervention; that is, if Levels I, II and III are required, all three were received
- completed *many* of the needed intervention activities; for example, in the suggested interventions under Level I, many of the suggestions would have been implemented

To receive a rating of *low,* the student/family must have:

- participated in *some* of the appropriate levels of intervention; that is, if Levels I, II and III are required, at least one was received
- completed *some* of the intervention activities; for example, in the suggested interventions under Level I, some of the suggestions would have been implemented

To receive a rating of *none,* the student/family must have:

- participated in *none* of the appropriate levels of intervention; that is, if Levels I, II and III are required, none were received
- completed *none* of the intervention activities; for example, in the suggested interventions under Level I, none of the suggestions would have been implemented

A sample of a completion of intervention form is shown in Figure 6.3.

Student # 032367   Version—Secondary

This student scored *0.20 on the substance abuse risk* assessment test which predicts a *medium* risk for substance abuse and scored *0.11 on the dropout risk* assessment which predicts a *low* risk for school dropout. Write the level of intervention completion (none = 0, low = 1, moderate = 2, high = 3) under the recommended level.

  1. How often angry?—very frequently
       Use Level I, Level II and Level III interventions.
          2   3   1

  2. Friends who use alcohol or drugs?—3 or 4
       Use Level I and Level II interventions.
          2   0

  3. Close adults who use alcohol or drugs frequently?—1 or 4

  4. Times high or drunk?—3 to 5 times

  5. Family against drugs?—a little against

  6. Parents know whereabouts?—seldom

  7. Use if a friend dared you?—not sure what I would do

  8. Times arrested?—1 to 2
       Use Level I and Level II interventions.
          2   2

  9. Ever suspended or expelled?—yes

10. Number of D's or F's?—1

11. Ever arrested?—no

12. Juvenile delinquency record?—false

13. Certified disability?—true

14. Times absent last semester?—00

15. Times moved or changed schools last year?—2

Figure 6.3 Sample Completion of Intervention Report.

THE QUESTIONNAIRE AND SUGGESTED INTERVENTIONS

Question 1

How often are you angry? (0) never, (1) sometimes, (2) frequently, (3) very frequently

If the student responds with a score of 2 or higher, you will be directed to one of the following interventions, which will be noted on the computerized score.

Level I

Interview the student for reasons, in order to select the appropriate intervention/s.

First, establish a caring and helpful environment/relationship with the student so that the student will trust you enough to give you information.

You may share some information about yourself, that you care about students, that you work on special programs, that you experienced some challenging times growing up, etc., whatever may be appropriate.

Suggestions for discussion topics include: Tell me about your day. Is there a particular time of the day you notice anger? Is there a particular situation/person (teacher, peer, parent, important relationship, etc.) that triggers anger for you? Have you gone through any family or relationship changes in the last few years?

This initial interview may show you what additional interventions, if any, are needed. For example, if a student's anger is a result of inadequate social skills, identifying and teaching particular skills may be helpful. If the anger is due to a family crisis, other responses will be more appropriate.

Level II

If indicated by the computer recommendation, or information gathered in the interview, assign the student to a mentor, counselor or peer assistant, who can provide ongoing support and monitoring of the student's situation. If your school does not have a mentoring program in place, this may be done informally. The mentor needs to have regularly scheduled contact with the student, and provide evidence that there is someone who cares. This might involve help with schoolwork or other problems, sending a birthday card and other little notes and occasional activities together.

Level II interventions may also include informal discussion and brainstorming of alternative behaviors and teaching of social skills or self-esteem fundamentals.

If no mentors are available at your site, consider referral to an outside group which offers mentors. Sample programs may include Big Sisters/Brothers, college or business mentoring programs.

Level III

Level III interventions will vary according to the reasons for the student's anger. Possible interventions are:

(*1*) If the student's anger is due to a crisis in her/his personal life — birth of a sibling, divorce, serious illness or death in the family, etc. — teach coping skills such as recognizing feelings of anger, control issues and depression; coming to terms with problems and learning to hope. Sample programs may include student individual or group counseling and STAGES. You can contact your county department of education or the equivalent to get the names, addresses and telephone numbers of firms that publish materials for prevention programs that you can use for Level III interventions.

(*2*) Teaching stress management skills may also be helpful. Sample programs may include STAR, STAGES, etc.

(*3*) If the student's anger is due to lack of social skills, teach communication skills, skills for making friends, etc., as appropriate. Sample programs may include STAR, etc.

(*4*) If the student's anger is due to deep-seated family or social problems, consider referral for individual and/or family counseling.

Question 2

How many adults do you know well that often drink alcohol? (0) none, (1) 1 to 4, (2) 5 to 9, (3) more than 9

If the student's response is 1 or higher, the following interventions may be recommended on your computer readout. Please note that with this question, a Level I response is necessary with a 1 response rather than a 2. It only takes *one* adult in the family who drinks alcohol often to put a child at risk.

Level I

Interview the student for reasons, in order to select the appropriate intervention/s.

First, establish a caring and helpful environment/relationship with the student so that the student will trust you enough to give you information.

You may share some information about yourself, that you care about students, that you work on special programs, that you experienced some challenging times growing up, etc., whatever may be appropriate.

Suggestions for discussion topics include: Tell me about your day. What is it that you have noticed about alcohol? Who do you know that drinks often? How do you feel about that/what do you think about that? How does that person's drinking affect you/your family/your schoolwork? What happens when this person drinks? (Be sure to reassure the student you are there to help, and that there is someone who cares.) Have you or your family gone through any changes in the last few years? The information in this interview may be critical in checking for child abuse.

This initial interview may show you what additional interventions, if any, are needed.

Discovering what role the adults who drink often play in the student's life will determine what level of intervention to implement. If parents or other important figures are substance abusers, Level III responses will almost surely be needed. If the student's relationship to substance abusing adults is not very significant, Level II responses may be sufficient.

Level II

If indicated by the computer recommendation, or information gathered in the interview, assign the student to a mentor or counselor, who can provide ongoing support and monitoring of the student's situation. If your school does not have a mentoring program in place, this may be done informally. The mentor needs to have regularly scheduled contact with the student and provide evidence that there is someone who cares. This might involve help with schoolwork or other problems, sending a birthday card and other little notes and occasional activities together.

You may consider assigning the student to drug and alcohol education programs which provide information about the requirements of a healthy body, the physical and social effects of drug abuse, the symptoms of drug abuse and learning to say *no*, etc. Sample programs may include STAR, QUEST, OSS, DARE, PAL, etc.

Level III

Consider referring student and/or family to outside social agencies for family counseling and/or drug/alcohol programs. Sample programs may include AA, specialized community hospital programs, county programs, child protective services, etc.

If needed, refer student for special programs for the children of substance abusers, which can help the student to understand that she/he is not responsible for the behavior of substance abusing adults, and provide coping skills. Sample programs may include STAGES, Children Are People Too, BABES, as well as city and county programs.

If appropriate, arrange for teaching latchkey skills for the child whose parents are not able to care adequately for him/her. Sample programs may include checking with your county office of education, city programs, etc.

If the exposure to drug-abusing adults is so serious that a referral to child protective services (CPS) is indicated, keep in contact with the student as he/she proceeds through this process. Children often feel abandoned and at fault when CPS is involved. Reassure the child that she/he is courageous, and that telling the truth is important. The child is not responsible for the substance or other abuse! Involve administrators and other appropriate and available personnel in this decision. If there is evidence for such a referral from your initial interview with the student, you need to proceed directly to this level of intervention after the interview.

Question 3

How often are you afraid to express your anger to people? (0) never, (1) sometimes, (2) frequently, (3) always

If the student's response is 2 or higher, the following interventions may be recommended on your computer readout.

Level I

Interview the student for reasons, in order to select the appropriate intervention/s.

First, establish a caring and helpful environment/relationship with the student so that the student will trust you enough to give you information.

You may share some information about yourself, that you care about students, that you work on special programs, that you experienced some challenging times growing up, etc., whatever may be appropriate.

Suggestions for discussion topics include: Tell me about your day. What situations bring about anger for you? What do people do that really bothers you? How do you think people usually experience anger? What do you think about anger? What happens when people get angry? What is the worst thing you can think of that might happen to a person who expresses anger? What else? Who would be the most difficult person to show your anger to? What might happen? What do people do when they are really upset? Have you gone through any family changes in the past few years? What changes has your family experienced? This initial interview may show you what additional interventions, if any, are needed.

Level II

If a student's inability to express anger seems to be primarily a function of confusion about anger, whether from inadequate modeling, and/or a lack of information, provide education on appropriate and inappropriate expressions of anger. Explain that anger is a natural emotion. Brainstorm healthy ways of expressing and managing anger. You could model appropriate angry behavior. Infuse such modeling and discussion into the daily life of the classroom, monitoring the student's progress informally. Sample programs may include STAGES, etc.

You may want to consider the appropriateness of a simple behavior modification program for the student, such as a system of rewards for appropriate expressions of anger. Remember that an elaborate program need not be designed—the system may be as simple as an agreement between you and the student that you will send her/him a private signal of congratulations when she/he expresses anger appropriately.

Level III

If the student needs to learn to communicate thoughts and feelings assertively, use a communication skills program to teach these skills. Sample programs may include STAR, YES, PAL, etc.

If the student's fear of expressing anger is appropriate, as in the case of an abusive parent, refer to appropriate personnel and agencies — school administration, counselor and/or psychologist, child protective services, etc. — keeping in contact with the student as she/he goes through this often-confusing process. Reassure the child that she/he is not at fault and is a courageous person for sharing the truth with you. Let the child know you will not abandon him/her.

Question 4

How much do you feel your family is against drugs? (0) very much against, (1) quite a bit against, (2) a little against, (3) not against

If the student's response is 2 or higher, the following interventions may be recommended on your computer readout.

Level I

Interview the student for reasons, in order to select the appropriate intervention/s.

First, establish a caring and helpful environment/relationship with the student so that the student will trust you enough to give you information.

You may share some information about yourself, that you care about students, that you work on special programs, that you experienced some challenging times growing up, etc., whatever may be appropriate.

Suggestions for discussion topics include: Is she/he simply unaware of the family's attitude because the topic isn't discussed? Are the parents articulately in favor of drug use? How can you tell people in your family feel that way? What have you been told about drugs? What have you seen happen when people use drugs? Do you know anyone who might think drugs are OK? The responses will tell you what additional response, if any, is required.

Level II

Counsel with parents about the need for values clarification. Would parent education be appropriate and acceptable? Sample programs may include district and/or police department parent education programs, Neighborhoods in Action, Active Parenting, etc.

Consider assigning the student to drug and alcohol education programs which provide information about the requirements of a healthy body, the physical and social effects of drug abuse, the symptoms of drug abuse and learning to say *no*. Sample programs may include STAR, QUEST, OSS, DARE, PAL, etc.

Level III

If you note a crisis situation, consider referring student and/or family to outside social agencies for family counseling and/or drug/alcohol programs. Sample programs may include AA, specialized hospital programs, city and county programs, etc. Also, listen for signs of child abuse and make the appropriate reports, if necessary (including child protective services), reassuring the child as she/he goes through the process.

If indicated, refer student for special programs for the children of substance abusers, which can help the student to understand that she/he is not responsible for the behavior of substance abusing adults, and provide coping skills. Sample programs may include STAGES, Children Are People Too, BABES and other city and county programs.

If appropriate, arrange for teaching latchkey skills to the child whose parents are not able to care adequately for him/her. Sample programs: check on available city/county/district programs which best fit student's needs.

Question 5

When you are away from home, or after school, how often do your parents/guardians know where you are? (0) always, (1) usually, (2) seldom, (3) never

If the student's response is 2 or higher, the following interventions may be recommended on your computer printout.

Level I

Interview the student for reasons, in order to select the appropriate intervention/s.

First, establish a caring and helpful environment/relationship with the student so that the student will trust you enough to give you information.

You may share some information about yourself, that you care about students, that you work on special programs, that you experienced some challenging times growing up, etc., whatever may be appropriate.

Topics for discussion may include: Does the family have a child-care problem? Have the parents indicated that they don't care where the student is? Is there evidence that the parents feel they can't control the student? What would happen if your parents did know what you are doing? Has your family gone through any major changes in the last few years? How do people in your family feel? What do people in your family think about? What would happen if something happened to you while you were out? How does your family feel about your friends? At what age do you think kids can take care of themselves? How do you know that? The responses will tell you what additional response, if any, is required.

Level II

Interview the parents. The family may need referral to after-school-care programs such as latchkey programs operated by the YMCA/ YWCA, local colleges or the district, Girls' Club/Boys' Club, etc. Parents may need referral to district or outside programs for parent effectiveness training—need for setting limits, communicating with children, etc.

If indicated by the computer recommendation, or information gathered in the interview, assign the student to a mentor, counselor or peer assistant, who can provide ongoing support and monitoring of the student's situation. If your school does not have a mentoring program in place, this may be done informally. The mentor needs to have regularly scheduled contact with the student and provide evidence that there is someone who cares. This might involve help with schoolwork or other problems, sending a birthday card and other little notes and occasional activities together.

Level III

Lack of supervision may be so serious that a referral to child protective services is indicated because of neglect. Involve administrators and other appropriate and available personnel in this decision. If there is evidence for such a referral from your initial interview with the student, you need to proceed directly to this level of intervention after the interview.

The student may need close monitoring at school, having someone to check in with several times a day. The mentor should show care and concern in a benevolent manner.

Question 6

How often do you feel all alone? (3) always, (2) usually, (1) seldom, (0) never

If the student's response is 2 or higher, the following interventions may be recommended on your computer readout (note that the numbering is different on this question).

Level I

Interview the student for reasons, in order to select the appropriate intervention/s.

First, establish a caring and helpful environment/relationship with the student so that the student will trust you enough to give you information.

You may share some information about yourself, that you care about students, that you work on special programs, that you experienced some challenging times growing up, etc., whatever may be appropriate.

Topics for discussion may include: Tell me about your day. Is the student lonely due to problems making friends? If that is the problem, is it shyness, being new or the fact that something about the student's behavior causes his peers to reject him? Has your family gone through any changes in the last few years? How does it feel for you to be alone? What do you think about? What happens when you get home from school? What do you and your family do after school, in the evening, on the weekend? What kinds of things make people sad? What happens when people feel sad? (If you sense the student may be depressed, check with counselors, school psychologists, etc., for intervention on Level III.) Choose appropriate Level II and/or Level III interventions according to the results of this interview.

Level II

If indicated by the computer recommendation, or information gathered in the interview, assign the student to a mentor, counselor or peer assistant, who can provide ongoing support and monitoring of the student's situation. If your school does not have a mentoring program in place, this may be done informally. The mentor needs to have regularly scheduled contact with the student and provide evidence that there is someone who cares. This might involve help with schoolwork or other problems, sending a birthday card and other little notes and occasional activities together.

It may also be helpful to assign a special friend to the student. Your school may have a mechanism for doing this: leadership team, peer assistance team, PAL, etc. If not, make use of your contact with, and knowledge of, other students to find one who would enjoy doing this, and who would also be in contact with you or other mentors, so that the peer does not feel responsible for the identified student's behavior.

Level III

If the student has been through family changes and is feeling sad, she/he may not understand this natural emotion. Sample programs may include STAGES, etc., to help children manage reactions to changes. The need may be in the area of social skills. Sample programs may include STAR, Here's Looking at You 2000, etc., that can help a student learn assertive social skills to reach out to peers.

If the student seems depressed, referral of student to school/community counseling services may be necessary. Family referral to outside agencies may also be helpful. If the family has been through a major change, parenting resources through STAGES or other grief, adjustment or loss programs may be helpful.

Question 7

Do your parents/guardians listen to you and attempt to understand your problems? (0) always, (1) usually, (2) seldom, (3) never

If the student's response is 2 or higher, the following interventions may be recommended on your computer readout.

Level I

Interview the student for reasons, in order to select the appropriate intervention/s.

First, establish a caring and helpful environment/relationship with the student so that the student will trust you enough to give you information.

You may share some information about yourself, that you care about students, that you work on special programs, that you experienced some challenging times growing up, etc., whatever may be appropriate.

Topics for discussion may include: Whom do you share your thoughts and feelings with at school/home? What happens when you get home from school, in the evening, on the weekend? When do people in your family talk? What happens when people in your family talk together? How do you feel during the day? Check to see if parents' hectic work schedule makes it difficult to provide support. Has your family been through any big changes in the last few years? Is there evidence that parents are unaware of the importance of listening to their children? The student's response to these questions will suggest what level of intervention would be beneficial, if any.

Level II

It may be helpful to conduct a parent conference. The content will be a function of the results of the student interview and the responses the parent makes during this conference. It may be that the family is experiencing a crisis, or has many demands and needs referral to outside agencies. The parent may need/desire parent education. This education may simply take the form of the communication that occurs at this conference — the parent becomes aware of the student's feelings and understands the significance of her/his responsiveness. If more education is needed, it might be provided by the school counselor or psychologist, or by a district parenting class. Sample programs may include STAGES for parents, Active Parenting, city and county programs, etc.

Teaching the student social skills to express thoughts and feelings may be beneficial. Modeling, sharing and teaching social conversation and listening skills may be needed. Sample programs may include STAR, Here's Looking at You 2000, etc.

Level III

The student may be experiencing some kind of life crisis – birth of a sibling, serious illness or death of a family member or other significant person, family financial crisis, divorce, etc. If so, provide support and instruction in coping skills – such as recognizing feelings of anger, control issues and depression; coming to terms with problems and learning to hope. Sample programs may include student counseling groups, STAGES, grief and loss information, etc.

Referral to counseling – if the student is angry or depressed, it may be helpful to spend time with the school counselor or psychologist for additional support. It may also be important to refer the student and/or family for individual and/or family counseling or district/city/county programs.

Question 8

If a friend offered you a drug or alcohol and said that you're chicken if you don't try it, what would you do? (0) not try it, (1) not sure, (2) try it

If the student's response is 1 or higher, the following interventions may be recommended on your computer readout.

Level I

Interview the student for reasons, in order to select the appropriate intervention/s.

First, establish a caring and helpful environment/relationship with the student so that the student will trust you enough to give you information.

You may share some information about yourself, that you care about students, that you work on special programs, that you experienced some challenging times growing up, etc., whatever may be appropriate.

Topics for discussion may include: How many friends do you have? What do friends do together? What happens if a person does not have any friends? What does being a friend mean to you? Do you know what peer pressure is? How do most people handle peer pressure? Why do you think people have a hard time saying *no?* Have you and/or your family gone through any big changes in the last few years? The responses will suggest what additional interventions, if any, are needed.

Level II

If indicated by the computer recommendation, or information gathered in the interview, assign the student to a mentor, counselor or peer assistant, who can provide ongoing support and monitoring of the student's situation. If your school does not have a mentoring program in place, this may be done informally. The mentor needs to have regularly scheduled contact with the student and provide evidence that there is someone who cares. This might involve help with schoolwork or other problems, sending a birthday card and other little notes and occasional activities together.

Consider assigning the student to drug and alcohol education programs which provide information about the requirements of a healthy body, the physical and social effects of drug abuse, the symptoms of drug abuse and learning to say *no.* Sample programs may include STAR, QUEST, OSS, DARE, PAL, etc.

Level III

Consider training the student in refusal and assertiveness skills beyond those offered in standard drug education programs. Sample programs may include STAR, individual counseling, etc.

If the student's response is 3, that she/he would try it, proceed with all the interventions suggested above, and consider these additional responses.

Assign the student to a school counseling group focused upon special problems and/or substance abuse. If this is unavailable, consider individual counseling at school and/or individual or group counseling at an outside facility.

Conduct a parent conference, if you suspect the student already is (or may soon become) involved with drugs. The conference may reveal a need for parent education programs. Sample programs may include district or police department programs for parents about drug abuse, Neighborhoods in Action, district Tough Love programs, Active Parenting, etc.

If the student is experiencing a life crisis, consider teaching skills for coping – recognizing feelings of anger, control issues and depression; coming to terms with problems and learning to hope. Sample programs may include STAGES, city and county programs, etc.

Consider referral to outside programs or agencies aimed at student users or near users, such as those offered by some police and probation departments.

Question 9

Have you ever been sent to the principal's office for a behavior problem? (1) yes, (0) no

If student's response is *yes,* the following interventions may be recommended on your computer readout.

Level I

Interview the student for reasons, in order to select the appropriate intervention/s.

First, establish a caring and helpful environment/relationship with the student so that the student will trust you enough to give you information.

You may share some information about yourself, that you care about students, that you work on special programs, that you experienced some challenging times growing up, etc., whatever may be appropriate.

Topics for discussion may include: How many times have you been sent to the principal's office? What is your version of what happened (choose one or more occasions)? Tell me about the kids at school. What happens during your day, after school, evenings, weekends? Have your and/or your family gone through any big changes in the last few years? What kinds of things make you angry? How do people usually express anger? What happens to them? How are you doing in class? What do you think about your teacher? What does your teacher think about you? What subject(s) do you like/not like? What consequences do you have at school/home for seeing the principal?

The responses will guide your choice of any additional interventions.

Level II

If indicated by the computer recommendation, or information gathered in the interview, assign the student to a mentor, counselor or peer assistant, who can provide ongoing support and monitoring of the student's situation. If your school does not have a mentoring program in place, this may be done informally. The mentor needs to have regularly scheduled contact with the student and provide evidence that there is someone who cares. This might involve help with schoolwork or other problems, sending a birthday card and other little notes and occasional activities together.

Consider referral to a school counselor, if available. Consider a behavior modification program focused on reducing the number of incidents of misbehavior and/or referrals, rewarding the student for appropriate behavior, etc.

Hold a parent conference. Is behavior the same at home? If not, what does the parent think is wrong at school? If behavior is the same at home, offer help. If appropriate, discuss some of the following options as possible steps the family might take. Sample programs may include STAGES for parents, Active Parenting, district/city/county programs, etc.

Provide new responsibilities as alternative activities to replace the patterns that have gotten the student into trouble. Provide opportunities for involvement in clubs, scouts, etc. Give the student a special responsibility (something active) at school, and recognition for completion.

Provide academic assistance if behavior problems are related to academic problems. Sample programs may include tutoring, peer tutoring, ESL, changing student's program, referral to the student study team or help for parents on how to work with the child at home.

Level III

Provide instruction in social skills if a student's misbehavior reflects lack of knowledge in interpersonal communication, and/or lack of social skills that lead to aggressive responses. Consider special instruction in these areas: understanding one's own personality style, making friends, being a friend, communicating needs, etc. Sample programs may include STAR, PAL, etc.

If the behaviors seem connected to a lack of interpersonal skills and relationships with peers, consider assigning a special friend to the student to give the student recognition and extra attention. Sample programs may include peer assistance programs, PAL, etc.

Consider referral for individual and/or group counseling for the student and family counseling within the district/city/county, if the student's behavior is due to deep-seated family or social problems.

Monitor frequency and severity of referrals to the principal, to see if problems persist.

Question 10

How many D's and F's did you receive last semester/quarter? 1, 2, 3, 4, 5, 6

If the student's response is 2 or higher, the following interventions may be recommended on your computer readout.

Level I

Interview the student for reasons, in order to select the appropriate intervention/s.

First, establish a caring and helpful environment/relationship with the student so that the student will trust you enough to give you information.

You may share some information about yourself, that you care about students, that you work on special programs, that you experienced some challenging times growing up, etc., whatever may be appropriate.

Topics for discussion may include: What do you think of/feel about school? What do you think of your teacher? What is your favorite/least favorite subject? Tell me what happens after school, evenings, weekends. Have you and/or your family gone through any big changes? Who do you hang around with at school? What is the hardest thing about school? Is there anyone to help you at home? What year in school was your best/most difficult? You may need to check the cumulative file, especially for younger students. Is there a language or other learning difficulty? Responses to these questions will identify what, if any, interventions may be helpful.

Level II

If indicated by the computer recommendation, or information gathered in the interview, assign the student to a mentor, counselor or peer assistant, who can provide ongoing support and monitoring of the student's situation. If your school does not have a mentoring program in place, this may be done informally. The mentor needs to have regularly scheduled contact with the student and provide evidence that there is someone who cares. This might involve help with schoolwork or other problems, sending a birthday card and other little notes and occasional activities together.

Parent conference—explore the same topics you covered in the interview with the student. In addition, does parent appear to need help with parenting skills and/or training in how to help a child with schoolwork? You may be able to do this parent education during the conference. If more help is needed, refer the parent to school parenting and/or homework workshops, if available. Refer to outside programs if needed and available.

Provide academic assistance. Assign a tutor, if available, or guide student to outside tutoring programs. Arrange for, or provide instruction in, English as a second language, if needed.

Consider using a behavior modification program with the student, such as a daily contract for getting work done on time and correctly, with an appropriate system of positive responses.

Level III

Refer student to the student study team for evaluation and recommendations if there appear to be severe academic problems.

Refer student for counseling if the academic problems seem to be a function of personal problems. If the student is experiencing a life crisis, consider teaching skills for coping—recognizing feelings of anger, control issues and depression; coming to terms with problems and learning to hope. Sample programs may include STAGES, small group counseling, PAL, etc.

Question 11

Have you ever been suspended or expelled from school? (1) yes, (0) no

If the student's response is *yes,* the following interventions may be recommended on your computer readout.

Level I

Interview the student for reasons, in order to select the appropriate intervention/s.

First, establish a caring and helpful environment/relationship with the student so that the student will trust you enough to give you information.

You may share some information about yourself, that you care about students, that you work on special programs, that you experienced some challenging times growing up, etc., whatever may be appropriate.

Topics for discussion may include: What do you think of/feel about school? What happened to cause you to be suspended? How are things at home? When did things get tough here at school? How are your relationships going (friends, family, etc.)? Is there anything you feel really angry about now? Have you or your family been through any big changes in the last few years/this year? (Check cumulative file.) How many times have you been suspended? What happens at home when this occurs? The student's response will guide you in deciding which additional interventions, if any, are needed.

Level II

If indicated by the computer recommendations, or information gathered in the interview, assign the student to a mentor or counselor, who can provide ongoing support and monitoring of the student's situation. If your school does not have a mentoring program in place, this may be done informally. The mentor needs to have regularly scheduled contact with the student and provide evidence that there is someone who cares. This might involve help with schoolwork or other problems, sending a birthday card and other little notes and occasional activities together.

Assign student to a peer advisor if your school offers such a program, particularly if the suspension may be partially a function of a poor choice of friends. Sample programs may include peer assistance programs, PAL, etc.

Parent conference—explore the same topics you covered in the interview with the student. In addition, does the parent appear to need help with parenting skills and/or training in how to help a child with behavior/anger management, etc.? You may be able to do this parent education during the conference. If more help is needed, refer the parent to school parenting and/or district/city/county workshops, etc. Refer to outside programs if needed and available.

Level III

If indicated, arrange for instruction in social skills if student's misbehavior reflects lack of knowledge in interpersonal communication and/or lack of social skills. Consider special instruction in these areas: understanding one's own personality style, making friends, being a friend, communicating needs, etc. Sample programs may include STAR, PAL, etc.

Refer student to the student study team for evaluation and recommendations, if there appear to be severe academic/behavior problems.

Refer student/family for individual or group counseling if the expulsions or suspensions seem to be a function of personal problems. If the student is experiencing a life crisis, consider teaching skills for coping—recognizing feelings of anger, control issues and depression; coming to terms with problems and learning to hope. Sample programs may include STAGES, small group counseling, etc.

Question 12

Have you ever been disciplined for a behavior problem? (1) yes, (0) no

If the student's response is *yes,* the following interventions are recommended.

Level I

Interview the student for reasons, in order to select the appropriate intervention/s.

First, establish a caring and helpful environment/relationship with the student so that the student will trust you enough to give you information.

You may share some information about yourself, that you care about students, that you work on special programs, that you experienced some challenging times growing up, etc., whatever may be appropriate.

Topics for discussion may include: What do you think of/feel about school? What happened when you were in trouble? How many times this year were you disciplined for behavior problems? Has this happened in other years at school? What was your best year in school? What was it you liked about that year? What was your worst year? Did anything happen that stands out in your mind? Have you or family members gone through any big changes? What do you do after school, evenings, weekends? How do people in your family usually handle anger? What happens? Usually students who are disciplined at school have a lot on their minds. What is happening in your life? Who do you hang around with at school/after school? The responses will guide your choice of interventions.

Level II

If indicated by the computer recommendation, or information gathered in the interview, assign the student to a mentor or counselor, who can provide ongoing support and monitoring of the student's situation. If your school does not have a mentoring program in place, this may be done informally. The mentor needs to have regularly scheduled contact with the student, and provide evidence that there is someone who cares. This might involve help with schoolwork or other problems, sending a birthday card and other little notes and occasional activities together.

Monitor frequency and severity of problems, to see if problems persist. Consider referral to a school counselor, if available. Consider a behavior modification program focused on reducing the number of incidents of misbehavior and/or referrals, with appropriate rewards.

Hold a parent conference. Is behavior the same at home? If not, what does the parent think is wrong at school? If behavior is the same at home, offer help. If appropriate, discuss some of the following options as possible steps the family might take. Sample programs may include STAGES for parents, Active Parenting, district/city/county programs.

If the behaviors seem to be a cry for attention, consider assigning a student special friend to give the student recognition and extra attention. Sample programs may include PAL, peer assistance programs, etc.

Giving the student a special responsibility at school might also help.

Suggest new activities if the student needs alternative activities to replace the patterns that have gotten her/him into trouble. Provide opportunities for involvement in clubs, scouts, etc.

Level III

Arrange for instruction in social skills if the student's misbehavior reflects a lack of knowledge in interpersonal communication and/or social skills. Consider special instruction in understanding one's own personality style, making friends, being a friend, communicating needs, etc. Sample programs may include STAR, PAL, etc.

Refer student to the student study team for evaluation and recommendations if there appear to be severe academic/behavior problems.

Refer the student/family for individual or group counseling, if the behaviors seem to be a function of personal problems. If the student is experiencing a life crisis, consider teaching coping skills – recognizing feelings of anger, control issues and depression; coming to terms with problems and learning to hope. Sample programs may include STAGES, small group counseling, etc.

Question 13

How many times last semester were you absent? (responses will vary from 0 to 99)

This number is designed for schools where a high absence rate is typical. The critical number may be less than twenty in some schools;

consider the normal attendance profile for your school. If the student's response is 2 or higher, the following interventions may be recommended on your computer readout.

Level I

Interview the student for reasons, in order to select the appropriate intervention/s.

First, establish a caring and helpful environment/relationship with the student so that the student will trust you enough to give you information.

You may share some information about yourself, that you care about students, that you work on special programs, that you experienced some challenging times growing up, etc., whatever may be appropriate.

Topics for discussion may include: What kinds of things keep you at home? (Check cumulative file or other records for a pattern of excessive absences.) What do you think of school this year? What do you like/dislike? Tell me about your friends. What do you think of your teacher this year? What does your teacher think about you? Have you or a family member been through any big changes (new baby, financial, divorce, loss, moving, etc.)? What happens when you get sick? Who takes care of you? (Does the student have a neglected or undetected health problem? If indicated, consider additional interventions, working with your school nurse or community health programs.) How are things at home? (Check for any signs of abuse and make appropriate reports to your school team and child protective services.) Responses in this interview will direct you to other interventions, if any.

Level II

Monitor student absence. Consider a behavior modification program to improve attendance – some schools have special attendance clubs. Individual teachers can also design a program of attendance incentives.

Assign student to an adult mentor, to increase student's bonding to school – many students are convinced that, "Nobody cares whether I'm here or not. They probably don't even notice." If indicated by the computer recommendation or information gathered in the interview, assign the student to a mentor or counselor, who can provide ongoing support and monitoring of the student's situation. If your school does not have a mentoring program in place, this may be done informally. The mentor needs to have regularly scheduled contact with the student, and provide evidence that there is someone who cares. This might involve help with schoolwork or other problems, sending a birthday card and other little notes and occasional activities together.

Refer student or family to school nurse or outside health provider, if student has (or may have) unmet health needs.

If the behaviors seem to be a cry for attention, consider assigning a student special friend to give the student recognition and extra attention. Sample programs may include PAL, peer assistance programs, etc.

If the student indicates that she/he was absent for reasons other than illness, or for very minor complaints, Level III interventions are recommended.

Level III

If student absence is due to parental neglect, babysitting, etc., hold a parent conference, possible referral to district or site attendance personnel and/or SARB, report to child protective services, etc.

If absences seem related to emotional problems, consider referral for counseling. If student is experiencing a life crisis — serious illness or death in the family, divorce, birth of a sibling, etc. — consider teaching skills for coping. These include learning to recognize feelings of anger, control issues and depression; learning to come to terms with problems and learning to hope. Sample programs may include STAGES, STAR, individual or small group counseling, etc.

Question 14

How many times have you moved or changed schools in the previous year? 1, 2, 3, 4, 5, 6

If the student's response is 2 or higher, the following interventions may be recommended on your computer readout.

Level I

Interview the student for reasons, in order to select the appropriate intervention/s.

First, establish a caring and helpful environment/relationship with the student so that the student will trust you enough to give you information.

You may share some information about yourself, that you care about students, that you work on special programs, that you experienced some challenging times growing up, etc., whatever may be appropriate.

Topics for discussion may include: Sometimes it's hard for people to move. What is moving like for you? Which move did you like? What was the hardest move? A lot of people have a hard time making new friends. How have you done with making friends? What do you like to do with your friends? What kind of things do friends like to do here at this school? How are things going at home? What do you think of school and your teacher? Have you or other family members been through other big changes in the last year? When there are lots of changes it is sometimes hard on families. How are you doing? How is your workload here at school? How long do you spend on homework? The student's responses will determine the interventions you select, if any.

Level II

If indicated by the computer recommendation, or information gathered in the interview, assign the student to a mentor or counselor, who can provide ongoing support and monitoring of the student's situation. If your school does not have a mentoring program in place, this may be done informally. The mentor needs to have regularly scheduled contact with the student and provide evidence that there is someone who cares. This might involve help with schoolwork or other problems, sending a birthday card and other little notes and occasional activities together.

Level II interventions may also include informal discussion and brainstorming of alternative behaviors and teaching of social skills or self-esteem fundamentals. Sample programs may include STAR, etc.

If no mentors are available at your site, consider referral to an outside group which offers mentors. Sample programs may include Big Sisters/Brothers, college or business mentoring programs, etc.

It may also be helpful to assign a special friend to the student. Your school may have a mechanism for doing this—leadership team, peer assistance team, PAL, etc. If not, make use of your contact with, and knowledge of, the other students to find students who would enjoy doing this, and who would also be in contact with you or other mentors, so that the peer does not feel responsible for the student's behavior.

Level III

If the student has been through family changes and is feeling sad, she/he may not understand this natural emotion. Help may be available through such programs as STAGES to help children manage reactions to changes. The need may be in the area of social skills. Sample programs may include STAR, Here's Looking at You 2000, etc., that can help a student learn assertive social skills to reach out to peers.

Individual or group counseling programs may help this student to talk with others who have been through changes, and to learn coping skills.

If the student seems angry or depressed, referral of student to school/community counseling services may be necessary. Family referral to outside agencies may also be helpful. If the family has been through a major change, parenting resources through STAGES or other grief, adjustment or district/city/community loss programs may be helpful.

Chapter 7

DEVELOPING A PREVENTION AND RECOVERY PLAN FOR STUDENTS AT RISK

To develop a recovery and prevention plan, a school administration must:

- Gain staff and school board commitment to create a plan.
- Prepare a prevention and recovery strategy and plan.
- Create a dropout prevention and recovery delivery system.
- Implement the system.
- Evaluate the system's effectiveness.

GAINING STAFF AND BOARD COMMITMENT

The primary advantage of developing a plan for students at risk in the eyes of staff may be reduction of class disruptions and problem behavior. Many students at risk are seeking attention and want teachers to recognize their particular needs and situation. A plan that allows for special relationships with teachers and, perhaps, a school-within-a-school or some other means for giving students and teachers a friendly, informal educational environment, may well reduce problem student behavior. Other special attention, such as services from counselors and administrators, will help as well.

In a time of limited resources, it is important to develop options that do not require additional resources. In our recent experience, this is the essential concept in working with school staff to initiate at-risk programming. With limited time available, teachers and other staff need to be guided to the most powerful interventions, and they must be the key players in developing them.

Program goals should be based on what research indicates is critical for students.

- improved academic achievement
- improved self-concept
- improved communication about personal concerns
- improved problem-solving skills
- more realistic life expectations (Rogus and Wildenhaus, 1991)

We are presently working with staff at Santa Ana High School, in Santa Ana, California, to expand their dropout prevention program which is described in detail in Appendix E. Unexcused days of missed school were reduced from twelve to six a semester for participating students. Many strategies were included such as an alternative to suspension program. One of the most powerful alternatives requires students to work at a school for the physically handicapped. Many of the students up for suspension are gang members and some of them want to finish school. They want to get out of the gang world. They want to be able to get a job. These students tend to be good candidates for working with handicapped children. Like many at-risk students, they feel no one has more reason to be discouraged and bitter than they do. Seeing children with no arms tends to give them a new perspective, which leads to better academic achievement when they return to school. They have improved their self-concept by helping those with worse problems than theirs. They are able to talk about their personal problems after learning to talk about the problems of the handicapped. They are open to new approaches to solving some of their problems, and they have become more realistic about their life expectations.

The school board may be most impressed by the significant improvement in attendance and the resultant increase in operating funds. This will be particularly true of recovered dropouts who begin attending school, thereby raising average daily attendance funds. The board will also breathe easier knowing they have made an important effort to educate all the students in the district, even those who have difficulty fitting into the comprehensive school and standard curricula available.

Some districts may find that their planning is facilitated by dividing prevention and recovery activities. In that event, the model described in this chapter may well serve as the basis for structuring both activities.

Students give a variety of reasons for dropping out including "didn't see the value of school," "personal and family problems," "conflict with teachers" and "school is boring." Researchers characterize dropouts with descriptors such as "verbally deficient," "overage in grade," "lacking basic skills," "exhibiting disruptive behavior" and "withdrawn." It is clear that any effort to deal with such a variety of concerns must include a variety of strategies and services.

Perhaps the place to begin in planning is to look carefully at what each school offers in the delivery of skills—reading, mathematics, language, problem-solving and social skills—as well as the development of a positive self-image. This information can be gained by using an evaluation model that does not assume teachers are, in fact, doing in October what they wrote in a plan the previous April. In our experience, if teachers are told that administrators expect there will be differences between April and October, they will then proceed to tell it like it is. Since the reading booklets didn't arrive, the second objective has been skipped entirely, and so on. We use a pamphlet by Plakos (1978) as a means to find out exactly what is being taught. It provides a firm foundation of fact.

The planning outline shown in Figure 7.1 is being used in the Orange Unified School District, Orange, California. It was written by Roger Duthoy, former Assistant Superintendent for Secondary Schools.

During the 1990–1991 academic year the at-risk task force created an overall strategy for involving board members, school staff, students, parents, community members and a consultant in the creation of a district plan for identifying and serving students at risk.

We would also like to suggest the SWOP (strengths, weaknesses, opportunities and problems) analysis (Lewis, 1983). To use the model described in this chapter, you would study the comprehensive strategy in terms of major strengths, major weaknesses, opportunities for improvement and problems. Then you would include possibilities for action in the prevention and recovery plan for students at risk. After the plan has been implemented, there may be certain portions of it where there are unacceptable deviations or poor performance. These can be highlighted in a special short report or form that focuses upon proposed plan corrections or something similar.

A comprehensive strategy for improving instruction and services for students at risk could include these aspects, as articulated by Novak and Dougherty (1980).

(1) Centers on the student—The broad goal of any dropout prevention effort is to help students stay in school, while recovery activities

1.0 HISTORICAL DATA

1.1 Definition of a Dropout

A student in grades ten, eleven or twelve, who stops attending school prior to graduation for forty-five days or more, and who has not requested that his/her transcript (academic record) be sent to another school or institution.

1.2 Three-Year Statistics

$$\text{Three-year dropout rate} = \frac{(D1 + D2 + D3) \times 100}{E1}$$

where:
D1 = Tenth grade dropouts (class of 1990)
D2 = Eleventh grade dropouts (same class)
D3 = Twelfth grade dropouts (same class)
E1 = Total tenth grade enrollment

1.3

For Orange Unified, the 1988 three-year dropout rate is 21.3% (statistics are generated by the CBEDS report).

$$\frac{(110 + 177 + 218) \times 100}{2370} = 21.3\%$$

1.4 One-Year Statistics (class of 1989)

$$\text{One-year dropout rate} = \frac{(D1 + D2 + D3) \times 100}{E1 + E2 + E3}$$

where:
D1 = Tenth grade dropouts (class of 1991)
D2 = Eleventh grade dropouts (class of 1990)
D3 = Twelfth grade dropouts (class of 1989)
E1 = Total tenth grade enrollment
E2 = Total eleventh grade enrollment
E3 = Total twelfth grade enrollment

1.5

For Orange Unified, the 1989 one-year dropout rate is 8.7%. (statistics are generated by the CBEDS report).

$$\frac{(105 + 197 + 218) \times 100}{1892 + 2500 + 1612} = 8.7\%$$

Figure 7.1 Dropout Report to the Board of Education — Outline.

2.0 CHARACTERISTICS OF A POTENTIAL DROPOUT

   2.1   Frequently absent, truant from school

   2.2   From low-income home (AFDC)

   2.3   Transient family

   2.4   Poor grades (retained or failed secondary courses)

   2.5   Low basic skills ability (reading and mathematics)

   2.6   Behind in credits earned

   2.7   At-risk behaviors (poor citizenship, gangs, smoking, alcohol, drugs, sexually active, on probation, discipline problem at school, etc.)

   2.8   Low self-esteem (dress, friends, goals, lack of participation in school activities, etc.)

   2.9   Lack of attachment to school (no one at school knows them or, in their opinion, cares about them)

   2.10 Nonsupportive family (lack of supervision, discipline, communication, models at home)

3.0 CURRENT INTERVENTION STRATEGIES IN ORANGE UNIFIED

Elementary Programs

   3.1   DARE (drug abuse resistance education)

   3.2   BABES

   3.3   Project Self-Esteem

   3.4   Developmental kindergarten

   3.5   Saturday school

K–12 Programs

   3.6   CASA (very active drug and alcohol effort by parents, students and staff)

   3.7   PRIDE (parent to parent networking)

   3.8   Red Ribbon Week, awareness weeks

   3.9   Categorical programs (Chapter 1, GATE, ESL, etc.)

   3.10 Summer school program

Figure 7.1 (continued) *Dropout Report to the Board of Education – Outline.*

3.11 Successful Parents for Successful Kids conference

3.12 Migrant education program

3.13 School study teams

3.14 Special education programs, I.E.P. teams

3.15 Gang information workshops

3.16 Good working relationship with the Orange Police Department

3.17 SARB (school attendance review board)

3.18 Quest International (skills programs)

3.19 Home and hospital

3.20 Independent study program

3.21 Cocurricular programs (clubs, student government, etc.)

Secondary Programs

3.22 PAL (peer assistance leadership)

3.23 Athletic programs

3.24 Choices program

3.25 Pregnant minor program

3.26 Child development program

3.27 Continuation high school program

3.28 Middle school philosophy (homeroom, interdisciplinary teams, child centered, etc.)

3.29 Regional Occupation Program (ROP)

3.30 Opportunity class (grades seven through nine)

3.31 Work experience programs

3.32 Decision-making skills class

3.33 Summer recreation program

3.34 Rancho Santiago evening programs

3.35 Hispanic youth, leadership conference

3.36 Career day, college and university nights

3.37 Academy program (El Modena High School)

3.38 Olivecrest program

Figure 7.1 (continued) Dropout Report to the Board of Education — Outline.

seek to get students to return to a structured program of education and, often, work. The student may need help in improving the skill areas previously mentioned, dealing with a personal or family problem, understanding oneself or learning new job skills. As a district dropout coordinator mentioned to us, even in a district of 25,000 we work to help dropout-prone students one by one.

(2) *Serves all students* — Identification of each student's needs is the key concept, and, to the extent possible, programs are inclusive. At the same time, some groups of students may need additional attention to bring them to a satisfactory level in, for example, reading or social skills.

(3) *Offers a comprehensive scope of services* — The range of services must be as broad as the varied problems students have. These services might include instruction in basic and social skills, tutoring in areas of individual need, counseling to help work on personal problems, testing to identify areas of competence and interest, as well as developing a supportive learning environment.

(4) *Coordinates resources and personnel* — The services suggested in

Working on Writing.

the previous paragraph may all be available through a school district, but a potential dropout often would not know about them or how to get them. Hence, there is need for a staff member to coordinate the efforts of teachers, librarians, counselors, health staff and contact persons in business who can provide training and employment opportunities.

(5) *Incorporates feedback and evaluation into the system* – The evaluation aspect of a dropout plan is critical in that so much of the effort is one-on-one by its nature. It is very difficult to keep staff informed about what is working and what isn't unless a strong effort to evaluate is implemented. A case system is one way to organize the effort. In this approach, each student with special needs is dealt with by a team of professionals who diagnose needs and suggest treatment and/or remediation as appropriate. All of these efforts are recorded in a permanent folder or computer record.

With these characteristics of a comprehensive strategy in mind, and written up in a brief handout, an administrator can approach the school board for support to begin work on a specific district plan for dropout prevention and recovery. Once approval is gained, contact with key staff can be initiated, and the elements of a strategy and plan can be developed.

PREPARING A PREVENTION AND RECOVERY STRATEGY AND PLAN

One of the key strategies in developing a prevention and recovery strategy typically involves the creation (or utilization of an existing) task force where the members are selected because they are interested in helping students at risk. This is often done after some incident has occurred that has focused attention on some aspect of the at-risk issue. For example, a large K–12 district we served as a consultant used the publication of test scores that were unsatisfactory as a lever to generate interest in improving services for potential substances abusers and dropouts. The main tasks in such an effort, as outlined in Table 7.1, are:

- identifying types of participants
- selecting strategies which will bring key members of each group on to the task force
- choosing tasks for each group that they feel are appropriate to their status and skill levels

TABLE 7.1 *A conceptual model for developing an at-risk task force.*

PARTICIPANTS	STRATEGIES	TASKS
Parents	Obtain representation from key organizations	Recruit parents who will be able to influence board members
School Administrators	Select representatives who will be positive and who can influence their colleagues at other schools	Justification of budget for at-risk programs (some successful experience with an at-risk program)
Minorities	Representation of primary constituent groups is key, especially those that are likely to speak out at meetings	Speak from experience about an at-risk program that has helped them
Teachers	A critical group which needs to include teachers who have been successful in working with at-risk students	Utilize their knowledge and experience with at-risk programs in planning and in lobbying for budget support for programs
Students	Representation of groups that will receive much of the program help	Use experience to help task force members feel these programs will work
Consultants	Select one or two that have already built reputations in the district, or who are immediately credible	Ability to share program information which stresses good programs already operating; a vision for future programs that has support of key staff

A prevention and recovery plan should:
- be student centered to meet the unique needs of each individual
- offer a variety of services in education, guidance and support
- include all school levels from elementary through high school
- include activities and services from both the schools and the community

The plan should include both prevention and treatment efforts so that students who are predicted to drop out, as well as those who already have dropped out, are served well.

CREATION OF A DROPOUT PREVENTION AND RECOVERY DELIVERY SYSTEM

Step One—Gaining School Staff and Community Commitment

Once the appropriate district administrators become aware of the need for the district-wide dropout plan, they can schedule a school board meeting and make a presentation using materials from this book as well as other data describing the local situation. Some of the key considerations in developing support for the program are:

- The new effort must be perceived as better than what is now in place, or there is no advantage in adopting it.
- It must be compatible with present values and fit with existing operating procedures.
- It should be simple enough to learn to use, so staff feel the effort to learn to use it is worth the time it takes.
- It should be tried out on a small scale so that any problems can be worked out before many staff are involved.

Step Two—Assignment of Responsibility for Dropout Prevention and Recovery Strategy

The board will assign a district staff member responsibility for designing a strategy for reducing and recovering dropouts. The strategy should:

- Identify the target population to be served, perhaps by using a dropout prediction model such as the one seen in Chapter 4. Goals, staffing, method of operation and budget should be described. For recovery, advertising in the community—especially on popular radio stations—has proven effective. School and community agency staff may be able to offer suggestions for contacting dropouts as well.
- Goal statements should be written based on an assessment of need.
- Specific objectives that will implement the goals should be written, and staffing to implement the objectives should be assigned.
- Training for staff should be planned.

- Methods of operation should be described. To state the obvious, the same old approaches that have caused dropout in the first place should not be used. As we have indicated in the review of the literature on program size, small, relatively autonomous efforts should be considered where perhaps four to six teachers work with about 125 students.
- An adequate budget should be provided. Every student who drops out costs the district $3,000 per student (or whatever your average daily attendance rate is) and hence it is worth serious effort. If dropouts are recovered there will, in turn, be a financial advantage to the district. If this is not true in your state, then you should work for legislation to provide such an incentive.

Step Three—School/Community Resource Assessment

School and community resources need to be identified, written down and put in a format, such as a computerized data base program, so they can easily be updated.

- Probably the most important resource within the school is the staff that will be involved. If they aren't involved, how serious can the effort be? In particular, each school should consider the appointment of an outreach coordinator or some equivalent title. This person has demonstrated that they like your students at risk and their families as well. The job includes the coordination of the myriad tasks that need to be carried out at the school level, as well as the planning and implementation skills to bring the ideas to reality over a period of years. In California, the person playing this role is funded by the state in schools with a high dropout rate.
- Support staff within the school could include counselors, department chairs, librarians, reading and learning disabilities specialists, as well as clerical staff.
- Community agency staff and facilities should be included. In a large district this list could include over a hundred entries.
- Business and industry training and job placement opportunities should be provided for. One way to start this list is to contact your state's liaison in the governor's office for

the department of labor to identify your local private industry council (PIC).

Present students who should be served can be identified through a dropout prediction model such as the one described in Chapter 4. Identification of students who have dropped out is difficult but teachers can often recall them if they have a list of students from previous years to jog their memories.

An advisory committee should include people who can serve as consultants and linking agents from key industries and community service agencies that provide important connections to the district.

Chapter 3 provides information that can be helpful in assessing the needs of individual students. The model we like is similar to the individual education plan used in special education which uses a team of people who know the student. The individual education plan guides the team in making a diagnosis and recommending treatment to help the student.

Determining dropout prevention and recovery objectives requires the joint efforts of the school staff and the advisory committee. Factors to consider include the needs of each student, the curricula that can be made available to both groups of students and individuals (when that is necessary) and community opportunities, such as work experience and job training.

Key aspects of setting the objectives include an accurate determination of the commitment levels of the school staff as well as business and community agency staff. The plan must have up-to-date information about resources in the community and, especially, placement opportunities in industry for training and later employment.

IMPLEMENTATION OF THE DELIVERY SYSTEM

The techniques for meeting program objectives are a combination of approaches the staff knows how to carry out—such as guidance to individuals, small group and large group instruction—and extensive record keeping and other administrative activities. There are also some efforts where the staff will need training, such as individualized computer-assisted or computer-based instruction. A special new effort will probably be needed to establish contacts with local employers for work experience and job training for interested students. This will require the most staff time and effort and, most likely, have the greatest motivational effect on students.

Many districts begin their renewed dropout efforts with the appointment of a dropout prevention coordinator or director at the district level. In many of the cases we know about, this is a former principal. We suggest that this be a director level responsibility, which includes all services for students at risk. This would require careful integration with the work of the director of health services, who often has been given responsibility for substance abuse concerns. This director would then work with site principals and the outreach coordinators to make assignments for the myriad activities that need to be strengthened and initiated to carry out a serious plan. In California and a number of other states, school districts are now linking their efforts to those of community agencies to serve students and families in need. The New Beginnings project in San Diego, California, is an example of one such program.

NEW BEGINNINGS PROJECT

The purpose of the New Beginnings project is to develop pilot approaches which demonstrate how school districts and community agencies can learn to share information about students and their families, when those students and families are in serious need of public and private support. Participating agencies in the New Beginnings project include San Diego Unified School District, Hamilton Elementary School, and staff from the following agencies/programs: AFDC, Foster Children, Child Protective Services, GAIN, Probation and Public Housing.

Some of the data gathered for the project include:

(*1*) Number of households from Hamilton Elementary School that have family members who are receiving services from the participating agencies

(*2*) Percentage of households from Hamilton that have family members who are receiving services from the agencies

(3) Comparison of caseload percentage of households from Hamilton served by each agency and the county-wide average served by each agency
(4) Number of households from Hamilton that are served by more than one of the agencies
(5) Number of at-risk students from Hamilton served by each agency

The actual implementation of a dropout prevention and recovery program is such a complex task that we suggest each district modifies the steps in the model plan to fit district needs, and includes a schedule indicating who is responsible for carrying out the tasks.

The plan schedules can also serve as a conceptual model for formative and summative program evaluation, which administrators can use to make corrections in the multitude of activities involved in the effort.

EVALUATION OF SYSTEM EFFECTIVENESS

We have developed a model for dropout program evaluation based on the conceptual work of Novak and Dougherty. It centers on the student, serves all students, offers a comprehensive scope of services, coordinates resources and personnel and incorporates feedback and evaluation into the system. Also, the software pre/post test scores that result from the data entered into the SAR screens (seen in Chapter 5) can be averaged for classes of students, and used as an evaluation of each intervention, and, collectively, your program.

Centers on the Student

The broad goal of any dropout prevention effort is to help students stay in school, while recovery activities seek to get students to return to a structured program of education and, often, work. An effective evaluation could focus on formal assessment of the student, utilizing grades, test data and staff entries in the student's permanent record. Informal assessment might be developed from observation of student behavior, school record analysis and teacher interviews.

Serves All Students

Identification of each student's needs is the key concept, and, to the extent possible, programs are inclusive. At the same time, some groups of students may need additional attention to bring them to a satisfactory level in, for example, reading or social skills. We can typically build more support from teachers and parents for programs that serve all students, such as proficiency testing and analysis, than we can for services designed for a narrow group such as predicted dropouts. The key, then, is to set a minimal standard, such as the fortieth percentile in reading, and work to bring every student up to that level. Many of the difficulties faced by potential dropouts are problems to a lesser degree for other students.

Offers a Comprehensive Scope of Services

The range of services must be as broad as the varied problems of students. These services might include instruction in basic and social skills, tutoring in areas of individual need, counseling to help work on personal problems, testing to identify areas of competence and interest, as well as developing a supportive learning environment.

Coordinates Resources and Personnel

The comprehensive services suggested in the previous section may all be available through a school district but a potential dropout often would not know about them or how to get them. Hence, there is need for a staff member to coordinate the efforts of teachers, librarians, counselors, health staff and contact persons in business who can provide training and employment opportunities.

Incorporates Feedback and Evaluation into the System

The evaluation aspect of a dropout plan is critical in that so much of the effort is one-on-one. It is very difficult to keep staff informed about what is working and what isn't unless a strong effort to evaluate is implemented. A case system is one way to organize the effort. In this approach, each student with special needs is dealt with by a team of professionals who diagnose needs and suggest treatment and or remediation as appropriate. All of these efforts are recorded in a permanent folder or computer record.

POLICY RECOMMENDATION

Local school boards should consider assisting in the development of structure and resources to identify and recover any student who may have dropped out. They should assign staff to the task of convincing students who are not attending school to return to new options they find satisfactory. The focus in these options should be on major individual strengths and weaknesses, as well as opportunities for improvement of a positive student self-image. Boards should provide leadership in seeing that at-risk students are identified, assessed and served through coordination of resources and personnel in an effort to offer a comprehensive scope of services utilizing feedback and evaluation in a dropout reentry program.

Chapter 8

DROPOUT PREVENTION PROGRAMS

Dropout prevention programs are designed to motivate students who have characteristics such as poor attendance, low grades and other predictors of dropout described in Chapter 4, to stay in school. Programs are described for both elementary and secondary schools. Recent research on effective programs is cited. At the secondary level student participation is typically voluntary, and program settings are often informal and operated by a teacher-in-charge in a manner that emphasizes the uniqueness of each student. A strong effort is made to accommodate different learning styles and speeds. Many of the programs have 100 or fewer students and five or fewer teachers.

There are four areas that should be addressed in prevention efforts according to Natriello et al. (1988).

(1) Student success in school — This can be addressed through extra instructional assistance such as tutorial efforts and computer-assisted instruction.

(2) Positive student-adult relationships — These can be facilitated by creating smaller units within large schools; assigning students to a single adult for special guidance; pairing students with an older student; keeping instructional teams of teachers with groups of students who are at risk.

(3) Making school relevant — Most successful prevention programs offer the incentive of a job opportunity or work experience. Many of the newly designed vocational education programs are linking academic skills to vocational applications. The key, according to re-

search at Ohio State (Pritz, 1992), is efforts by staff to link basic skills instruction with work experience so students see the practical connections.

(4) *Reducing outside interferences*—Programs to reduce gang influence and recruiting can help, as can efforts to reduce substance abuse, those that care for girls who become pregnant and those that help students cope with abuse which occurs in their homes.

STUDY SKILLS PROGRAMS

The National Association of Secondary School Principals (NASSP) and the National Association of Elementary School Principals (NAESP) are now offering ʰᵐ*Study Skills* for at-risk students. The Comprehensive Risk Assessment software complements these interventions perfectly. Together they are an important new source of materials for at-risk students. NASSP is a large (42,000 members) organization, and their support offers important credibility to the system of identification, placement and use of the ʰᵐ*Study Skills* instructional materials. The print materials serve grades five through thirteen and cover the following areas.

- *Learning to learn* provides skills for perceiving, organizing, making sense of and using ideas and data.
- *Learning style* gives insight into students' own style of learning and provides practice in their learning style strengths.
- *Cooperative learning* includes many activities that support cooperative learning strategies.
- *Listening skills* are used throughout the study skills programs.
- *Creative problem solving* provides strategies for solving problems effectively and imaginatively.
- *Adaptability* supports the development of adaptability by helping students to learn skills for managing and making sense of new conditions, ideas and information.
- *Personal management* teaches scheduling and goal-setting skills and offers instruction in studying and "testwiseness."

RIGOROUS ACADEMIC PROGRAMS

One of the important findings in recent program development for at-risk students is the possibility that many of these students can respond successfully to a rigorous academic program. For example, Ventures in Education is a nonprofit organization that operates in thirty-nine high schools nationally with 4,100 participating students. The K–12 curriculum stresses mathematics, reading and science. Of the 1,000 program students graduating in 1991, 94 percent enrolled in four-year colleges and universities (Staff, 1992b). This is in contrast to 40 percent of students who typically attend four-year institutions in a given year.

Ventures programs operate in urban, suburban and rural settings. The high school curriculum frequently includes four years each of English, mathematics, science and social studies, and two years of a foreign language. The programs also include advanced placement courses, summer workshops, enriched curricula and a commitment to counseling for each student.

Since we often read that about 25 percent of at-risk students are gifted, these data should not surprise us. Nor is Ventures in Education the only group stressing a rigorous curriculum for at-risk students. The Accelerated Schools program guided by Professor Henry Levin of Stanford University has a similar goal. It seeks to accelerate learning, so that students improve basic skills achievement as well as enhancing their problem-solving capabilities (Levin and Hopfenberg, 1991). It is used in more than fifty schools, many of them in Illinois. Upward Bound, which we helped to start in 1966, has been using a similar approach with 20,000 students a year, and is very successful.

COMMUNITY SERVICE LEARNING

Community service is a time-honored tradition in the United States. Programs of community-service learning combine service with learning activities. Students are asked to "learn and develop through active participation in thoughtfully organized service experiences that meet actual community needs and that are coordinated in collaboration with the school and community . . . there is structured time for a student to think, talk or write about what the student did and saw during the actual service activity" (Duckenfield and Swanson, 1992).

To date, the research on service learning is encouraging. A review of the studies so far indicates that students improve in social, personal and academic development (Conrad and Hedin, 1991). In the area of social development, the studies show participants gain an increased sense of personal and social responsibility. They also have more positive attitudes toward others. Personal development outcomes indicate more active exploration of careers, enhanced self-esteem and growth in moral and ego development. Academic improvement is seen in greater mastery of skills and content directly related to their service experiences, as well as more complex patterns of thought.

What are some stories of the impact of service learning for at-risk youth?

Dianne Scott, principal of Overbrook High School in Philadelphia, tells us how she assigned her 120 most at-risk ninth graders a three-hour-per-week community service placement. Attendance improved from 70 to 89 percent for these students.

Patty Goldstein, director of Project Success in Reading, Pennsylvania, had a class of likely dropouts who raised their overall grade point average from 2.1 to 2.9, in part from the impact of a community service requirement. Both of these stories and the following information are taken from Duckenfield and Swanson (1992), an excellent booklet available from the National Dropout Prevention Center at Clemson University.

There are four levels of service learning integration into a school curriculum.

- Level one incorporates service learning as an extracurricular activity.
- Level two utilizes a curricular unit of service learning as part of another course.
- Level three of implementation is the introduction of a full course, mandatory or elective, on service learning.
- Level four is school-wide integration into a number of courses where, for example, science students might teach nutrition to the elderly, and industrial arts students could build ramps for the handicapped.

To successfully introduce service learning, a district should do a needs assessment to determine community, student and parent interest. Promising projects should be selected, and students should be trained to succeed. A key component is time for students to reflect upon their service, and discuss their experiences. Successful service learning has been implemented in all grade levels. A number of school districts have already decided to require service learning and more are in the process of doing so. Check with your county office of education for more details.

ELEMENTARY SCHOOL PROGRAMS

Much of What We Do Now Is Not Supported by Recent Research

One example is retaining students at grade level. In some urban school districts the majority of students have been retained at least once by the time they complete elementary school. This is a false positive as they say in the medical world. It is true that the scores for these students may go up the next year, but this is the result of a year of maturation. The long-term effect on these students tends to be negative (Gottfredson, 1988). Even more widely practiced are pullout programs. They are somewhat better than retention, because students tend not to fall behind any further, especially in math, in the early grades (Carter, 1984).

What Programs Do Work?

Preschool and full-day kindergarten programs show good effects soon and late, that is, in the early grades, and then much later in outcomes such as graduation from high school and lower delinquency levels (Berrueta-Clement et al., 1984). The best research results come from continuous progress programs according to a new study by staff at Johns Hopkins. Slavin and his colleagues (1989) used the following criteria.

(*1*) The program had to be one that could be replicated by schools other than those in which it was developed.

(*2*) It had to have been evaluated for at least a semester and compared

Puppets Developed by Irvine Unified School District, Irvine, California.

to a control group, or it had to have shown convincing evidence of year-to-year gains.

(3) The program had to provide effects in reading and/or mathematics of at least 25 percent of an individual standard deviation.

In the minds of the researchers, this last criterion meant it had to have educational as well as statistical significance. To practitioners it is important because many of the programs they have heard about were eliminated by this rigorous standard.

In continous progress programs, students proceed at their own pace through a well-defined sequence of instructional objectives, and are taught in small groups at similar skill levels. The students may come from different homerooms or even grade levels. Examples of continuous progress programs are:

- *DISTAR,* K–6, reading and math. Teacher instructs small groups using highly structured, scripted lessons. Students are assessed frequently and regrouped as needed.
- *U-SAIL,* 1–9, reading and math. Combines continuous progress, individualized activities, and adapts to existing curriculum and materials.
- *PEGASUS-PACE,* K–8, reading. Students proceed through seventeen reading levels where they are frequently assessed and regrouped.
- *ECRI,* 1–6, reading. Teacher instructs small groups and uses frequent mastery checks.
- *Project INSTRUCT,* K–3, reading. Cross-grade grouping according to reading skills; students proceed through skills at their own pace.
- *GEMS,* K–12, reading. Students work in small groups or individually on materials at their own levels; includes frequent assessment, mastery tests and corrective instruction.

Cooperative learning programs were also found to be effective. In cooperative learning, students work in small teams to master material, and are rewarded based on the individual performance and cooperation of all team members. Cooperative learning approaches include:

- *Team accelerated instruction,* 3–6, math. Students work on programmed materials in mixed-ability teams, while teachers teach same-ability teaching groups.

- *Cooperative integrated reading and composition,* 3–5, reading and writing. Students work in mixed-ability teams on partner reading, story grammar, summarization, vocabulary, reading comprehension, spelling and writing, while teacher teaches reading groups.
- *Student teams – achievement divisions,* 3–5, math. Students work in mixed-ability teams, and are rewarded based on achievement of team members.
- *Companion reading,* 1 only, reading. Students engage in structured peer tutoring using phonetic materials, whole-class teaching.

Remedial tutoring programs tend to utilize older students and/or volunteers in one-on-one tutoring. Programs include:

- *Training for turnabout volunteers,* 1–6, reading and math, tutors from 7–9. Cross-age tutoring where tutors are training in preservice and in-service classes. They do not use programmed material and tutees are tutored forty minutes a day, four days a week. In-service training is offered on the fifth day.
- *School volunteer development project,* 2–6, reading and math. Community volunteer tutors work two to four hours a week per volunteer. Volunteers tutor students thirty minutes a day, four days a week.
- *Success controlled optimal reading experience (SCORE),* 1–6, reading and math. Each student is tutored fifteen minutes per day by older students or volunteers.

Computer-assisted instruction (CAI) has had mixed results. Drill and practice for ten minutes per day, following use of CAI for instruction, has had the best results. Slavin's data indicate the best vendor is Computer Curriculum Corporation, based on studies in Los Angeles Unified (1–6, math and 3–6, reading and language), Lafayette Parish (3–6, math) and Merrimak Education Center (2–9, reading). We are also very impressed with the results achieved in Azusa Unified School District using WICAT, as reported in Chapter 16.

SECONDARY SCHOOL PROGRAMS

In secondary schools, student participation is typically voluntary and program settings are often informal and operated by a teacher-in-charge in a manner that emphasizes the uniqueness of each student. A strong effort is made to accommodate different learning styles and speeds. Many of the programs have 100 or fewer students and five or less teachers. Successful programs often:

- Offer alternative curricula to interest the students.
- Provide a supportive environment to meet the holistic needs of the student.
- Emphasize self-awareness, interpersonal skill building and developing responsibility for one's behavior.
- Provide academic and other experiences which lead to early and frequent success (Florida Center for Dropout Prevention, 1986).

Dr. Nancy Peck, director of the Florida Center for Dropout Prevention, suggests that in addition to these items, districts develop plans that are comprehensive (K–12); emphasize collaboration with the community, business and parents; have open communication, as in a task force; offer transferable skills and counseling; utilize structural change as needed; have an assessment and placement capability; and conduct periodic evaluations.

Some program options include:

- resource tutorial models
- school-within-a-school
- separate alternative school
- self-contained alternative class
- school without walls
- street academy and agency-based learning center
- community- and business-based learning centers

Program components of successful programs include:

- strong sense of affiliation, where the student feels she/he has joined
- encouragement of early and frequent successes
- clear, explicit and attainable goals
- experiential learning component that may include observation of interesting activities, volunteer service and paid work
- a self-knowledge dimension that helps students understand the needs of others, and behave as responsible members of a group
- an emphasis on completion of remedial work as a way to start

TABLE 8.1 Sources for successful programs.

GROUP	INITIALS
National Diffusion Network	NDN
State department of education (where located)	SDE
California State Department of Education	CSDE
Florida Center for Dropout Prevention	FCDP
National Center for Research in Vocational Education	NCRVE
National Council on Effective Secondary Schools	NCESS

academically, followed by standard academic content, often taught in nontraditional ways
- integration of content areas with an emphasis on material the student can make immediate use of in personal or work situations (Raywid, 1982)

Schooling for at-risk students should be interesting enough to get the attention of alienated students. In this regard, many districts are turning to computer-based instruction as an important option. It should avoid the repetition found in many remedial programs, and it should help students make a connection to school staff.

A number of successful programs are described here. Each has been identified by an impartial group or a staff member in the appropriate state department of education as a strong example of its type. Program type definitions are taken from the Florida manual (Florida Center for Dropout Prevention, 1986). The identifying groups and their initials are shown in Table 8.1.

RESOURCE/TUTORIAL MODELS

Resource/tutorial models consist of the delivery of periodic services to students including counseling, tutorial services or career education. Referral for services may be made by students, teachers or counselors.

Discovery through Reading[1]

Discovery through Reading delivers rapid skill development for second and third grade students who are having difficulty in their regular

[1]Identified by NDN. Contact Dorothy Neff, Project Director, Clarkston Community Schools, 6590 Middle Lake Road, Clarkston, MI 48016, 313-625-3330.

classrooms. Specially trained teachers work with a tutoring load of thirty students whom they see in pairs throughout the week. The teachers are trained to focus upon six tasks that each student can readily complete in each session. The environment is not threatening, and the student competes with her/himself. Performance is reinforced with concrete rewards, and graphed immediately so progress is visible.

The discovery teachers utilize tutoring sessions which occur twice a week for forty-five minutes. Evaluation gains are impressive, with the greatest gains measured in second grade.

SCHOOL-WITHIN-A-SCHOOL

A school-within-a-school is a semiautonomous, nontraditional educational program housed within a larger school, or in a separate facility with strong administrative ties to the parent school. Students may attend the alternative program the entire day or part-time. The program may be located in regular K–12 schools, vocational schools, adult education centers or on community college campuses.

Peninsula Academies Program[2]

The Peninsula Academies program helps educationally disadvantaged youth overcome the handicaps of low academic achievement and lack of skills. This is accomplished through a high school level curriculum related to work, especially computers and electronics. Emphasis is placed on English, mathematics and science. Students are also exposed to jobs with the promise of employment at the completion of the program.

The initial two programs are located at Menlo-Atherton (computer) and Sequoia (electronics) High Schools. They accommodate 100 students each, beginning with tenth graders, having begun with thirty students in 1981. Five reports conducted by the American Institutes of Research indicate the academies have been very successful and the state of California is now supporting a series of new academies in other locations. One of our pilot CRA schools, El Modena High School, has an Academy program.

[2]Identified by NCRVE. Contact Jim Wood, Academy Program, El Modena High School, 3920 Spring Street, Orange, CA 92669, 714-997-6331.

Media Academy[3]

Fremont High School, in Oakland, California, has created a school-within-a-school called the Media Academy, which focuses on increasing the engagement of black and Hispanic students at risk. It is modeled after the Peninsula Academies approach and utilizes exposure to occupations in media. Students major in journalism for three years, and produce the school newspaper, the yearbook and a Spanish-English newspaper distributed to neighborhood residents. Students also have contact with production operations at local newspapers, radio and TV stations (Smith, 1989).

Motivating factors for students include creation of an environment where competence is important. Extrinsic rewards, such as future occupational opportunities, are present. Intrinsic rewards, like being part of the action at the Academy, are appealing. Social support is strong in the three-year program, and students feel ownership because they really are given responsibilities in producing news articles and editorials.

SEPARATE ALTERNATIVE SCHOOL

A separate alternative school is a nontraditional alternative program which has its own facility and an autonomous administrative structure.

Evergreen Alternative Learning Program[4]

The Evergreen program is for students of many different interests, levels and abilities. Students elect to attend in order to catch up with their class when they have fewer credits than they need to graduate, or perhaps, to take more responsibility for directing their own learning. Whatever their age or need, there is an emphasis on developing strong personal relations between teachers and students. Learning to cooperate and make group decisions is a key part of the program, as is building a program that works for each student. Some students seek part-

[3]Identified by NCESS. Contact Steve O'Donoghue, Fremont High School, Oakland Unified School District, Oakland, CA, 415-261-3240.
[4]Identified by FCDP. Contact Roy Morris, Jr., Coordinator, Evergreen Alternative Learning Center, 13905 N. E. 28th Street, Vancouver, WA 98662.

time employment, while others are focused on seeking academic independence.

Extensive use of community resources is frequent, and learners may work alone or in groups. They may learn entirely from books, or from field study, television, films, records or other experiences and resource people.

SELF-CONTAINED ALTERNATIVE CLASS

A self-contained alternative class is a program consisting of one classroom housed in a traditional school. Students may participate in the program for all or part of the day.

Dropout Prevention Program[5]

The Hillsborough Dropout Prevention program serves high-risk students through a peer counseling class and periodic tutorial and counseling services. Students are enrolled in regular classes in their high school and, when they or a staff member see the need, they are referred to the program.

The program staff place identified students with a team of staff who have demonstrated a caring and supportive interest in high-risk students. The team consists of the student's regular classroom teachers, a dropout prevention specialist and a counselor.

SCHOOL WITHOUT WALLS

A school without walls is a model that utilizes experiential learning sites outside of a school setting. Sites may include workplaces in the community, museums, parks, wilderness areas and bodies of water.

Panama City Marine Institute[6]

The Panama City Marine Institute program is nonresidential and designed for students in grades eight through twelve who are first time

[5]Identified by FSDE. Contact Mr. Kelly Lyles, Hillsborough County Schools, P.O. Box 3408, Tampa, FL 33601, 813-272-4404.
[6]Identified by FCDP. Contact Larry W. Schmidt, Director, 222 East Beach Drive, Panama City, FL 32401, 904-763-0748; or Ms. Addie Adams, Bay County School, P.O. Box 820, Panama City, FL 32402.

offenders, chronic truants or who have shown severe behavior problems in their regular school. It includes basic, remedial and vocational education components delivered under contract by Bay County Schools. The activities include scuba diving, boat repair, yachtsmanship and other marine-related occupational skills.

Students may prepare for the GED or take classes in order to receive credits toward a regular diploma. Individual and group counseling is a key component and utilizes ten hours a week of the program. Employability skills and family counseling are also available.

STREET ACADEMY AND AGENCY-BASED LEARNING CENTERS

Street academy and agency-based learning centers are small program delivery sites located in the community. They serve alienated students, dropouts and students who work.

Project 50-50[7]

Project 50-50 is a computer technology program for secondary students who gain computer application skills while improving their ability to function socially and to improve their academic performance. It has been especially appropriate for ethnic minorities, females and low-income youth. It is an industry/education partnership model with four components that incorporate the computer as a subject of study, as a tool, as a career possibility and as a metaphor for topics such as map reading and orienteering.

Adoption of the model involves a school linking to a local business, training teachers and carrying out some curriculum development in order to implement the program. Project students show an increase in computer skills and self-esteem in comparison with nonproject students. They also show increased interest in math, science and technology.

One of the most successful dropout prevention programs that we know about is a self-contained alternative class at Rowland High

[7]Identified by NDN and FCDP. Contact Deborah J. Miles, NDN Coordinator, French River Teacher Center, North Oxford, MA 01537, 617-987-1626.

School, Rowland, California. It is described in a report by Lori Marie Wasson in Appendix C. We trust you will find it as interesting as we do. There are few programs where we have such a simple model and powerful, quantitative results to indicate its success.

POLICY RECOMMENDATION

Each district should consider developing dropout prevention programs that are designed to motivate students who have the characteristics of dropouts, such as poor attendance and low grades, to stay in school. Rather than retention or pullout programs, emphasis should be given to continuous progress programs, where students proceed at their own pace through a well-defined sequence of instructional objectives, and are taught in small groups at similar skill levels. The students may come from different homerooms or even grade levels.

Chapter 9

DROPOUT RETRIEVAL PROGRAMS

The goal of dropout retrieval programs is to provide educational activities that will lead to a high school diploma or its equivalent for students who have dropped out of school. In order to operate successful retrieval programs one needs:

- to develop a tracking system that will serve to identify and locate dropouts
- to develop procedures to recruit dropouts and provide them with options which motivate them at a location they find acceptable
- to develop linkages to community agencies and industries which allow students to receive services and to make job training and employment possible (Florida Center for Dropout Prevention, 1986)

CHANGING PROGRAMS TO MEET STUDENT NEEDS

One of the most significant adaptations a district can make is to offer classes in the late afternoon and evening so that dropouts can work and still attend. Los Angeles Unified School District now keeps its adult schools open until 10 P.M. to accommodate student needs. There are many teachers who would like to work afternoons and evenings. All graduate education courses in the California State University system, as in many universities, are offered between 4 and 10 P.M. to accommodate teachers, so it seems fair that some K–12 teachers could work those hours to accommodate their students.

Perhaps the biggest opportunity for schools is working with the business community to develop training and job placements. We see a readiness on the part of both school districts and businesses to do far more than the traditional vocational education. This results from business leaders' concern about our lack of competitiveness in the world-wide industrial competition. The Business Advisory Commission calls for businesses to:

- Join in mentor programs that link students to particular businesses or trades.
- See to it that every job is an opportunity to develop character and self-esteem.
- Develop networks with organizations that specialize in working with at-risk youth.
- Develop transportation options that make it possible for youth without cars to work.
- Support schools that are well managed.
- Form partnerships, compacts, private industry councils and other links between business and schools (Business Advisory Commission, 1985).

In California dropout prevention and recovery programs are linked to vocational education programs directed at pregnant teenagers, single adults with children (many are dropouts) and Job Training and Partnership Act projects. The public schools at the K–12 level offer these possibilities in many states.

Program Options

- high school with special features
- vocational/technical school with GED options
- school-based program with work experience and basic skills
- adult, evening or community-based program leading to a diploma or GED
- community-based program offering an academic component, job training and placement
- alternative school with nontraditional curricula and organizational structure

Program Components

- clearly defined procedures for identification and recruitment of students

- individual assessment of each student to determine skill levels
- delivery of academic content and basic skills
- competency-based instruction leading to a high school diploma
- employability skills training
- computer-based instruction, such as PLATO, offering full curriculum
- computer-assisted instruction, such as Computer Curriculum Corporation, and supplementing teachers
- supervised internships, work experience and job placements
- counseling and advisement
- attendance incentive programs
- Job Training Partnership Act (JTPA) programs
- business/school partnership programs
- child care services for students with children
- field experiences
- tutoring
- career exploration

A number of successful programs are described in this chapter. Each has been identified by an impartial group or a staff member in the appropriate state department of education as a strong example of its type. Program type definitions are taken from the Florida manual (Florida Center for Dropout Prevention, 1986). The identifying groups and their initials are shown in Table 8.1.

HIGH SCHOOL WITH SPECIAL FEATURES

Highline Satellite School[8]

Highline's purpose is to provide students who are out of school with two alternatives, a half-day program emphasizing vocational opportunity, and a route back to traditional high school graduation. The program offers preparation for the GED from 8 A.M. to NOON, NOON to 3 P.M. and from 5 to 8 P.M. Students take four courses, and can also earn work credit for their employment outside school.

---

[8]Identified by SDE. Contact Barbara Birch, Principal, 440 South 186th Street, Seattle, WA 98148, 206-433-2574.

Special features include operation from 7:30 A.M. to 8:30 P.M. to accommodate a diverse student population, child care for those who need it and special programs for middle school students. Students tend to have attendance, behavior or child care problems and may be self-referred. They may also be guided to the school by parents, guardians, school or community agency staff. The program is funded by regular district funds supplemented by vocational education monies. It operates in a former elementary school and serves 500 students with twelve certificated staff, two administrators and six other staff.

VOCATIONAL/TECHNICAL SCHOOL WITH GED OPTIONS

Connecticut, through its vocational/technical school system, provides bilingual vocational training programs which offer job-entry and trade related skills taught bilingually; job-specific language using an English as a second language approach; preventive counseling and life coping skills; case management of trainees' problems such as child care and transportation; and job development and placement. For more information, contact the Connecticut Department of Education.

SCHOOL-BASED PROGRAM WITH WORK EXPERIENCE AND BASIC SKILLS

Orange County Minority Youth Dropout Project[9]

The program recruits dropouts back into a school-based setting and works with potential dropouts as well. It serves black students in grades five, seven and ten, as well as postsecondary students. It is self-contained and interacts with the regular school curriculum. The program provides structured work experience through public/private sector partnerships.

A second aspect of the program focuses on identification of elementary students who are potential dropouts, and training teachers to work with them to prevent dropout. Activities include tutoring, attendance incentive experiences, field experiences, employability skill training and career exploration.

---

[9]Identified by FCDP. Contact Vera E. Williams, Administrator, 410 South Woods Avenue #551, Orlando, FL 32805, 305-423-3093.

Upon program completion the staff carries out follow-up using both telephone contact and individual conferences.

ADULT, EVENING OR COMMUNITY-BASED PROGRAM LEADING TO A DIPLOMA OR GED

Educational Clinics Incorporated[10]

This dropout recovery program has been operating since 1968 and is funded by the state of Washington. It utilizes a clinic approach which begins with a diagnosis of student academic skills and develops a complete program of basic skills, reading, math, language arts, science and social studies. Employment skills are also featured including developing positive work attitudes, as well as locating and applying for jobs.

The program is located in a business district and has a business and community advisory committee. Students progress at their own pace, and classes are offered throughout the year, four hours a day, five days a week. Upon reaching their appropriate grade level, students may return to their regular school or take the GED.

COMMUNITY-BASED PROGRAM OFFERING AN ACADEMIC COMPONENT, JOB TRAINING AND PLACEMENT

70001 Training and Employment Institute[11]

A private, nonprofit public service corporation, 70001 operates more than sixty projects in twenty states. The focus is on dropout prevention using a highly structured curriculum called the Comprehensive Competencies program. Job training is a key component, as is placement. Young people aged sixteen to twenty-one are served. They receive preemployment training, motivational activities, leadership training and personal development activities. Students' academic backgrounds are evaluated upon entry, and individual educational plans are prepared to meet their needs.

[10]Identified by FCDP. Contact Educational Clinics Incorporated, 1414 Alaskan Way, Suite 515, Seattle, WA 98101, 206-622-6980.
[11]Identified by NCRVE and FCDP. Contact 70001 Training and Employment Institute, West Wing, Suite 300, 600 Maryland Avenue, SW, Washington, D.C. 20024, 202-484-0103.

There are about 5,000 students in the program at any given time, and 82 percent have completed it successfully. Some 92 percent have been placed in jobs through the program. Programs are operated either directly by 70001, or through community-based organizations. Financial support comes from JTPA and corporations.

ALTERNATIVE SCHOOL WITH NONTRADITIONAL CURRICULA AND ORGANIZATIONAL STRUCTURE

Career Opportunity Center[12]

This year-round alternative school is designed to help dropouts, sixteen years of age and older, to complete a diploma or pass the GED. It is an open-entry, open-exit program where each student is encouraged to talk to her/his instructor in each content area once a week. Courses are competency-based and use a contract specifying tasks to be completed. It is signed by both the student and the instructor. There are no grades, and credit is earned when the contracts are completed. Many of the courses are based on the adult performance level (APL) literacy approach.

POLICY RECOMMENDATION

Each district should consider developing a dropout retrieval program that is designed to:

- Develop a tracking system that will serve to identify and locate dropouts.
- Develop procedures to recruit dropouts, and provide them with options which motivate them at a location they find acceptable.
- Develop linkages to community agencies and industries which allow students to receive services and make job training and employment possible.

[12]Identified by FCDP. Contact Carolyn Conklin, Director, Career Opportunity Center, 2542 Junction Road, Kansas City, KA 66106.

Chapter 10

PREPARING FOR YOUTH APPRENTICESHIP PROGRAMS

We choose to call apprenticeship programs work-directed learning. This phrase seems to capture the essence of what makes the programs succeed. As we discuss the many definitions and models, we will indicate how each is work-directed learning, whether they are school-based or work-based programs. These include, to name a few: experience-based career education programs (unpaid experience in naturally occurring jobs); cooperative education or co-op programs (school-supervised experience in paid jobs); two + two or tech-prep programs (last two years of high school and two years of community college organized around a career theme); career academies (a school-within-a-school where a team of teachers offers a career-related academic curriculum to students in grades ten through twelve or nine through twelve); youth apprenticeships, where candidates spend an increasing amount of their time on the job, and most of their training and tasks are directly job related.

David Savage, writing in the *Los Angeles Times* on December 29, 1992, indicated that the Clinton administration is going to focus on apprenticeships, and will dramatically increase funding for students who are interested in preparing for jobs through this approach. If funding can be found, there may be as many as 300,000 apprenticeships created, at a cost of $1 billion from 1993–1996. This is welcome news to those of us who have been working to help at-risk students for many years. As a nation we are better prepared to work on the youth apprenticeship problem than it might at first appear.

There is, however, a semantic problem. Some key groups object to calling these programs youth apprenticeships. People in business and in unions where there are existing apprenticeships suspect the new programs will not be the traditional high-quality apprenticeships where

133

proven candidates in their mid-twenties are selected, and there is a contract between a job candidate and a master of a trade, craft or skill, under specified conditions which include full-time pay. Women and minorities do not want to call them youth apprenticeships because they have not had access to the existing programs, which have historically favored white males. Perhaps the most potent group objecting to the name are middle-class parents who believe their children will not have access to the benefits of middle-class life if they are connected to a youth apprenticeship program and do not attend college. Perhaps in time we can develop youth apprenticeship models that will be more widely accepted in our society.

The phrase work-directed learning (WDL) seems to capture the essence of what makes the programs succeed, without being offensive. As we discuss the many definitions and models, we will indicate how each is work-directed learning, whether they are school-based or work-based programs. These include, to name a few: experience-based career education programs (unpaid experience in naturally occurring jobs); cooperative education or co-op programs (school-supervised experience in paid jobs); two + two or tech-prep programs (last two years of high school and two years of community college organized around a career theme); career academies (a school-within-a-school where a team of teachers offers a career-related academic curriculum to students in grades ten through twelve or nine through twelve).

Work-directed learning not only captures the essence of the school-to-work transition programs, it also sums up what motivates professional students. Our own students, who are teachers learning to be school administrators, are absolutely work directed in their motivation. Professionals who are mainly interested in learning about and improving their own practice are also work-directed learners. The desire to become competent and succeed in one's chosen work is a powerful motivator.

Work-directed learning programs recognize the need to provide job-specific and job-related training for the 75 percent of students who do not go on to a four-year college. They require collaboration between business, labor and education, something that has been more readily achieved in Germany and Japan than in the United States. California's regional occupational programs, begun in 1967, are a notable exception. Perhaps the time has now come for their more complete development in this country; many of us will work to help this come about. Perhaps we have attempted to move too quickly to achieve the difficult new understandings and relationships between schools, unions and employers in the past. As the proverb says, "It is hard by the yard but a cinch by the inch."

WHAT IS A YOUTH APPRENTICESHIP PROGRAM?

One definition, contained in proposed federal legislation, speaks of a youth apprenticeship program as one which:

- integrates academic instruction and work-based learning (the community classroom concept)
- provides for work-site learning and paid work experience
- is offered to students beginning in the eleventh or twelfth grade
- results in receipt of a high school diploma or certificate of competency
- leads to permanent employment or to entry to a postsecondary program (U.S. Congress, proposed legislation, 1992)

The legislation indicates there should be a written agreement between the employer, the local education agency, the student and the parent which defines their roles and responsibilities in the program. Participating schools are asked to provide career exploration opportunities, and academic programs that prepare students to participate in the apprenticeship. Employers are asked to assist schools in developing curricula that are relevant to the workplace, to take primary responsibility for ensuring the success of the work-site learning and work experience (community classroom) and to provide the school with information about each student's performance. An advisory council should be established to review the various apprenticeship programs under its purview, to ensure that they mesh with local labor demands and provide broad-based competencies and transferable skills that will allow the student to progress to more responsible positions in the appropriate trade or industry.

PROGRAM CHARACTERISTICS

Academic instruction should consist of a program of study that meets state expectations, including proficiency in English, mathematics, history, science and geography. There should be modifications to curriculum to insure relevance to the workplace.

Work-based learning should consist of instruction in occupationally specific knowledge, skills and abilities accepted as industry standards. It should also include a planned program of job training with specific identification of the tasks to be mastered. It should include the development of sound work habits and behaviors, and training in the use of resources, working effectively with coworkers and utilization of appropriate technologies.

Work-site learning and experience should take at least 20–50 percent of the student's time in the first year of the program, and increase to 40–70 percent in the second year. This time should be used to help the student meet the academic requirements of the school and workplace, get appropriate job training and meet other workplace requirements, such as the use of various technologies.

The written agreement should include a commitment on the part of the student to achieve specific academic standards, to remain in school and attend regularly, to avoid alcohol and drug abuse and to meet work-site requirements.

Parents should be asked to commit to support of their children's school and workplace requirements.

Employers are asked to help students acquire skills and knowledge in an orderly sequence, to provide them with a mentor at the work site and to employ them after successful conclusion of the apprenticeship, if that is feasible. Coastline Regional Occupational program in Costa Mesa, California, has data indicating that in 1991–1992, 74 of 141 (52 percent) employers hired participants. More than 90 percent of participants seeking employment were placed in jobs, or in further training leading to a job. Therefore, it seems wise to ask employers to carefully consider hiring trainees, but not to make it a requirement. Often, the individual goes to work for another firm in the same industry.

The school should work to coordinate the successful operation of the program, and to offer a high school diploma and a certificate of competency specifying the standards the student has met in the program. The agreement may include a second educational organization and post-secondary training. There should be provision for a wage scale, a schedule of hours of work expected in both the school and work-site portions of the program and provision for termination of the agreement.

Improving Basic Skills.

The school should also be responsible for advising the student about occupational and career opportunities, work experience requirements and possibilities for postsecondary education and career specialization. Advisement should also include job descriptions of potential positions, and information about how job-related competencies will be assessed.

Many of the existing programs help educationally disadvantaged youth overcome the handicaps of low academic achievement and lack of skills. This is accomplished through a high school level curriculum related to work, especially computers and electronics. Emphasis is placed on English, mathematics and science, as well as job experience, with the promise of employment at the successful completion of the program.

In a general way, then, we can say that the problem is our lack of linkage to the world of employment. We need to consider establishing structures that can hire instructors with business and industry experience, as the regional occupational programs do. Linkage can be increased as businesses are forced to change to the low supervision, employee-as-problem-solver approach to keep up with technological change. They will have to find ways to work more closely with the schools. This will lead to enhanced authority for teachers and they, in turn, will have more to offer their students in terms of job recommendations and skill training that will help them advance in their jobs.

Some analysts see a different vision, which places the burden for employee skill preparation on business employees. In our experience this is not likely. In the early 1980s two model academy programs were developed at Menlo-Atherton (computer) and Sequoia (electronics) High Schools in Redwood City and Menlo Park, California. They accommodated 100 students each, beginning with tenth graders. Many of the faculty in the beginning were employees from the participating firms. Over time, it became clear that the employees liked their regular work more than teaching high school students.

We further recall efforts to convert teachers into computer programmers in several school districts in the early 1980s. Some districts decided that the way to get good software for schools was to train teachers who knew the curricula to develop the software. The teachers did, in some cases, learn to program and make software but they, like the business employees, turned out to like their regular teaching work more than software development. Those who did like programming went to work for software companies.

We see little future in attempting to turn the task of preparing our secondary students over to business employees for most of their academic preparation.

HOW CAN WE BUILD YOUTH
APPRENTICESHIP PROGRAMS?

If we see a youth apprenticeship where most participants get a good job at the completion of the program as our goal, how can we move in that direction?

- *Step one* — Connect our program building efforts to existing programs that have built a foundation for a more potent connection to the business world.
- *Step two* — Make sure the program offers the student sound foundations in core academic areas such as reading, writing and computation, and teaches students to solve problems, just as they will have to do on the job.
- *Step three* — Look for employers who lack problem-solving employees, and get them to make a strong commitment to help train students and to provide adult mentors on the job. When the program meets employers' needs, as the regional occupational programs do (400,000 participants), employers become very positive and seek the candidates out.
- *Step four* — Adopt an incremental change approach, where you begin with the present situation and move toward stronger linkages as the school and employer learn to work together. Many of our present vocational education programs are good beginnings to work from.

Here are five principles to keep in mind for building school-to-work programs.

(*1*) Programs should use work-based learning methods that build on school learning, and are connected to schools.

(*2*) School-based programs should build upon work experiences.

(*3*) Experience-based teaching in classrooms should develop cognitive as well as practical skills.

(*4*) School-to-work linkages should reward school learning and effort with good jobs.

(*5*) Credentialing procedures should identify clear standards and certify attainment (Rosenbaum, 1992).

Powerful youth apprenticeships take a long time to build. The interim steps will provide our students with better access to good jobs than they may have at present.

Chapter 11

MOVING TOWARD YOUTH APPRENTICESHIPS

There have been major changes in vocational education in recent years. Essentially, the new programs teach academic skills as well as vocational skills, and the best programs use problem solving in their courses. Often the new programs link high school and community college efforts, since many of the vocational skill areas require training that is only available at the college level. This is especially true in fields that use expensive technology. The chapter closes with a description of regional occupational centers and programs which base their course offerings on current and future labor market demands.

In California, we have had success with what have become known as academy programs, but they have been funded at a low level due to inadequate public interest. About 4,000 students a year participate in these programs.

Career academies began in Philadelphia in 1969 at Thomas Edison High School with the Electrical Academy. Other academies were initiated in Philadelphia, as they were in Pittsburgh. The initial two model programs we know about in California are located at Menlo-Atherton (computer) and Sequoia (electronics) High Schools in Redwood City and Menlo Park, California. Five reports conducted by the American Institutes of Research indicate the academies have been very successful, and the state of California attempted to find adequate funds to support a series of new academies in other locations. There were about fifty academies in California in early 1993 (Stern, 1992). A leading example, the Oakland Health and Bioscience Academy at Oakland Tech-

141

nical High School, achieves an attendance rate of 96 percent and more than 80 percent of its graduates meet the entrance requirements of the University of California. This is a hopeful record in Oakland Unified School District, where less than 20 percent of the graduates meet the requirements.

You can obtain a video titled *Rising to Potential through Vocational Education* from South Carolina ETV for $49.95 by calling 1-800-553-7752. It presents ten of the new style programs which are federally funded demonstration sites. There is an accompanying publication, *Vocational Education for the 21st Century,* which can be obtained from the National Dropout Prevention Center by calling 1-800-656-2599.

Several of the programs described below have been influenced by the academy model. The ten demonstration projects were funded by the U.S. Office of Vocational and Adult Education in 1989.

Certain themes are apparent as one reads these program descriptions. They are:

- The projects are customer driven, as administrators work to make the program fit the needs of the student.
- Academic material is taught in the context of the workplace.
- Curriculum is integrated to support workplace needs and understandings.
- Guidance and counseling are offered to help students succeed in the workplace.
- There is recognition that job expectations have increased in recent years, and students now need more advanced communication skills, math proficiency and problem-solving skills.
- There is typically provision for parental and family involvement.
- There is a shift from industry to information and service placements.
- Many of the placements are for women, minorities and immigrants, the majority of new workers.

Feedback from these projects is encouraging. Often a retention and graduation rate of 90 percent or more is being reported for students who were at risk and likely to drop out prior to program entry.

EXAMPLES OF SUCCESSFUL PROGRAMS

The following program profiles are taken from *Vocational Education for the 21st Century,* and are the ones seen in the video.

Bilingual Vocational Education[13]

Bilingual vocational education is a collaborative effort based in Richmond, Virginia. The program is located in two school district technical centers and one high school. It is designed for refugee students with limited English proficiency. The program focuses on increasing English skills, personal confidence and job-readiness skills. Students are mainstreamed into regular vocational education classes, and can receive help from bilingual teacher aides, tutoring and counseling services. Some students may spend half a day at their home high school for ESL instruction and independent living classes, and the other half at a technical school where they take vocational education classes.

The program serves students ages sixteen to twenty-one who are nonliterate or semiliterate in their native languages, as well as refugee students who are too old to learn English and complete high school by their eighteenth birthday.

Business Technology Academies Program[14]

The Business Technology Academies program is a collaborative effort between Carlmont and Woodside High Schools in the Sequoia Union High School District. In this three-year program, students receive instruction in language arts, mathematics, social studies and business technology from the same team of instructors for the three-year period. These are provided in a block while students are mainstreamed for electives and other school activities. Computer literacy and computer-assisted instruction are provided through state-of-the-art

[13]Contact Mary Jo Bateman, 1010 N. Thompson Street, Richmond, VA 23230.
[14]Contact Dr. Marilyn Raby, Director, Curriculum Services, Sequoia Union High School District, 480 James Avenue, Redwood City, CA 94062.

interactive technology. Each student is matched with a local industry volunteer mentor and, during their senior year, students may qualify for work experience through paid summer employment.

The program serves under-achieving, low-income students from ages fifteen to eighteen who have shown irregular attendance and a poor academic record, but who are willing to try to change their performance.

The Community Career Centers[15]

The Catonsville and Rosedale Community Centers could be described as educational halfway houses designed to assist dropouts and potential dropouts between fourteen and twenty-one years of age. They are helped to obtain jobs, return to school, pass GED examinations or join the military forces. Students are given an assessment that leads to a competency-based program including academic instruction, counseling and renovation and repair of center building and grounds. Social and emotional growth are nurtured through mentoring, parent involvement, development of social skills, self-concept enhancement and adventure activities. Students are exposed to educational and employment possibilities, and are tracked so they can be given assistance, if necessary, after they leave the centers.

Guidance in Retaining Adolescent Dropouts (GRADS)[16]

GRADS is a cooperative effort including the Central Area Vocational Technical School and the Oklahoma Child Service Demonstration Center in Cushing. Students spend a half-day at the vocational center and the other half at one of the sixteen feeder high schools. An assessment leads to individualized vocational instruction that includes basic skills and occupational instruction in a resource room utilizing computer-managed instruction and tutoring. Instructional materials are available for differing reading levels, and important material is color coded to assist students. Student progress is monitored weekly, and instructional and behavioral changes are made as they are needed. Per-

[15]Contact Don Hardesty, Rosedale Community Career Center, 8200 Old Philadelphia Road, Baltimore, MD 21237.
[16]Contact Celia Myers, Central Area Vocational Technical School, 123 E. Broadway, Cushing, OK 74023.

sonal and career counseling are provided, as are adult and peer mentoring.

GRADS serves students aged fifteen to nineteen with a history of low grades, high absenteeism, discipline referrals, suspensions and expulsions.

Lifelong Options Program[17]

The program is a collaborative effort between the National Dropout Prevention Center, the Center on Education and Training for Employment at Ohio State University and three school districts. It includes:

(1) Occupational experiences, such as vocational education, entrepreneurial experiences and on-the-job training
(2) Academic instruction individualized for basic skills and integrated with the occupational component
(3) Intensive individual and group counseling with emphasis on self-concept and character development
(4) Employability training with classroom instruction and real-life experiences
(5) Life-coping skills training for decision making, conflict resolution and interpersonal skills development

Lifelong Options has been implemented in rural, suburban and urban districts for students likely to drop out.

Youth Experiencing Success (YES)[18]

YES is located at the Center of Applied Technology South in Anne Arundel County, Maryland. Students divide their time between their home high school, where they receive required academic instruction, and the center, where they are involved in vocational education. Community-based educational experiences allow students to receive academic credit in English or social studies while receiving on-the-job training from a business or professional sponsor. Students also receive

[17]Contact Jay Smink, Executive Director, National Dropout Prevention Center, 205 Martin Street, Clemson University, Clemson, SC 29634.
[18]Contact Karl Behringer, Anne Arundel County Public Schools, 2644 Riva Road, Annapolis, MD 21401.

counseling and work on personal and social skills. The program serves students aged fourteen to twenty.

Changing How Our Pupils Succeed (CHOPS)[19]

CHOPS is a school-within-a-school located in the McFatter Vocational Technical School in Broward County, Florida. Students receive block instruction in basic academic subjects by computer-managed instruction (WICAT), and take classes in their chosen occupational areas before or after their academic classes. Intensive counseling and group counseling are both available as are job training and personal/social skills development. At the completion of the program students earn both a vocational certificate and a high school diploma. Students aged fifteen to twenty are served.

Oconee Alternative School Is Super (OASIS)[20]

Students receive core academic instruction in small classes, with computer-assisted instruction available. They also receive individual and group counseling and employability skills training. If they wish, they can also attend Hamilton Career Center for half-day vocational courses or get on-the-job training. Students operate a business producing and selling outdoor furniture.

North Dakota Project COFFEE Vocational Training Program[21]

This North Dakota program serves at-risk students from four Indian reservations using the Cooperative Federation for Educational Experiences (COFFEE) model. Students spend two hours a day working on mathematics, English and reading skills. A partnership with businesses and industries allows opportunities for field trips, tours and work experiences. Individual and group counseling is available, and training in preemployment skills — including values clarification, com-

[19]Contact Annette Zylinski, Wright Administration Center, 5th Floor, 600 SE 3rd Avenue, Ft. Lauderdale, FL 33301.
[20]Contact Louis Holleman, School District of Oconee County, N. College and N. Broad Streets, P.O. Box 220, Walhalla, SC 29691.
[21]Contact Jerry Bodine, State Board for Vocational Education, 15th Floor, State Capitol, 600 East Boulevard Avenue, Bismarck, ND 58505.

munications skills, decision making, conflict resolution and interpersonal relations—is offered. Physical education, mentoring, on-the-job placement and employment training are also offered. Students served are from fourteen to twenty-two.

Preparing At-Risk Youth for Employment[22]

This program of vocational training and support serves students from twenty-three high schools and other programs in Detroit. Students spend half a day receiving their academic program at their sending school, and half a day in vocational programs at several centers throughout the city. The vocational programs lead to certificates and local business and industry staff help design the programs. Students who begin in the tenth grade can take a three-year program where they work twenty hours a week for pay. Tutoring and counseling are available, as are basic reading and mathematics help.

Students aged fifteen to nineteen who have low grades and scores are eligible if they spend the previous year in an alternative program.

Student Transition and Retention Program (STAR)[23]

STAR is a cooperative California effort including Rancho Santiago Community College, Santa Ana Unified School District and Central County Regional Occupational program. It operates from the College Centennial Education Center and offers a high school diploma on an individual or small group basis. The curriculum is delivered after a careful assessment of student needs, and can serve students who need basic high school subjects, and those who need English as a second language. Vocational courses are available for those who speak English, as are employability and life-skills training. Students are given assistance in obtaining jobs, including bus passes and child care, for example. They can also transfer into the regular college curriculum. The program serves students from seventeen to twenty-one who are referred by the school district.

[22]Contact Dr. Stanley Waldon, Office of Vocational-Technical Education, 5057 Woodward #804, Detroit, MI 48202.
[23]Contact Dr. Adrienne Sims, STAR Program, Rancho Santiago College, 2900 Edinger Avenue, Santa Ana, CA 92704.

Technical Alternative High School[24]

This program in New York serves students who are emotionally handicapped. They receive a half-day of vocationally related academic course work, together with vocational education the rest of the day. An individual education plan is developed for each student appropriate for his or her capability. They are given the option of pursuing a high school diploma, a GED, occupational assessment and exploration, employability training, supervised work experience and intensive counseling. The social skills curriculum focuses upon personal skills and human adjustment. A behavior modification approach is used to guide students toward independence and successful behavior.

The program serves students aged fourteen to twenty-one who are two years below grade level, have low-average to average intelligence and who exhibit moodiness, withdrawl, depression, denial and poor self-concept.

Vocational Mentoring Program[25]

The Vocational Mentoring program in Portland, Oregon, includes Grant High School, the chamber of commerce, Good Samaritan Hospital and Legacy Health Systems. It includes a bridge program for eighth graders entering high school, and a partnership project to help students prepare for entry-level jobs. There is a vocational mentoring program which includes vocational/technical training, and academic courses taught at the hospital where there is also a career exploration alternative. Students explore patient care, administration, nutrition services and other hospital activities. Counseling is available from hospital staff. The other half-day is spent at the high school in required courses.

The program serves students aged fourteen to twenty-one who are one to four years below grade level, have low grades, discipline referrals and come from dysfunctional families.

---

[24]Contact Dr. Stephen Jambor, BOCES Mid-Westchester Center, 65 Grasslands Road, Valhalla, NY 10595.
[25]Contact Kelvin Webster, Grant High School, 2245 NE 36th Avenue, Portland, OR 97212.

COMMON ELEMENTS IN SUCCESSFUL PROGRAMS

These new programs have been built around some common approaches. These include a careful needs assessment of total district needs, a willingness to design a comprehensive program (even child care in Santa Ana), a program that serves a diverse population (even special education students in Westchester), program evaluation to determine success, a commitment to provide necessary resources, sufficient flexibility to allow program staff to operate somewhat autonomously and adequate time for planning and implementation of the program. In several of the projects there is on-the-job training that can lead to a job with the business or agency providing the training.

In a survey of the program directors, the following factors were identified as keys to program success.

- People make the difference, especially caring people who like at-risk students.
- The program must be realistic and lead to jobs.
- A variety of community resources are called into play.
- Programs can operate in many different settings, often settings very different from a comprehensive high school.
- Programs must meet the diverse needs of the student participants, including language deficiencies, learning disabilities, emotional handicaps, substance abuse problems, low self-esteem and low academic achievement.
- Strong district commitment is needed, as is a clear vision of the need for vocational opportunities and adequate resources.
- Perhaps most of all, program autonomy and student and staff participation in operating the program are needed.

The link to community colleges is very important in that more than half of all new jobs created between now and the year 2000 will require education beyond high school. The directors of the ten demonstration projects found they were doing two things at once to help the at-risk students. They had to be flexible enough to create a program that would meet the students' personal need for self-esteem and bonding, while at the same time providing training that could lead to employment. The projects succeeded to the extent that they met student needs, but no project met the needs of all students, or served all the students who needed help.

This latter factor is one of the most difficult for teachers and administrators to come to terms with. We have been working as consultants in a high school for the past several years where the majority of students are at risk of dropping out. The teachers are stretched to the very limit of their energy and there is no way that all needy students can be helped. In fact, we had to become very tough about admission to our program for it to succeed at all.

In the first year of the program about eighty students were identified and placed in a large alternative classroom with a teacher and an aide. They were not able to make a difference for these students and the program was terminated. It was run by a teacher who was full of energy but not good at recruiting other teachers to help her. There was no program in the second year. In year three, we recruited another teacher who was well liked by the staff, and she has been able to recruit five other teachers to help her for several hours a week each. We are trying to restrict the program to thirty students, so it can have a positive impact and survive. It is a continuing struggle, however. A high-level district administrator came by the principal's office while we were designing the program, and when the principal said it would be for thirty students the district administrator immediately said "Its got to have more students . . . there are hundreds here that need it." That is true, but even thirty will not be served unless the participants are restricted. The single most effective dropout prevention program we know about, at Rowland High School, Rowland, California, has one teacher and twenty students.

Hard choices need to be made for prevention programs to succeed. In this case, we are using the keyboard version of our Comprehensive Risk Assessment software to select the most needy students for interventions, as described in Chapters 5 and 6. These are the candidates. Then the principal, the vice-principal for discipline and the teacher who directs the program decide which students will be admitted on the basis of what interventions they need – according to the software report – and which teachers they have recruited who can deliver various interventions. The bottom line is teacher availability. It seems much like a medical model. You have to restrict the students you work with to those who can be helped by the specialists you have available.

REGIONAL OCCUPATIONAL PROGRAMS (INTERNSHIPS)

Undoubtedly the best accepted model (400,000 participants a year) for training high school students and adults for entry level careers is ROP (regional occupational programs) funded by the state of California. Most of the training in these internship-like programs is carried out at the work site in businesses, industries and in schools for youth and adults. These programs have been in operation since 1967 and there are now seventy-two of them. Costs of the ROPs are covered by reimbursement for student attendance.

Training in the ROPs is coordinated from regional occupational centers, and it includes upgrading of skills (29 percent) and advanced training (18 percent), as well as career preparation (53 percent). They operate under three types of governing structures: joint power agreements between two or more districts, county boards of education and single (large) districts. An ROP internship can lead directly to a paid apprenticeship or full-time employment, and it supplements offerings in high schools, community colleges and adult education programs.

The community-based courses in business and industry are typically offered in community facilities which are used without charge. Some courses are taught in local high schools as well. Instructors from business and industry have vocational teaching credentials which are based on years of experience in their field rather than educational background, although some have good educational backgrounds. The instructor has three roles.

- Recruit students.
- Conduct the training of the students.
- Help place the students into appropriate jobs.

Students receive high school credit for the courses, and classes typically meet from five to twelve hours a week. In the Coastline ROP in Costa Mesa, California, 61 percent of the students are from high schools, and 39 percent are adults returning for training. They offer the courses shown in Figure 11.1.

Who Attends ROP?

ROP courses are open to people sixteen and over with priority given to high school seniors, juniors and adults in the area served by the ROP.

Animal Science

Animal Health Care

Automotive

Auto Body Repair/Refinishing
Auto Tune-Up and Emissions
    Inspection
Automotive Brakes/Front End
    Steering and Suspension
Automotive Occupations

Business

Banking Occupations
Business Office—Cooperative
Business Office Skills
Computer Software Applications
Computerized Accounting
Computerized Accounting—
    Advanced
Data Entry
Desktop Publishing (adults)
Legal Secretary (adults)
Lotus 1-2-3 (adults)
Office Skills and Procedures
    (adults)
Office Skills and Procedures
    (high school students)
Small Business Ownership/
    Management
Word Processing
Word Processing—Advanced
Word Processing (adults)

Communication

Video/Television Production
    Assistant

Floral Design

Floral Design
Floral Design—Advanced

Graphics/Printing/Drafting

Commercial Art (photography)
Computer-Aided Drafting
Drafting Occupations
    (mechanical/electrical/
    architectural)
Graphic Arts/Printing
Technical Illustration

Technical Illustration with
    Computer Applications

Health

Dental Assistant (back office)
Dental Radiology (X-ray)
Health Occupations
Medical Assistant (core)
Medical Assistant (front office)
Medical Assistant (back office)
Medical Transcription
Nurse Assistant Precertification/
    Home Health Aide
    Precertification

Industrial Technology

Computer Repair and
    Maintenance I
Electronic Assembly
Electronic Test Technician I
Electronic Test Technician II
Home, Condominium and
    Apartment Repair
Machine Tool Operations

Marketing

Grocery Cashiering (certificate
    program)
Grocery Occupations—Cooperative
Merchandising—Advanced—
    Cooperative
Retail Sales and Merchandising

Service Occupations

Careers with Children
Careers with Children—Cooperative
Cook/Chef Assistant
Cook/Chef Assistant—Cooperative
Cosmetology
Food Services—Cooperative
Hospitality Occupations
Instructional Assistant/Job Coach
Manicuring
Service and Manufacturing
    Occupations (special needs)
Service and Manufacturing
    Occupations—Cooperative
    (special needs)

Figure 11.1 Courses Offered by Coastline ROP.

152

Students attending these courses receive up-to-date skills that lead to employment, or, in some cases, to college attendance. Students are given placement assistance by the instructors and by job placement specialists. High school students pay no fee and adults pay $35 per course.

Linking to Community Colleges

Coastline ROP has developed matriculation agreements with all of the community colleges in its service area.

Golden West College

Students who complete the courses listed with a grade of C or better will receive advanced placement, and may receive credit by examination.

- Computer-Aided Drafting
- Computerized Accounting
- Computer Software Applications
- Word Processing

Students who complete the courses listed with a letter grade of A or B may receive advanced placement.

- Health Occupations/Basic Nurse Assistant
- Certified Nurse Assistant

Irvine Valley College

Students who complete this course with a letter grade of A or B will receive advanced placement, and may receive credit by examination.

- Computer-Aided Drafting

Orange Coast College

Students who complete the courses listed with a letter grade of A or B will receive advanced placement, and may receive credit by examination.

- Construction Carpentry

- Drafting Occupations
- Machine Tool Operations
- Medical Transcription
- Electronic Assembly
- Video/Television Production Assistant

Students who complete the courses listed with a grade of C or better will receive college credit and advanced placement.

- Health Occupations
- Basic Nurse Assistant
- Certified Nurse Assistant

High school students who complete this course with a letter grade of A or B may have EC 105, Preschool Aide (three units), waived.

- Careers with Children (252 hours)

Students who complete the courses listed with a letter grade of A or B will receive college credit.

- Computer Software Applications
- Word Processing
- Computerized Accounting

Rancho Santiago College

Students who complete the courses listed with a letter grade of A or B will receive advanced placement, and may receive credit by examination.

- Automotive Occupations
- Electronic Assembly
- Machine Tool Operations

Saddleback College

Students who complete the courses listed with a letter grade of A or B will receive advanced placement, and may receive credit by examination.

- Auto Body Repair and Refinishing
- Computer Repair and Maintenance I and II

- Computerized Accounting
- Graphic Arts/Printing
- Small Business Ownership/Management
- Automotive Occupations
- Computer Software Applications
- Electronic Test Technician I and II
- Word Processing

Students who complete this course with a letter grade of A or B may have Cooperative Work Experience 168 (three units) for Option II (infant/toddler) of the Child Development Certificate waived.

- Careers with Children (252 hours)

Students who complete this course with a letter grade of A or B may have Cooperative Work Experience 168 (three units) for Option II (infant/toddler) and Option III (school age) of the Child Development Certificate waived.

- Careers with Children—Cooperative

Students who complete the courses listed with a letter grade of A or B may receive advanced placement.

- Health Occupations/Basic Nurse Assistant
- Certified Nurse Assistant

Each of these courses has a two-page written agreement that spells out the student options for receiving various levels of credit as the work is transferred into different courses where the student may wish to apply them. This detail indicates an unusual amount of collaboration between the ROP and the two-year institutions.

NEW DEVELOPMENTS

A youth apprenticeship program, one form of work-directed learning, is one which

- integrates academic instruction and work-based learning
- provides for work-site learning and paid work experience
- is offered to students beginning in the eleventh or twelfth grade

- results in receipt of a high school diploma or certificate of competency
- utilizes national skill standards
- builds upon existing education/training programs and existing articulation and community networks

Several California ROPs are adapting their programs so students will be paid by the employer. This in turn will make them eligible to participate in the youth apprenticeship funding that will be supported by the Clinton administration. They are also beginning to develop certificates of competence and letters of qualification which build on the extensive progress that has already been made in California and nationally in the use of national skill standards.

The current cooperative training programs at the Coastline Regional Occupational Program (ROP) will be altered to address the paid apprenticeship requirement that will be in upcoming federal legislation. Existing industry-based national skill standards, such as those in computer-aided drafting, are already in place at Orange Coast Community College, and are being put in place at other participating community colleges. Certification of skill competencies included in the current high school/secondary education reform will be addressed. Students who complete a program will receive appropriate documents of skill standard certification, and employers at apprenticeship placement sites will be provided with complete skill standard competency manuals so the industry experience will dovetail with, and build upon, the school site program.

The current articulation agreements, tech prep program development and other current means of providing seamless transitions to technical programs at Orange Coast Community College or other coast community college district programs, will become the platform for school-to-college transition articulation. Students will have access to the next level of technical training, higher level work-based learning experience, and will be able to give consideration to further education at California State University, Fullerton, and other institutions, for baccalaureate work and beyond.

Student, faculty, business, industry/labor principals and community/education leaders will evaluate the process described previously, develop written documents regarding the process and make consultants available for communities across the county to establish similar youth apprenticeship transitions.

PRINCIPLES FOR CONNECTING SCHOOL AND WORK

To understand how our education system needs to relate to business and industry, we must first understand the changes that are taking place in the world of work. If there is little change in the technologies used in business and industry, as there has been historically, there is a gently moving timetable for education to adjust to the changes.

If, on the other hand, the pace of technological change accelerates, as it has in the last several decades, education must speed up the pace of adaptation.

There is a second principle operating as well. The U.S. mass production system has historically utilized production workers with little training, thus minimizing the need for apprenticeship programs. Quality control has been accomplished through close supervision and careful management. Rapid technological change, shortened product life cycles and increased foreign competition, have led firms to change to a different approach, requiring more highly trained workers and fewer supervisors (Rosenbaum, 1992).

These changes have led to the need for apprenticeships and related training approaches that require workers to use higher-order cognitive skills, and to engage in problem solving as they work.

As Rosenbaum indicates, between 1975 and 1990 jobs that require these higher skills increased at two-and-one-half times the rate of jobs requiring lower skill levels. This trend will continue into the coming decade.

What, specifically, are these higher-order skills? Foundation skills include reading, writing, mathematics, listening and speaking. Complex reasoning skills are needed for defining and solving problems, critical thinking, knowledge acquisition and evaluating problem solutions (Stasz et al., 1990).

It seems clear that more highly trained employees will require a greater investment on the part of employers. This will, in time, lead them to make a greater commitment to keep their highly trained employees for a longer period of time. It will also lead to a greater business interest and investment in training programs such as apprenticeships and related work-directed learning programs.

Who will train our 75 percent of students who are not headed for a four-year college? Most likely our present and future teachers. Some business leaders argue that many of our teachers don't care about these students, and that we should introduce a voucher system to force them out of education by eliminating schools that are not chosen by parents, and presumably, the teachers in those schools.

ARE U.S. TEACHERS THE PROBLEM?

Before we leap into the voucher approach, we need to use some higher-order thinking skills and see if the problem is our teachers. It is helpful to look at successful models for preparing students for the work force, such as those in Germany and Japan, to understand where the problem is.

In both Germany and Japan, employers are closely linked to schools through a variety of mechanisms that allow them to influence school curricula, and to participate in the skill certification process. In Germany, for example, students spend one or two days a week in school and the rest of the week at a work site. Their apprenticeships last two to four years, and lead to immediate employment upon completion at about age eighteen. There is close collaboration between the school, union and business in the skill identification and certification process.

Consequently, employers take the recommendations of schools and teachers seriously when it comes to deciding which students to hire. This has a wonderful effect on the teachers, for they now have compelling authority when dealing with students who are going to be dependent upon them for job placement. This is easy for me to understand as a professor of educational administration, for I have the same authority. My students need my recommendation in order to become administrators in the schools.

Chapter 12

WORK-DIRECTED LEARNING

Work-directed learning seeks to use the motivation of competence in one's chosen work to provide students with purpose and drive as they prepare themselves for future accomplishment. It includes school-based and work-based learning, and is, perhaps, the single greatest motivating force in U.S. society. Work-directed learning propositions are offered as part of a conceptual model that uses many paths to achieve its goal of preparing young people to obtain and advance in good jobs. The chapter concludes with the description of a complete apprentice training curriculum produced in an interactive, multimedia format by the Industrial Training Corporation.

PURPOSE OF WORK-DIRECTED LEARNING

The purpose of work-directed learning is to use the desire for competence and income to motivate the learner.

Program Propositions

(*1*) If the learner sees a connection between what is to be learned and increased income/competence, she/he will be motivated to complete the program.

(2) The learner is more likely to obtain a job and advance in his/her career if problem solving is integrated into the school-based and work-based aspects of the program.

(*3*) Both school- and work-based learning should include content knowledge, a variety of instructional approaches, planning strategies, problem-solving strategies and learning strategies.

School-Based Propositions

(*1*) School-based learning should include content that leads to a diploma or a certificate of competence.

(*2*) School-based learning should be built around existing career preparation courses, and be revised regularly. It should be designed so that an increasing proportion of student time is spent at the work site, and be based on a written agreement signed by the student and representatives from the school and work sites.

(*3*) School-based learning should begin as early as is possible, and not later than age sixteen. It should include life-coping and wellness skills, employability skills for getting and keeping a job, and each student should be guided by a teacher/advisor.

Work-Based Propositions

(*1*) Work-based learning should be integrated with school-based learning at the earliest opportunity in the school curriculum, and no later than grade eleven.

(*2*) Work-based learning should offer occupationally specific knowledge and skills, utilize sequenced learning, include a mentor from the job site and result in a job placement.

Work-directed learning is a generic concept encompassing programs based both in schools and at work sites. It uses many paths to achieve its goal of preparing young people to obtain and advance in good jobs.

We move now to some specific suggestions for implementing work-directed learning. Berryman (1992) has outlined a four-part learning paradigm which influenced the conceptual base for our work-directed learning model. The method section (taxonomy of teaching methods) was developed by Peterson (1992). We apply concepts to a present-day apprenticeship program later in the chapter, so that the reader can see the types of changes that could be made as they seek to offer employment-bound training (the curriculum) in a delivery system (instruction) that utilizes the new generic approach focusing upon problem solving and critical thinking.

HOW STUDENTS LEARN

There are four types of knowledge students use in the learning environment. These include:

(*1*) Content knowledge, such as conceptual and factual knowledge, and procedures that relate to the field of interest, whether it be electronics, machine repair, accounting or English

(*2*) Planning strategies such as assessing needs, predicting future needs and goal setting

(*3*) Problem-solving strategies which are based on successful experience and include problem identification, listing of alternative solutions, selection of a solution, implementation of the solution and evaluation of effectiveness

(*4*) Learning strategies which include learning to learn, identifying one's learning style, cooperative learning, listening skills and adapting to new situations

Principles to Guide Instruction

- *Increasing complexity*—Tasks the students are asked to perform are increasingly complex as they move through the training experience.
- *Increasing diversity*—Tasks the students carry out are increasingly diverse and require more and varied skills.
- *Global before local skills*—Students should get a feel for the overall product or big picture prior to being asked to develop individual parts of the whole.
- *Context*—Work to carry out instruction in a context that facilitates what you are teaching. For example, teach writing where you have access to an electronic bulletin board where the students can write messages to each other.
- *Use of experts*—If you are teaching about using experts, go to a setting where the students can see an expert at work, or show a videotape of an expert working.
- *Intrinsic motivation*—Intrinsic motivation comes from inside us and often follows extrinsic motivation, such as pleasing someone. To help students understand this, invite someone to class, like an athlete, who plays hard because it's fun.

- *Cooperative learning* – In cooperative learning, students work together to solve problems and carry out tasks. It is easy to demonstrate this with two students at a computer. Typically, they will naturally cooperate to accomplish a task.
- *Competitive learning* – To make competitive learning constructive, the students should compete in using a sound process, rather than in terms of the product being produced. Realistically, the easiest thing for students to understand is a combination of competitive and cooperative learning, as in teams working together to make a presentation and get a high grade.

As we begin to think of the curriculum we need for work-directed learning, particularly apprenticeship programs, it is appropriate to review program requirements.

ACADEMIC CURRICULUM AND INSTRUCTION

The academic curriculum should consist of a program of study that meets state expectations, including proficiency in English, mathematics, history, science and geography. There should also be modifications to the delivery of instruction to insure relevance to the workplace, especially in the areas of critical thinking and problem solving. Even if little change is made in curriculum, modifying instructional approaches to use problem solving and critical thinking is an important step.

There are other areas that also need to be included in the revised curriculum. These include basic skills [such as ^hm^*Study Skills* for at-risk students developed by the National Association of Secondary School Principals (NASSP)] for example:

- *Learning to learn* – This includes skills for perceiving, organizing, making sense of and using ideas and data.
- *Learning style* – This gives insight into student's own style of learning, and provides practice in learning style strengths.
- *Cooperative learning* – This includes many activities that support cooperative learning strategies.
- *Listening skills* – These are used throughout each study skills program.

- *Creative problem solving* — This includes strategies for solving problems effectively and imaginatively.
- *Adaptability* — This supports the development of adaptability by helping students learn skills for managing and making sense of new conditions, ideas and information.
- *Personal management* — This teaches scheduling and goal-setting skills, and offers instruction in studying and testwiseness.

The NASSP study skills materials are being used in more than 7,000 classrooms nationally, and are designed for at-risk students. Our suggestion would be to train the academic core teachers (English, mathematics, history, science and geography) to use these strategies as they teach their regular content. This is the manner in which they are typically implemented in classrooms.

VOCATIONAL EDUCATION

Since most high schools have existing vocational education programs, it makes sense to build the internship/apprenticeship curriculum around the present vocational education courses if they are leading to jobs. If they are not, perhaps a supplementary structure, such as that of California's regional occupational programs, needs to be put in place. Vocational education courses frequently include trade and industrial education, business education, agriculture, home economics, marketing education and technical education. This will require some serious revision, however, since many existing vocational education courses do not reflect the new emphasis on problem solving and critical thinking that are crucial in preparing students for the higher-level cognitive requirements of the present and future job market.

At this point, decision makers need to carefully consider whether the present teachers are willing and able to revise existing courses to reflect higher-order thinking skills. It may be that teachers whose present courses already reflect these strategies should play this role. You might use a math teacher, for example, who has been teaching problem solving for years, as a consultant to the vocational education teachers for this task.

This is a serious issue in that one of the main purposes of the Vocational and Applied Technology Education Act Amendments of 1990 was to introduce problem solving and critical thinking into the vocational education curriculum. The old curriculum, dumbed down to the supposed level of the vocational education students, did not work. Only one-third of the students who completed the curriculum got jobs, in part because employers had learned that those students had a hard time learning to use new machines and technologies.

OCCUPATIONALLY SPECIFIC KNOWLEDGE

Work-based learning should consist of instruction in occupationally specific knowledge, skills and abilities accepted by industry standards. It should also include a planned program of job training, with specific identification of the tasks to be mastered. It would include the development of sound work habits and behaviors, training in the use of resources, working effectively with coworkers and utilization of appropriate technologies.

Work-site learning and experience should take 20–50 percent of the student's time in the first year of the program, and increase to 40–70 percent in the second year. This time should be used to help the student meet

- the academic requirements of the workplace
- appropriate job training requirements
- other workplace requirements, such as the use of various technologies

The balance of the student's time should be used to meet the academic and other school diploma requirements. Disagreement over the allocation of time may lead to the development of a supplementary structure, as in regional occupational programs, where 50 percent or more of the student's time is directed to the needs of the work site.

Since there are many controversial features in a program oriented to the work site, a written agreement should be used to ensure completion of program requirements. The written agreement should include a commitment on the part of the student to achieve specific academic standards, to remain in school and attend regularly, to avoid alcohol and drug abuse and to meet work-site requirements. In practice, the California ROPs have found little problem in students living up to these regulations, since all the other people at the work site want to keep their jobs and tend not to violate them. Programs that are not employment oriented will have greater difficulties, because students do not see the job and income payoffs for following the rules.

Parents should be asked to commit to support of students' school and workplace requirements.

Employers are asked to help students acquire skills and knowledge in an orderly sequence, to provide them with a mentor at the work site and to employ them after successful conclusion of the apprenticeship.

LIFE-COPING AND WELLNESS SKILLS

Life-coping skills are taught throughout the curriculum in the Irvine Unified School District, Irvine, California. The program has been carefully evaluated and shown to be successful, and is part of a K–12 curriculum for drug prevention. The skills shown in Table 12.1 are taught in the tenth grade.

CERTIFICATE OF COMPETENCY

The school should work to coordinate the successful operation of the program, and to offer a high school diploma and a certificate of competency specifying the standards the student has met. The agreement may include a second educational organization and postsecondary training. There should be provision for a wage scale, a schedule of hours of work expected in both the school and work-site portions of the program and provision for termination of the agreement.

The school should also be responsible for advising the student about occupational and career opportunities, work experience requirements and possibilities for postsecondary education and career specialization. Advisement should also include information about how job-related competencies will be assessed, and job descriptions of potential positions.

WORK-BASED LEARNING

A decade ago, one could make a case for teachers' concerns that employers had too narrow a view of the skills students need. Increas-

TABLE 12.1 Life-coping skills, grade ten.

LIFE SKILLS Coping with Anger and Depression	WELLNESS SKILLS Use and Misuse of Substances
Integrating six stages and reactions of change Applying knowledge of reactions to change Integrating knowledge of resources Integrating skills to cope with denial Integrating the effects of anger Utilizing assertion skills to deal with anger Integrating the effects of bargaining Utilizing assertive refusal to cope with bargaining Integrating the understanding of depression Accepting and integrating reactions to STAGES Integrating skills to understand hope	Recognizing alcohol dependency Recognizing effects of marijuana use Understanding alcohol and marijuana Physical and mental effects of alcohol Learning about effect of other substances on self and others Differentiating between prescription and nonprescription drugs Learning about misconceptions and myths of alcohol and alcoholism Examining factors that influence decision not to use Analyzing the influence of advertising Developing resistance, peer and media Benefits of giving up tobacco and other substances
Effective Problem Solving	**Family Health**
Developing effective problem-solving skills Understanding difference between fact and belief Developing awareness of rational/ irrational beliefs Differentiating between rational/ irrational beliefs Developing the skill of problem solving Developing understanding of self talk Developing the skill of brainstorming Developing skills of alternative solution Understanding the consequences of brainstorming Recognizing skill of listing alternatives Recognizing consequences in problem solving Practicing implementing plan	Recognizing family influences and differences Learning how the family meets basic needs Locating community resources and family assistance Developing awareness of individual rights and responsibilities in relationships Recognizing dysfunctions within families Identifying/preventing abuse Identifying proper steps in solving family problems
	Personal Health
	Achieving and maintaining health Understanding how health choices affect quality of life Understanding when health changes require professional assistance

ingly, employers recognize the need for broader skills, especially those that lead to improved problem solving. Consequently, it is easier now for high school teachers to link to local employers, and to feel good about the training students are receiving. This is a key factor leading to improved opportunities for apprenticeship development at the current time.

The big question now becomes "What curriculum can we deliver that is sound academically, that is presented in an interesting manner, that is relevant to the work site and that therefore meets students' needs?"

Preparing a Problem for Class.

A youth apprenticeship program is one which

- integrates academic instruction and work-based learning
- provides for work-site learning and paid work experience
- is offered to students beginning in the eleventh or twelfth grade
- results in receipt of a high school diploma or certificate of competency
- leads, as appropriate, to entry into a postsecondary program or permanent employment

Next we suggest the types of changes that could be made as one seeks to offer employment-bound training (the curriculum) with a delivery system (instruction) that utilizes the new generic approach focusing upon problem solving and critical thinking.

Perhaps the most complete work-based learning materials are those developed by the Industrial Training Corporation (Staff, 1992a). These materials are in an interactive videodisc format and are used widely across the country for apprenticeship and other on-site training. We will describe this entire curriculum in order to give you an idea of the materials available, and also an indication of the types of apprenticeships that presently exist in business and industry in the U.S. The youth apprenticeships we design should flow into these apprenticeships if we are truly interested in creating a system of school-to-work transition. These (adult) apprenticeships are highly regarded by the business community, and to the extent we can integrate our efforts with them we strengthen the chances of our programs being adopted by businesses. This is not to say that adult apprenticeships cannot be improved by adding problem solving and critical thinking.

You may recall from Chapter 1 that we described a paradigm for introducing an expert system, the one described in Chapter 5, which is used to identify students at risk and place them in interventions. We believe that successful change comes about incrementally. The existing apprenticeship system is not going to disappear quickly. It has grown to its present state over decades, and it has served the top-down corporations well. Now we are in a new era that requires us to move toward bottom-up collaboration at the work site between well-trained, technologically literate workers and a slender few managers. It should help school staff, as they look for possible locations for new apprenticeships, to see curricula from across the country, especially those for which multimedia materials have been developed.

APPRENTICESHIP TRAINING MATERIALS

Reading through the examples of apprenticeship materials, it is apparent that any apprentice-to-be will need a solid high school education to complete many of the lessons. Since schools depend upon employers to make apprenticeship programs work, it behooves the schools to send well-prepared students into apprenticeship programs. Otherwise the employers will drop the programs.

The training material examples cover fundamentals, quality, safety, mechanical, electrical/electronic and instrumentation areas of technical skills. Concepts from the work-directed learning model are labeled A, application ideas are labeled B and examples from the various training modules are labeled C.

Fundamentals

Materials covering fundamentals include work practice, proper tool use, mathematics, reading and writing.

Applied Mathematics—Thirty-Two to Forty-Eight Hours of Training

A. Content knowledge is conceptual. Factual knowledge and procedures relate to the field of interest, whether it be electronics, machine repair, accounting or English.

B. This applied math module is a good example of the appropriate use of content knowledge if the instructor continually connects the material to skills and procedures in the balance of the training curriculum.

C. Lesson one: whole number operations
Lesson two: fractions
Lesson three: decimals
Lesson four: math operations—percent, ratio and proportion, graphs
Lesson five: math operations—positive and negative numbers, powers and roots

Lesson six: algebra—using common industrial formulas
Lesson seven: measurement/unit analysis
Lesson eight: geometry and trigonometry—length, area, volume and angle calculations

Hand Tools and Measuring Instruments—
Eight to Twelve Hours of Training

A. Work to carry out instruction in a context that facilitates what you are teaching. For example, teach writing where you have access to an electronic bulletin board where the students can write messages to each other.

B. This instruction could easily be implemented in a shop or laboratory to give it relevance.

C. Lesson one: hand tools
Lesson two: precision measuring instruments

Interpersonal Skills—Four to Six Hours of Training

A. Personal management teaches scheduling and goal-setting skills, and offers instruction in studying and test-taking ability.

B. Communication skills and team building are a good place to work on scheduling and goal setting.

C. Lesson one: communication skills, including team effectiveness and problem solving

Reading and Writing Enhancement—Twenty-Four to
Thirty-Six Hours of Training

A. Learning strategies for reading and writing enhancement include learning to learn, identifying one's learning style, cooperative learning, listening skills and adapting to new situations.

B. Reading and writing enhancement training is a good place to focus on learning to learn, as, for instance, students begin to realize that procedures and instructions are in a process of continual change. The efficient thing to do is learn how to learn to use new procedures.

C. Lesson one: reading and writing procedures and instructions
Lesson two: reading and writing forms and applications

Lesson three: reading and writing logs and memos
Lesson four: reading and writing workplace information documents
Lesson five: reading and writing reference materials
Lesson six: reading and writing technical manuals

Quality

Training materials on issues of quality emphasize comprehensive training in statistical process control and predictive maintenance.

Rotating Equipment, Predictive Maintenance and Alignment— Twenty-Eight to Forty-Two Hours of Training

B. Listening/speaking teaching methods, such as discussion, debate and oral reports, would be appropriate in a module such as rotating equipment.

C. Lesson one: principles and practices of predictive maintenance
Lesson two: vibration analysis
Lesson three: lubricant and trend analysis
Lesson four: techniques for extending bearing life
Lesson five: principles of reverse double-dial alignment
Lesson six: reverse double-dial alignment procedure
Lesson seven: computerized and laser alignment

Statistical Process Control—Twenty-Eight to Forty-Two Hours of Training

A. Planning strategies such as assessing needs, predicting future needs, goal setting, and problem solving are taught.

B. One can easily imagine an instructor asking students to learn planning strategies as they learn to use statistical process control skills. Control charts allow us to measure the difference between our accuracy now, and our target accuracy, for example.

C. Lesson one: introduction to statistical process control
Lesson two: introduction to control charts
Lesson three: control charts for variables
Lesson four: control charts for attributes
Lesson five: advanced control charts

Lesson six: machine- and process-capability studies
Lesson seven: problem-solving techniques

Safety

Safety lessons focus on giving students practice in making decisions and taking action in potentially dangerous situations. Watching/doing approaches such as inquiry, demonstration, simulation and field trips would fit nicely into the safety modules below.

Electrical Safety—Eight to Twelve Hours of Training

C. Lesson one: electrical safety awareness
Lesson two: lockout/tagout

Respiratory Protection—Eight to Twelve Hours of Training

C. Lesson one: air purifying respirators
Lesson two: atmosphere supplying respirators

Rigging and Lifting—Twelve to Eighteen Hours of Training

A. If you are teaching about using experts, go to a setting where the students can see an expert at work, or show a videotape of an expert working.

B. In this module, the instructor makes sure the students actually watch an operator using the equipment, prior to operating it.

C. Lesson one: hand-operated equipment
Lesson two: forklifts and cranes
Lesson three: ladders and scaffolding

Underground Storage Tank Health and Safety—Sixteen to Twenty-Four Hours of Training

C. Lesson one: petroleum products
Lesson two: exposure and oxygen depletion
Lesson three: underground storage tank site physical hazards
Lesson four: protecting, monitoring and planning

Mechanical

Mechanical training materials focus on troubleshooting mechanical problems in real-life situations with hands-on practice in a safe environment. Watching/doing methods, such as hands-on, are made to order for troubleshooting as students learn how to solve mechanical problems.

Air Compressor Repair—Eight to Twelve Hours of Training

C. Lesson one: reciprocating compressors—principles and troubleshooting
Lesson two: reciprocating compressors—disassembly, inspection and repair

Centrifugal Pump Repair—Eight to Twelve Hours of Training

C. Lesson one: centrifugal pumps—principles and troubleshooting
Lesson two: centrifugal pumps—disassembly, inspection and repair

Hand Tools and Measuring Instruments—Eight to Twelve Hours of Training

C. Lesson one: hand tools
Lesson two: precision measuring instruments

Industrial Hydraulic Power—Twenty to Thirty Hours of Training

C. Lesson one: hydraulic system operation
Lesson two: hydraulic pumps, pumping principles and accumulators
Lesson three: pressure controls
Lesson four: directional flow controls
Lesson five: hydraulic actuators

Mechanical Seals—Four to Six Hours of Training

C. Participants are trained to understand the functions and operation of mechanical seals, and to repair common seals.

Pipefitting—Sixteen to Twenty-Four Hours of Training

C. Lesson one: pipefitting materials and layout
Lesson two: tubing and threaded pipe
Lesson three: preparing piping installation
Lesson four: lagging and insulation

Rigging and Lifting—Twelve to Eighteen Hours of Training

C. Lesson one: hand-operated equipment
Lesson two: forklifts and cranes
Lesson three: ladders and scaffolding

Rotating Equipment, Predictive Maintenance and Alignment— Twenty-Eight to Forty-Two Hours of Training

A. Adaptability training supports the development of adaptability by helping students to learn skills for managing and making sense of new conditions, ideas and information.
B. Adaptability can be demonstrated nicely in a predictive/maintenance module, where students can learn the old approach along with the new, and where they may come to realize how valuable it is to a company to have employees that can adapt quickly to new approaches.
C. Lesson one: principles and practices of predictive maintenance
Lesson two: vibration analysis
Lesson three: lubricant and trend analysis
Lesson four: techniques for extending bearing life
Lesson five: principles of reverse double-dial alignment
Lesson six: reverse double-dial alignment procedure
Lesson seven: computerized and laser alignment

Valve Repair—Eight to Twelve Hours of Training

C. Lesson one: gate valve repair
Lesson two: globe and control valve repair

Electrical/Electronic

The electrical/electronic materials move from routine installation to troubleshooting complex digital systems. Reading/writing methods ranging from the use of textbooks and chalkboard, to peer review and peer tutoring, all seem appropriate as students move through the electronic modules. Programmed instruction would be a fine way to introduce the complex systems at the end of the training series.

Digital Electronic Theory—Sixteen to Twenty-Four Hours of Training

A. Intrinsic motivation comes from inside us and often follows extrinsic motivation, such as the desire to please someone. To help students understand this, invite someone to class, like an athlete, who plays hard because it's fun.

B. Frequently the person who teaches electronic theory is a good example of intrinsic motivation. They have played with circuits and codes for their own enjoyment since they first encountered them.

C. Lesson one: binary logic circuits
Lesson two: codes, encoders, decoders and flip-flops
Lesson three: counters and shift registers
Lesson four: data transmission, conversion and storage

Electric Motors—Sixteen to Twenty-Four Hours of Training

A. Students are asked to perform increasingly complex tasks as they move through the training experience.

B. These modules on electric motors have been designed so they move toward increasing complexity.

C. Lesson one: AC motors – theory and routine testing
Lesson two: AC motors – maintenance
Lesson three: AC motors – variable speed motor theory and maintenance
Lesson four: DC motors – theory and maintenance

Electrical Control Equipment—Twenty to Thirty Hours of Training

C. Lesson one: fuses and molded case circuit breakers
   Lesson two: limit switches
   Lesson three: switches, coils and overload relays
   Lesson four: motor starters
   Lesson five: troubleshooting electrical control circuits

Electrical/Electronic Test Instruments—Twelve to
Eighteen Hours of Training

C. Lesson one: the multimeter
   Lesson two: the megohmmeter, clamp-on ammeter and wheatstone bridge
   Lesson three: the oscilloscope

Electrical/Electronic Theory—Twenty-Eight to
Forty-Two Hours of Training

A. In cooperative learning, students work together to solve problems and carry out tasks. It is easy to demonstrate this with two students at a computer. Typically, they will naturally cooperate to accomplish a task.

B. These theoretical materials present the instructor with a fine opportunity to place a theory-oriented student with several students who are not so oriented, to demonstrate their problem-solving capabilities.

C. Lesson one: AC/DC theory—Ohm's law and DC circuits
   Lesson two: AC/DC theory—characteristics of AC circuits
   Lesson three: AC/DC theory—three-phase AC systems
   Lesson four: solid-state theory—semiconductors and diodes
   Lesson five: solid-state theory—rectifiers and filters
   Lesson six: solid-state theory—transistors, SCRs and triacs
   Lesson seven: introduction to digital electronics

Electrical Print Reading—Eight to Twelve Hours of Training

C. Lesson one: wiring, single-line and building electrical diagrams
   Lesson two: ladder diagrams

Electrical Safety—Eight to Twelve Hours of Training

C. Lesson one: electrical safety awareness
Lesson two: lockout/tagout

Electrical Switchgear—Twelve to Eighteen Hours of Training

C. Lesson one: bus work and circuit breaker
Lesson two: circuit breaker testing and maintenance
Lesson three: protective relays

*Modicon 984 Basic Training—Sixteen to
Twenty-Four Hours of Training*

A. Problem-solving strategies are typically based on successful experience, and include problem finding, problem identification, listing of alternative solutions, selection of a solution, implementation of the solution and evaluation of effectiveness.

B. Troubleshooting is a fine opportunity for working on the difficult skill of problem finding.

C. Lesson one: system hardware
Lesson two: software configuration
Lesson three: programming
Lesson four: system troubleshooting

Programmable Controllers—Sixteen to Twenty-Four Hours of Training

A. To make this competitive learning module constructive, students should compete in using a sound process, rather than in terms of the product being produced. Realistically, the easiest thing for students to understand is a combination of competitive and cooperative learning, as in teams working together to make a presentation and get a high grade.

B. A nice opportunity for competition presents itself in this advanced material on troubleshooting.

C. Lesson one: principles of operation
Lesson two: interpreting ladder logic
Lesson three: troubleshooting strategies
Lesson four: troubleshooting simulations

Soldering—Twelve to Eighteen Hours of Training

C. Lesson one: introduction to soldering
Lesson two: the component board

Instrumentation

The materials in the instrumentation section focus upon instrumentation and control, using computers and calibration test equipment. Students should get a feel for the overall product or big picture prior to being asked to develop individual parts of the whole. The section on instrumentation is a good example of presenting general principles and the big picture before moving to local skills, such as calibrating test equipment.

Analyzers—Sixteen to Twenty-Four Hours of Training

A. Each of the study skills programs starts with listening skills and uses them throughout.

B. Listening skills can be developed nicely around content that lends itself to lecture, such as the module on analysis and analyzers.

C. Lesson one: principles and process analysis
Lesson two: physical process analyzers
Lesson three: composition analyzers
Lesson four: automated product sampling

Control Valves—Sixteen to Twenty-Four Hours of Training

C. Lesson one: body types and trim
Lesson two: actuators and positioners
Lesson three: body and trim maintenance
Lesson four: actuator and positioner maintenance

Controller Tuning—Four to Six Hours of Training

C. These materials cover basic instrument control, including the proportional, integral and derivative control modes.

Digital Instrumentation—Eight to Twelve Hours of Training

C. Lesson one: smart transmitters
Lesson two: single-loop digital controllers

Electronic Maintenance—Twenty to Thirty Hours of Training

A. Learning to learn skills are useful for perceiving, organizing, making sense of and using ideas and data.

B. A good place to teach learning to learn is an area like transmitters and controllers, where constantly improving technology makes change and new learning almost continual.

C. Lesson one: pressure and temperature transmitters
Lesson two: flow transmitters
Lesson three: level and weight transmitters
Lesson four: transducers, recorders and annunciators
Lesson five: electronic controllers

Fundamentals of Industrial Measurement—Sixteen to Twenty-Four Hours of Training

C. Lesson one: pressure measurement
Lesson two: flow measurement
Lesson three: temperature measurement
Lesson four: level measurement

Industrial Process Control—Eight to Twelve Hours of Training

C. Lesson one: single-loop control
Lesson two: multiple-loop control

Instrument Calibration—Twenty to Thirty Hours of Training

A. Instrument calibration can give insight into students' own styles of learning, and provides practice in their learning style strengths.

B. A set of concepts like calibration principles presents a good opportunity for students to come to understand there are many different learning styles, including reading alone, reading and discussing with a partner and dividing content among a group and having each member teach her/his materials to the others.

C. Lesson one: calibration principles
Lesson two: calibrating pressure and differential pressure instruments
Lesson three: calibrating temperature instruments
Lesson four: calibrating flow instruments
Lesson five: calibrating level instruments

Interpreting Process Control Diagrams—Four to Six Hours of Training

C. This lesson is designed to introduce participants to industrial process control, instruments and control functions.

Process Operations—Twelve to Eighteen Hours of Training

C. Lesson one: heating and cooling systems
Lesson two: distillation columns
Lesson three: batch-process systems

*Test Instruments and Devices—Sixteen to
Twenty-Four Hours of Training*

C. Lesson one: pneumatic and hydraulic test devices
Lesson two: electronic test devices
Lesson three: frequency and temperature test devices
Lesson four: analog and digital oscilloscopes

Troubleshooting—Twelve to Sixteen Hours of Training

A. Troubleshooting teaches creative problem-solving strategies for solving problems effectively and imaginatively.

B. Creative problem solving would fit naturally into this module on troubleshooting since troubleshooting is problem solving.

C. Lesson one: troubleshooting single-loop control systems
Lesson two: troubleshooting multi-loop control systems
Lesson three: troubleshooting distributed control systems

KEY PROBLEMS

To make these lessons and similar training opportunities available to students, we have significant problems to solve. Among them are the legal status of the participants. Some states use a top-down approach. In Wisconsin, for example, they have passed legislation dealing with the legal status of apprentices. Issues, such as child labor laws and compensation, have been clarified. Other states, such as New York, operate from the bottom up, and they work to solve these and other issues by creating models at the local level which will become legislation in time.

Enlisting employers is the most difficult challenge of all. Firms that do not hire teenagers, or spend much money on training their adult employees, are not likely to participate. It is therefore important to locate firms that are more training oriented. It seems likely that tax incentives will be offered in the years ahead that focus on apprenticeships and other entry-level training opportunities for students still in their teens. The development of work-directed learning systems will be critical. In such systems we will integrate the many components discussed in these chapters, just as the many components in a school system are linked together to facilitate student movement through the system.

WHERE WE SHOULD BE GOING

We need a vision of future apprenticeships. The apprenticeships we have just described offer the content of the present with a delivery system of the future that is problem solving oriented and uses critical thinking skills. This is another example of two steps forward and one step back. This approach is similar to our experience in attempting to get teachers to use scanners to identify and place students at risk in interventions. We retreated to a model where teachers don't have to use scanners, but rather, they enter data by typing it into the computer. The day will come when future teachers are comfortable with the scanner approach.

Most U.S. vocational education teachers hold traditional views, and it will take incremental steps to bring new concepts into their curricula. Employment-bound programming, such as traditional apprenticeship materials, are still visible. But new approaches with more generic training will come. These approaches will be proposed no doubt as part of a restructuring effort. There will still be a present employment/task emphasis, but some of the new courses will be designed to emphasize problem solving, and some will meet college admission requirements, a benefit for those students who change their minds and decide to attend a four-year college. It's the kind of compromise that allows the system to work.

We close the chapter with some recommendations for federal policy seen throughout Rosenbaum (1992).

> The nation needs a system to which all young people have access, not just those who meet income guidelines or other specially defined populations. Narrow targeting, which stigmatizes and marginalizes programs, should be replaced with more universal eligibility criteria.

> We must build a system, not just fund a series of demonstration projects. Neither employers nor schools nor young people need another short-term program layered on top of the already overwhelming welter of education reform initiatives.

> We must place new emphasis on career education and guidance. Career education should become part of the K–12 curriculum so that our children have a rich understanding of the industries that drive our economy and the occupational opportunities within them. Guidance counseling in high school should be about careers, not just about college choices.

> The system must be rooted in the commitment of quality employers to provide work and learning opportunities for young people. This would open up the possibility of using jobs and training as an incentive to hard work and achievement in school. And it would connect young people to the labor market in a more systematic and beneficial way.

> A broad, diverse set of career pathways must be available for young people wanting to explore and then enter different industries, occupations and specializations. No single program design will answer the needs of all communities, employers, schools and young people.

> Curricula and teaching strategies must emphasize active, contextual learning, broad rather than narrow skill training and the integration of academic and vocational education. The pedagogy of school-and-work integration should reflect cognitive science research on the power of learning-by-doing and should recognize the growing importance of higher-order thinking skills to productive employment and citizenship.

> The system must not foreclose the possibility of higher education. The "school-to-work transition" is a misnomer. The end of compulsory schooling can no longer serve as the end of formal learning. Instead, the

system should encourage a rich set of routes to lifelong learning in workplaces and educational institutions. Increasingly, we must think in terms of "school-and-work integration."

An effective system must generate and disseminate more—and more systematic—labor market information upon which students and employers can base their career preparation and hiring decisions. Employers should have easier access to useful information on student achievement, and better ways to judge applicants' skills and competencies. Students should have more complete knowledge of the performance of different public and private training providers, and the employment and income prospects of different careers. Policymakers and public at-large need more accurate information on the career trajectories of young people after they leave school.

Chapter 13

ESTABLISHING AND IMPROVING A PEER ASSISTANCE PROGRAM

In this chapter we make suggestions for key elements to consider in starting a new peer assistance/counseling program, or enhancing the one you have. They include Peer Assistant software, a list of relevant materials for schools, a list of risk factors and recommended interventions, a model sponsoring agency for a county- or city-wide peer assistance program, a sample parent letter and return form, a peer assistant report form, a risk assessment survey, paper and pencil short form, a teacher referral form and a curriculum guide.

One critical resource for a school seeking to reduce dropouts is the school's own students. Most school staff are familiar with the use of students as peer tutors, especially the use of older students to help younger students. This model suggests the use of same-age students with their peers to help them become aware of the great risks they run by engaging in behaviors that lead to dropout, such as the use of alcohol and drugs.

PEER ASSISTANT SOFTWARE

The purpose of the Peer Assistant software is to provide a student who has been trained to use the software as a tool for carrying on a somewhat intimate conversation with another student who has been referred by a classroom teacher as a potential student at risk. Two-thirds of substance abusers eventually drop out of school, so this software, which is directed toward substance abuse, is really quite relevant for dropout prevention.

Figures 13.1 through 13.17 show screens from the Peer Assistant software.

Before the peer assistant and the at-risk student have been placed in front of an Apple II, Macintosh or IBM-compatible computer to see the software, the school staff member in charge should follow these steps.

(*1*) If your school has an operating peer assistance program or the equivalent, go to the next step. If you do not have a program, you should see that a letter is sent home to the parent/guardian of the student who has been referred by a teacher as one who may be at risk of dropping out or becoming a substance abuser. Copies of a parent permission letter, return form and peer assistant report form are included in this chapter (see Figures 13.18, 13.19 and 13.20).

(*2*) Peer assistance leaders should be identified, and trained to use this software. At the minimum, this should include having the student sit and view the program on the computer you are using with the teacher or counselor in charge. There should be role playing of possible difficult or confusing responses that at-risk students might make.

(*3*) If your school does not have a peer assistance program or the equivalent, and you would like to develop one, you can purchase a training manual by Dr. Barbara Varenhorst titled *Curriculum Guide for Student Peer Assistance Training.* You can purchase this book, and the other items mentioned in this chapter, from Guidance Resources, Irvine Unified School District, 5050 Barranca Parkway, Irvine, CA 92714.

This program is designed as a peer counseling instrument to be used in programs which have a focus on factors of teenage substance abuse. This program is not intended to predict substance dependency in an individual. Rather, it is intended to be used as a part of a larger substance abuse program by trained peer counselors under adult supervision.

Press <return> to continue

Figure 13.1 Screen One.

Interview questions' instructions:

Respond to the following multiple choice questions by entering the number of the answer which best describes how you view yourself.

Press <return> to continue

Figure 13.2 Screen Two.

I view myself as:

1. A nonuser of drugs or alcohol
2. An occasional user (that is, you have used drugs or alcohol within the last year, but not on an average of once a week)
3. A frequent user of drugs and alcohol (that is you have used marijuana or illegal drugs, prescription drugs or alcohol an average of one or more times a week during the past year)

Please Enter a number

Figure 13.3 Screen Three.

How important is it to you to get good grades in school?

1. Very important
2. Quite important
3. A little important
4. Not important

Please Enter a number

Figure 13.4 Screen Four.

```
Do you learn anything from drug prevention activities at school?

1. Very frequently

2. Frequently

3. Sometimes

4. Not at all

Please Enter a number
```

Figure 13.5 Screen Five.

```
How many of your closest friends use alcohol or other drugs?

1. None

2. One or two

3. Three or four

4. Five or more

Please Enter a number
```

Figure 13.6 Screen Six.

```
How much do some other members of your family drink or use drugs?

1. Not at all

2. Sometimes

3. Frequently

4. Very frequently

Please Enter a number
```

Figure 13.7 Screen Seven.

How much do you think your family is against drug and alcohol use?

1. Very much against
2. Quite a bit against
3. A little bit against

Please Enter a number

Figure 13.8 *Screen Eight.*

How many days have you been absent from school in the past year?

1. Zero to five times
2. Six to ten times
3. Eleven to fifteen times
4. Sixteen or more times

Please Enter a number

Figure 13.9 *Screen Nine.*

How many D's or F's did you receive in the last marking period?

1. None
2. One or two
3. Three or four
4. Five or more

Please Enter a number

Figure 13.10 *Screen Ten.*

How many times have you moved to a new residence (home) in the past year?

1. None
2. One or two times
3. Three or four times
4. Five or more times

Please Enter a number

Figure 13.11 Screen Eleven.

Based upon the responses which have been entered into the computer during the interview section of this program, the score total is _____ .

This compares with scores on the following chart:

 9 to 16 Low potential

17 to 25 Medium potential

26 to 35 High potential

Please <return> to continue

Figure 13.12 Screen Twelve.

Instructions: the following questions are designed to be the starting point for peer discussions.

Recently, a midwestern state surveyed 7,000 employers to find out what their number one concern was when hiring new employees. The overwhelming majority put substance abuse in first place.

Press <return> to continue

Figure 13.13 Screen Thirteen.

There is a growing trend nationwide by employers to require drug testing as a condition of employment. These tests routinely look at both illegal and prescription drug levels, as well as alcohol levels in the human body. Recognizing that the effects of substance abuse stay with the body for long periods of time:

1. What kind of employment do you hope to have as an adult?
2. How will you react to employment opportunities that require you to submit a urine, blood or hair sample for drug analysis? What are some of the alternatives in this situation?
3. What are five advantages of working with other employees who are abuse free?
4. List five ways that activities you participate in outside of your job affect the company and its employees while you are on the job.

Press <return> to continue

Figure 13.14 Screen Fourteen.

By the year 2000, employment opportunities for high school dropouts will be severely restricted. Traditional areas of employment for dropouts and undereducated persons are being increasingly automated, or those activities are being filled by higher-qualified persons as the trend toward underemployment continues. Suppose, for the purpose of these questions, that you have chosen to drop out of high school.

As a dropout:

1. Describe the type of life that you would like to live as an adult.
2. Describe a picture of what you consider to be an ideal family life.
3. List five kinds of long-term or steady employment opportunities that would be available to you.
4. Give three examples of ways that you might be able to improve your future while working full time.

Press <return> to continue

Figure 13.15 *Screen Fifteen.*

Ancient saying states that:

People can be measured by the friends that they associate with.

1. What percentage of your friends (those people that you frequently associate with) do not use or experiment with drugs?
2. What changes would you have to make in your life to establish firm friendships with five more persons who are not substance abusers?
3. What value do you see in high school graduation based on your observations of the lives of others who have graduated? Why?
4. What changes would you have to make in your life to establish firm friendships with five or more persons whom you feel will graduate from high school?
5. What percentage of your friends do you think will graduate from high school?
6. What actions would you have to take to set an example with your friends, family and relatives, as a person who will become a successful, dependency-free adult? Are you willing to try? Why?

Press <return> to continue

Figure 13.16 Screen Sixteen.

This concludes the discussion program.

This starts you on the pathway to success.

PLEASE REMOVE THIS DISK FROM THE COMPUTER DISK

DRIVE NOW AND TURN OFF THE COMPUTER.

COPYRIGHT © SAR, INC. 1990

Figure 13.17 Screen Seventeen.

Dear Parents:

As you are aware, drug abuse has become a serious problem across our nation. Research shows that many users begin using drugs as early as elementary school. Schools and parents need to unite to prevent the continual spread of drug abuse, so that students are given the opportunity to reach their learning potential.

We know you share our interest in eliminating drug abuse in our community. Therefore we are asking you to give permission for your child to participate in this project. Thank you for your cooperation and support in this matter.

Sincerely,

Assistant Superintendent

Figure 13.18 Sample Parent Letter.

(4) Select your at-risk students for participation in the use of the Peer Assistant software. If your school already has a means for identifying at-risk students you should use it, or you can use the results of the Comprehensive Risk Assessment software. This software is designed to identify students who are potential substance abusers and potential dropouts. This is critical, but districts find they also need to set up effective interventions in order to assist students at risk. Irvine Unified School District has developed many such interventions which have been carefully evaluated and found to be effective. These are now for sale. Your district no doubt has a number of interventions that are also effective. Finally, districts need a quick and reliable way to place students, who have been identified, into these interventions. We can now do this with the Comprehensive Risk Assessment software. Lists of students for placement into interventions are printed out, and these are then sent to student study teams, or the equivalent, for a final decision

about placement. This saves precious teacher time. The study team then needs to initiate a tracking and follow-up system to make sure the students actually attend the interventions, and that they are improving. This is judged by entering new data about their performance each semester and printing out their new, and hopefully improved, risk scores. At the end of the year you can have your staff complete the intervention completion questionnaire and identify why some interventions have been effective, and why some need to be improved or eliminated.

(5) The staff member in charge then arranges for pairs of students to meet and view the Peer Assistant software with the peer assistance leader playing the role of host.

Dear Administrator:

I have read the above letter and I give my permission for my son/daughter _____ to participate in the Peer Assistance program. I understand my child will participate in a computerized survey with another student to learn about the risk involved in drug use. It is my further understanding that:

- The student peer assistants are trained to keep information confidential and to respect student participants' privacy.
- Interview data will be thrown away.
- Students will be identified only by number.
- Students will not be labeled.
- Student participation will not affect school performance.

Parent Signature _____

Date _____

Figure 13.19 Sample Return Form.

```
                           Report


Name of Peer Adviser _____


Name of Peer Assistant _____


Name of Student Participant _____


What were the key problem areas discussed?




What suggestions were discussed?




Signatures


Peer Adviser _____


Peer Assistant _____


Student Participant _____


Date of Report _____
```

Figure 13.20 Sample Peer Assistant Report Form.

(6) If the at-risk student scores as a moderate- or high-risk individual when his/her score is reported in the software program, the peer assistance leader should indicate this to the staff member in charge. Many schools like to use an informal, verbal report in this situation in order to keep the process low-key and nonthreatening. The Peer Assistant software is designed so that it does not save student responses, nor does it print them out. We feel this also reduces the likelihood of the process being perceived as threatening by the student at risk.

(7) Once the moderate- and high-risk students have been referred to the staff member in charge, she/he refers them to the principal or his/her designee for appropriate assistance. Chapter 6 describes dozens of approaches for working with at-risk students using various interventions.

(8) If you decide to establish a peer assistance program, one or two of your teachers will need to be trained to be trainers of the student peer assistance leaders. The training focuses upon the following areas.
- communications
- listening
- decision making
- problem solving
- understanding teenage issues
- referral system policies and procedures
- the role of the peer assistant

Write to Irvine Unified at the previously listed address for more information about this training.

LIST OF RELEVANT MATERIALS FOR SCHOOLS

Middle and High School Materials

Real Friends, a book young people can read and use for self and peer facilitation, was written by Dr. Barbara Varenhorst, formerly from Palo Alto Unified School District; order from Harper and Row Publishers, Keystone Industrial Park, Scranton, PA 18512.

Caring and Sharing: Becoming a Peer Facilitator, a student handbook for learning helping skills, was written by Robert D. Myrick and

Tom Erney; order from Educational Media Corporation, P.O. Box 21211, Minneapolis, MN 55421.

Telesis includes peer counseling and training curriculum with workbooks in English, Spanish, Laotian, Cambodian and Vietnamese. The curriculum addresses self-awareness, group dynamics, decision making, pharmacology, communication, counseling and peer leadership; order from Telesis Corporation, 3180 University Avenue, Suite 640, San Diego, CA 92104.

Additional Junior High and Middle School Materials

Starting Conflict Manager Programs tells how to set up a school program to reduce conflict; *Training Middle School Conflict Managers* tells how to train middle school students to help other students reduce conflict; order both from Community Boards Center for Policy and Training, 148 Ninth Street, San Francisco, CA 94103.

Just Say "NO" Guide is for adult leaders of Just Say "NO" clubs; order from Just Say "NO" Foundation, 1777 N. California Blvd. # 200, Walnut Creek, CA 94596.

Elementary School Materials

Project Self-Esteem, a personal/social skills curriculum for second through sixth grade students taught by teams of parent volunteers or teachers, was written by Sandy McDaniel and Peggy Bielen; order from Enhancing Education, P.O. Box 16001, Newport Beach, CA 92656.

Training Elementary School Conflict Managers tells how to train elementary school students to help other students reduce conflict; order from Community Boards Center for Policy and Training, 148 Ninth Street, San Francisco, CA 94103.

Just Say "NO" Guide is for adult leaders of Just Say "NO" clubs; order from Just Say "NO" Foundation, 1777 N. California Blvd. # 200, Walnut Creek, CA 94596.

High School Materials

Choices: A Teen Woman's Journal for Self Awareness and Personal Planning, and *Challenges: A Young Man's Journal for Self Awareness and Personal Planning* were designed to assist young women and men to develop skills in the areas of goal setting and decision making. Written by Bingham, Edmandson and Stryker, they are appropriate for youth and as a training guide for adults; order from Mission Publications, P.O. Box 25, El Toro, CA 92630.

Middle and Elementary School Materials

STAR Curriculum, a social skills curriculum of fifty lessons for sixth to eighth grade students, was written by Guidance Resources staff, Irvine USD; order from Guidance Resources, Irvine Unified School District, 5050 Barranca Parkway, Irvine, CA 92714.

STAR Kit, containing one curriculum, fifteen student workbooks, one set of task cards, audiotapes, workbook, activity cards and one student and one parent handbook, was written by Guidance Resources staff, Irvine USD; order from Guidance Resources, Irvine Unified School District, 5050 Barranca Parkway, Irvine, CA 92714.

Friends Can Be Good Medicine, a K–12 curriculum about relationships and well-being, was written by staff at the California Department of Mental Health; order from California Department of Mental Health, Publications Unit, 1600 9th Street, Sacramento, CA 95814.

More Teachable Moments, a K–12 curriculum which helps develop expert listening skills using student and teacher awareness of the ways we sometimes do not listen, was written by Cliff Durfee; order from LIVE, LOVE AND LAUGH, P.O. Box 9432, San Diego, CA 92109.

Grades Three, Five and Seven Materials

Y.E.S. Curriculum is a unique model prevention curriculum designed to help infuse current anti-drug/gang messages into subject area curricula; order from Orange County Department of Education, Media Services Unit, P.O. Box 9050, Costa Mesa, CA 92628.

RISK FACTORS AND RECOMMENDED INTERVENTIONS

This is a more complete list of risk factors than are used in the Comprehensive Risk Assessment system described in Chapter 5. The questions that are also used in that system are marked with an asterisk (*). The interventions following each question would be recommended, if the student response was that given in parentheses.

(1) With whom do you live? (any answer other than two parents)
  - Interview student to determine any associated problems.
  - If indicated, teach coping skills for major change, i.e., STAGES (Irvine Unified School District, 1987).
  - If indicated, provide parent support group or refer for counseling.

*(2) How important is it to you to get good grades in school? (not important)
  - Interview student to determine reason.
  - Check school records for grades and achievement.
  - If indicated, refer for special education screening.
  - If indicated, teach study skills.
  - If indicated, conduct activities to increase student's bonding to school, i.e., opportunities for recognition.

(3) Do you ever argue with teachers? (often or very often)
  - Interview to determine reason.
  - If indicated, train in STAR assertive communication, GOAL accountability or PLUS problem-solving skills.
  - Train teacher(s) in cooperative discipline.

*(4) Are you absent from school when you are not sick? (4–7 days)
  - Interview to determine reason.
  - If indicated, implement school bonding activities, i.e., assign to a staff mentor.
  - Monitor and/or contract for school attendance.

*(5) Have you ever been suspended or expelled from school? (yes)
  - Interview for dates and specifics.
  - If indicated, monitor student behavior and/or increase school bonding.

(6) What do you learn from school prevention activities? (nothing or a little)
  - Interview for reason.
  - If student is high risk (has several risk factors), provide secondary drug prevention activities, i.e., more intense drug education/counseling in small group.

(7) How many times have you used a prescription drug without a doctor? (2–6 or more times)
  • Provide specialized drug education/counseling in small group.

(8) Where did you learn most of what you know about drugs? (answer other than school or parents)
  • If indicated, provide correct drug education information.
  • Train parents in how to talk to youth about drugs.

*(9) How many of your close friends use alcohol or drugs? (3–5 or more)
  • Compare to student's own level of use.
  • If indicated, teach STAR peer-refusal skills.
  • Provide opportunities for interaction with nonusing peers.

*(10) How many times have you used marijuana? (once a week for past three months)
  • Provide specialized drug education/counseling in small group.

*(11) What would you do if a friend asked you to use marijuana? (I'm not sure or I would try it)
  • Interview for reason.
  • If indicated, teach STAR refusal skills.

*(12) How often do you feel angry? (often or very often)
  • Interview for reason.
  • Provide opportunity for counseling.
  • If indicated, teach STAGES coping and anger management skills.
  • If indicated, teach STAR or PLUS relaxation skills.

(13) How often do you argue with your family? (often or very often)
  • Interview for reason.
  • If indicated, refer for family counseling.
  • If indicated, refer parents for education on family communication.

*(14) How much are your parents against your use of drugs? (not at all or mildly)
  • Interview for reason.
  • If indicated, refer parents for education on clarifying/ communicating values.
  • If indicated, counsel student on being responsible for self.

*(*15*) How much do adults you are close to, use drugs? (often or very often)
- Interview to determine relationship (parents, siblings or other) and impact.
- If indicated, provide student counseling support for family member's use.
- If indicated, counsel student on being responsible for self.

(*16*) How often do you smoke cigarettes? (one or more a day)
- Educate about risk factors for drug abuse.

*(*17*) Have you ever been arrested? (yes)

(*18*) How old were you the first time you were arrested? (any answer)
- Interview for reason and date.
- If indicated, monitor for antisocial tendencies.
- Create opportunities for prosocial behavior.
- If indicated, teach GOAL or PLUS self-control skills.

(*19*) How old were you when you had your first alcoholic drink (more than a sip)? (under fifteen years)
- Educate about risk factors for drug abuse.

(*20*) How often did you drink last year? (once a week or every day)
- Educate about risk factors for drug abuse.

*(*21*) How many times have you been drunk or high? (three or more times)
- Provide drug education and counseling.
- If indicated, provide opportunities for alternative high experiences.

*(*22*) When you are away from home, after school and in the evening, how often do your parents know where you are? (seldom or never)
- Interview for specifics.
- If indicated, refer parents for education on limit setting.

(*23*) If you had a personal problem, with whom would you talk? (not mother or father)
- Interview for extent and balance in student's support system.
- If indicated, refer parents and youth to improve communication skills.

(*24*) Does your family have rules, and are they enforced? (none or a few)

- Interview for outcomes of rule enforcement.
- If indicated, refer parents for education on limit setting.
- If indicated, counsel student on self-discipline skills.

(25) How many times have you tried illegal drugs? (three or more times)
  - Educate on risk factors for drug abuse.

THE ORANGE COUNTY SUBSTANCE ABUSE PREVENTION NETWORK

The Orange County Substance Abuse Prevention Network is a coalition of public/private agencies and organizations providing substance abuse prevention and treatment services in Orange County, California. Participants include parents, educators, treatment providers, law enforcement officers and social service representatives. It is a model sponsoring agency for a county- or city-wide peer assistance program which tries to answer such community questions as:

- How can we keep children from experimenting with drugs in today's chemically oriented society?
- What can we do if a child is experimenting with drugs?
- Where can we go for help?

The stated objectives of the Orange County program are:

- Coordinate county-wide prevention efforts.
- Participate in the planning and funding of drug abuse prevention projects for Orange County.
- Provide training and technical assistance.
- Seek legislative support and funding for prevention projects.
- Participate in regional, state and national prevention planning efforts.

The program's participating agencies include:

- Agape Counseling and Therapy Services
- Breakaway Health Corp.
- Care Action
- Center for Creative Alternatives
- Center for Family Counseling

- National Council on Alcoholism
- Neidhardt, Ryan & Waln Counseling Associates
- Orange County Alcohol Program
- Orange County Drug Abuse Services
- Orange County Just Say "NO" clubs
- Orange County Trauma Society
- PAL program
- Phoenix House
- Charter Hospital, Long Beach
- CompCare–Care Units
- Cypress Police Department
- Junior League of Orange County
- KIDS of Southern California
- Project NODS
- Project Self-Esteem
- Psycho Neurological Institute
- Second Chance Adolescent Program
- Straight Talk Clinic, Inc.
- Western Center for Drug-Free Schools
- Youth and Family Recovery Center

Parent groups participating in the program are:

- CASA, North Orange County
- CASA, Orange County Unified School District
- Irvine Chemical People
- Parents Who Care, Newport Beach
- Parents Who Care, Tustin
- PRIDE, Newport Mesa

Chapter 14

PARENT INVOLVEMENT

This chapter includes an overview of the San Bernardino Unified School District's plan for the use of categorical funds for disadvantaged youth. It then presents a case study of the Riley Elementary School and its successful efforts to improve student performance and bring it up to the district average, even though Riley has a greater proportion of disadvantaged students than the district does overall. The focus at Riley was on reading and language arts improvement. The support teacher program and implementation of whole language are likely reasons for the improvement. The Riley staff also focused much of their energy on parent involvement, and there has been a remarkable improvement in student performance.

San Bernardino City Unified School District is the eleventh largest school district in California. The student population is nearing 540,000 and is continuing to grow. The district includes Hispanic, Caucasian, African American and Asian students, and smaller numbers of other ethnic groups.

The purpose of the San Bernardino City Unified School District's master plan for categorical programs was to provide a framework for making maximum use of categorical funds in order to have a significant, positive effect on the achievement of educationally disadvantaged youth. The master plan for categorical programs was developed by a forty-two member task force. The task force members were divided into five committees that were asked to address program, instruction, parent involvement, change and evaluation issues.

The subcommittee for parent/community involvement was asked to look at and define types and amounts of parent involvement needed to positively impact student achievement, and to define specific strategies for achieving parent involvement.

One-on-One Instruction.

The subcommittee sought to foster the idea of collaboration among students, staff, parents and community as an essential ingredient to educational success. They were also determined to show that parents and community play an essential role in the success of students, and that both should be actively involved in the education of students.

To support the subcommittee's work, the board of education adopted the following policy on parent involvement. Its key provisions were:

- Establish and maintain a PTA program.
- Establish and maintain a school site and/or school advisory council where appropriate.
- Include parent participation in the program and curriculum development.
- Help parents develop parenting skills.
- Provide parents with the knowledge of techniques designed to assist their children in learning at home.
- Promote clear two-way communication between school and family about school programs and student's progress.
- Involve parents, with appropriate training, in instructional support roles at the school.

- Support parents as decision makers and help them develop their leadership in governance, advisory and advocacy roles.
- Establish a parent center with materials and books for parent use.
- Develop a family support team to assist parents with resolutions of those home problems that interfere with student learning.
- Develop a home/school agreement delineating home, school and student responsibilities.

RILEY ELEMENTARY SCHOOL

At the Riley Elementary School, the San Bernardino master plan was translated into an initiative to improve reading. As the initiative got underway, the school's principal, James E. Riley, prepared a report on the work. This is his report.

Riley's primary focus of 1990–1993 will be reading improvement. We want all students to become independent readers with a love and joy of all literature-based reading. The full implementation of all materials provided by the Houghton-Mifflin Literature series, including listening, speaking, reading and writing skills, in conjunction with the language arts portfolios for each student, should prove very beneficial.

In addition, use of Chapter 1 and school-based coordination money provided a Slavin model reading program in grades one through three, to help accomplish our goals. Staff development will be an integral part of the program.

Riley needs to continue emphasis on problem solving and higher-level thinking skills in math, and to continue to implement the science recommendation of the program quality review.

Riley School is a pilot school for categorical programs in the San Bernardino City Unified School District. Many innovative programs have been implemented, including a very comprehensive parent education program.

The purpose of the San Bernardino City Unified School District's master plan is to provide a framework for making maximum use of categorical funds in order to have a significant, positive effect on the achievement of educationally disadvantaged youth.

The principle underlying the parent education component in the master plan is that parents and community play an essential role in the success of students, and the goal of the plan is to actively involve parents and community in the education of students.

The innovative project's allowance is intended to promote program improvement, as well as to give more local flexibility in providing Chapter 1 services. Part of the innovation funds are used to encourage innovative approaches to parent involvement, or rewards to, or expanded use of, an exemplary parental involvement program.

Parent Involvement Program

In 1990–1991, Riley School began to implement the district master plan for categorical programs. There are many components to the parent education program that began in 1990–1991. They include:

- *First grade parent club meetings* — First grade parent club meetings are held monthly and are conducted by the reading support teachers. They are designed to instruct parents in language arts strategies they can use with their children at home.
- *Home/school agreements* — As part of the master plan, home/school agreements were designed to involve parents in taking an active role in their children's education, and to take responsibility for ensuring their child's attendance and homework responsibilities.
- *Parent library* — With some of the Chapter 1 innovation funds, library books were purchased for checkout to parents of first and second grade students. These books are checked out on a weekly basis.
- *School advisory, school site and bilingual advisory councils* — Councils are mandated for schools. These councils are in place and are very well attended. Also, we have representatives who attend the district advisory council on a monthly basis.
- *Parent volunteers* — Historically, Riley School has had a fair number of volunteers who give time within the classroom. The number of volunteers, although lower than it was ten years ago, is still relatively high, and volunteers are a viable part of the instructional program.

In 1991–1992 our parent education program expanded to include:

- *Take-home computers*—The objectives of the program are to improve basic skills, increase parent involvement in the school program, encourage increased time on task in academic subjects and encourage computer literacy and confidence. The take-home computer program targets second grade students who have been involved in the reading support program. Parents and students are trained together in the use of the computer, as well as the software that is provided. The computers are taken home during the student's offtrack time. Older, inexpensive computers are utilized.
- *Family reading style classes*—These classes are held in the fall and spring, and are targeted for all parents and students. Parents are taught different ways of reading to their children, as well as providing an environment conducive to reading.
- *Literacy/ESL class*—Many Riley parents are semiliterate or illiterate. To compensate, literacy classes are held for parents every Thursday from 10 A.M. to NOON at the Feldheym Library. Dr. Ann Freeman, director of the literacy program, conducts these classes. Also, ESL classes are held at the library on a weekly basis for parents with limited English proficiency.
- *CASA*—The community and school alliance program is a joint effort between the community and the schools to generate grants for teachers for specific school projects. At Riley we have a CASA grant for kindergarten students. It is a listen and learn story tape project. Story tapes and books are sent home with students, and are checked out on a weekly basis.
- *The family support worker*—The family support worker is the liaison between community and school. The family support worker makes home visits and phone calls to families in at-risk environments.
- *The family support team*—This team consists of the program facilitator, vice-principal, family support worker, counselor, Chapter 1 nurse, health aide and sociological services worker. The family support team looks very closely at students in grades K–2, who are referred by their classroom teacher for absences, homework, tardies, clothing, glasses and behavior. The team provides a variety of family support assistance.

- *PRICE*—This is a parent education workshop to help parents build self-esteem within their children, and to give parents strategies in working with their children in the areas of discipline and self-esteem.
- *Monitoring performance results*—The third year of the pilot program, 1992–1993, will encompass program evaluation. We will take an in-depth look at the implementation of the reading support program and the whole language program. We will look at ways to fine-tune existing programs. And we will disseminate and expand the programs throughout the grade levels, as well as bring them into other schools.

Progress toward Meeting Three-Year Objectives

Continuous-Reading is a set of materials, published by Houghton-Mifflin in 1990, which allows the school to implement its whole language curriculum. Continuous-Reading is the reading portion of the program. There were 269 continuous students at Riley with pretest scores on the Individual Tests of Academic Skills (ITAS). ITAS is a standardized test given to assess achievement in reading, language and mathematics. Their average pretest score in reading was 36.0. The average posttest score was 38.1, a gain of 2.1.

Table 14.1 shows the gain or loss at each grade level (raw score at grade one) compared to the district average gain or loss.

At all grade levels (except third grade) Riley students showed significantly greater gains (or less loss) than the district as a whole.

The support teacher program and implementation of whole language are likely reasons for the improvement. At grade one, continuous stu-

TABLE 14.1 Reading scores.

GRADE	RILEY	DISTRICT
1	43.3	49.5 (raw score)
2	−2.9	−4.3
3	−3.2	−0.8
4	+5.9	+2.2
5	+3.5	−1.4
6	+4.0	+2.3
all	+2.1	−0.4

```
┌─────────────────────────────────────────────────────────────┐
│                      Questionnaire                          │
│ Parent Involvement in Our School:                           │
│ ─────────────────────────────────────────────────────────  │
│   Parent Name            Address            Telephone       │
│ ─────────────────────────────────────────────────────────  │
│   Child's Name        Track and Grade                       │
│ Indicate your response to each of the following statements  │
│ by circling either "Yes" or "No."                           │
│ 1. Yes   No   There should be many school activities that   │
│ involve students, parents and teachers, such as reading     │
│ enrichment programs and recognition assemblies to honor     │
│ student achievement.                                        │
│ 2. Yes   No   Parents should be encouraged to work in the   │
│ school as volunteers.                                       │
│ 3. Yes   No   Parents should supervise children with        │
│ homework.                                                   │
│ 4. Yes   No   Parents should be able to schedule visits to  │
│ the school during the day to understand the kinds of        │
│ experiences their child is having in school.                │
│ 5. Yes   No   Should there be parent education classes and  │
│ opportunities to teach parents how to help their children   │
│ benefit from school? If yes, which would you like to        │
│ participate in this year?                                   │
│ _____Parent club meetings                                  │
│ _____Parent library checkout                               │
│ _____Take-home computer                                    │
│ _____Parent advisory committee                             │
│ _____Classroom volunteer                                   │
│ _____Literacy classes                                      │
│ _____ESL classes                                           │
│ _____PRICE—self-esteem/positive reinforcement             │
│ Would you like to know more about access to services? If    │
│ so, please check those you are interested in.               │
│ _____Health                                                │
│       • shots                                               │
│       • physicals                                           │
│       • care of teeth                                       │
│       • care of eyes/ears                                   │
│ _____Sociological services                                 │
│       • clothing/shoes                                      │
│       • emergency food                                      │
│       • housing                                             │
│ _____Counseling for parents/child                          │
└─────────────────────────────────────────────────────────────┘
```

Figure 14.1 Parent Questionnaire.

dents averaged 43.3 in total reading, which was up from last year's 41 NCE average and only 6.2 below the district's NCE average.

When one considers that the Riley School population is one of the most economically depressed populations in all of southern California, and that the large majority of students begin here with little or no exposure to books, these scores are remarkable. Further, these students did not have the highly successful whole language experience in kindergarten that this year's kindergarten had. We would expect even better results next year because of the kindergarten program.

When we began, not many people thought we could make this kind of progress because of the at-risk environment in the Riley area. The doubters included many teachers. There are no doubters any more at Riley Elementary School.

Figure 14.1 is a questionnaire which is sent to parents to help gauge their needs and interests, and the effectiveness of the program.

Chapter 15

DATA-BASED CHANGE: THE HOMEWORK CLUB[26]

The data-based change protocol has been developed to assist administrators in introducing new programs into schools. The model allows the change agent to predict staff reaction, and to plan for a successful response to the change proposal.

The homework club model helps school staff to create a rich, student-centered environment which allows each child to reach his/her potential. This program is responsive to the particular language needs of the children and families involved. The program is an intervention plan to enhance academic achievement of identified at-risk youth through collaborative efforts at the K–6 level.

The homework club intervention project specifically addresses the needs of identified Chapter 1 students at Glenelder Elementary School in the Hacienda La Puente Unified School District, La Puente, California. Our mission is to develop appropriate extended day activities for low-achieving students, especially those from minority communities. This model is designed to provide targeted students with the opportunity for equal access and achievement in all curricula. This school site has an 80 percent Chapter 1 population.

The intervention is built upon collaborative partnerships which include administration, teachers, parents and students. These partnerships focus on four specific areas: student academic performance, personality characteristics, home environment and home support.

[26]This chapter was written by Cynthia J. Dixon and Arlene G. Reyes, of Glenelder Elementary School, Hacienda La Puente Unified School District, La Puente, CA.

STUDENT ACADEMIC PERFORMANCE

Students attend after-school homework club three times a week. Students participate in activities geared toward supporting each homeroom homework policy, and the core curriculum. The Chapter 1 teacher facilitates after-school sessions, and keeps in close communication with regular classroom teachers to ensure consistency. This area is assessed through self-image and attitude, teacher observation, anecdotal records and report cards.

PERSONALITY CHARACTERISTICS

Students participate in a two-day "Be a Better Student" seminar specifically designed to meet the needs of various interests and learning styles. Students also participate in the Junior Achievement program in order to gain an understanding of how those personal learning styles relate to the community, the workplace, the business world and self. Students are given the chance to recognize the influence that time, effort and a positive self-image have on their school performance. Students are able to define their own potential, and not be limited by language differences or the expectations of others.

HOME ENVIRONMENT

Parents of identified and targeted students participate in at least two parent education sessions designed to assist parents in creating a supportive home environment conducive to academic successes: i.e., how to utilize existing systems, how to advocate for the needs of their children and how to meet their own needs. The Chapter 1 resource teacher organizes the parent education meetings, to be held in the morning and evening to ensure attendance by working parents. The student homework assessment tool, shown in Figure 15.1, is completed by a parent of each student enrolled in the program. The resource teacher adjusts extended day sessions to meet the needs of the students being serviced according to the student homework assessment tool.

A New Skill.

Student Homework Assessment

Student Name _____

Evaluator/Tutor _____

Age _____ Grade _____

School_____

Teacher _____

Telephone _____

Parent Name _____

Background Information _____

_____

_____

Academic Performance (based on observation, report cards and teacher conferences)

_____

_____

My child's favorite academic subject is _____

My child is a competent reader. Yes _____ No _____

Comments _____

My child performs competently in mathematics computation.

Yes _____ No _____

Comments _____

My child performs competently mathematics applications and problem

solving. Yes _____ No _____

Comments _____

My child's school has a homework policy and I am aware of it.

Yes _____ No _____ (attach a copy if possible)

Comments _____

_____

_____

Student Name _____

Date _____

Figure 15.1 Student Homework Assessment Tool.

Student Homework Assessment

Behaviors: Please respond as accurately as possible to these behaviors in order to help us assess where we may be able to assist the student. Score 5 points for each response.

Personality Characteristics:

____ My child is a "self-starter."
____ My child is an organized person regarding space and time.
____ My child likes school and his/her teachers.
____ My child is easily distracted (add).
____ My child tends to wait until the last minute to get things done.
____ My child is easily overwhelmed by multilevel tasks.

Home Environment:

____ There is a designed "quiet place" in our home for completing homework.
____ My child has access to materials required to complete homework such as: pen/pencils, paper, index cards, folders.
____ There are additional materials and equipment such as: typewriter, computer, staplers, scissors.
____ We have encyclopedias, dictionaries and atlases.

Home Support:

____ There is a daily period set aside in our home for completing homework (no TV or telephone calls).
____ I feel capable of assisting my child with his/her homework assignments.
____ I am available during the time my child needs to work on his/her homework.
____ I understand that the assignments are for my child and not me.
____ Family trips and outings have given my child a strong experiential background.
____ Transportation to the library/tutoring is provided.

Figure 15.1 (continued) Student Homework Assessment Tool.

HOME SUPPORT

The site principal, resource teacher, classroom teachers and instructional aides organize three family nights designed to assist parents and students in creating a comprehensive support system with informal enrichment activities that improve confidence and promote success throughout their school careers. Lessons include ideas and models that can be used to incorporate experiences outside school, and may pull from the community, such as library trips, museum visits, family outings and cultural events. Not only do these sessions promote family support, but they encourage parents and extended family members to serve as teachers and role models in the home. Parents learn how to build on the child's existing strengths, and learn to challenge and encourage children to develop and pursue their own interests.

The following change model is designed to help administrators gather the information they need to carry out the school improvement they are seeking to implement. It is based on *Initiating and Responding to Change,* which was written by Dr. William L. Callison, and has been used successfully by scores of our students over the past fifteen years.

INITIATING AND RESPONDING TO CHANGE

Organizations reacting to pressures for initiating and responding to change must develop strategies for change.

Strategies for change may be interpreted as including, but not limited to, dissemination (and provisions for utilization) of pertinent information regarding all aspects of plans; ways of identifying and handling internal environmental constraints, as well as facilitating influences; ways of identifying potential opposition, conflict and tensions, and of resolving them advantageously; appropriate means of helping individuals, organizations and agencies to effect needed change in their perspectives; and procedures for implementing the proposed change.

Concept—Change is multifaceted, and the organization must possess the mechanisms to identify, categorize and handle the multiple sources of impetus for change. The administrator recognizes multiple sources for change.

It was recognized that changes in attitudes, expectations, beliefs and operations were necessary to accomplish the goals and objectives established for Glenelder Elementary. Every education employee at our site, including site administrator, teacher, instructional aide and resource teacher, intensified efforts to make this happen, and therefore, specific strategies were developed and implemented to ensure that all students had an opportunity to succeed as they went through the education system.

This intervention program specifically addressed the needs of identified Chapter 1 students whose achievement level was historically low, and who were primarily from minority communities. The district does not always provide adequately for these students. The homework club is a detailed effort to educate disenfranchised students through alternative, extended day activities which supplement regular classroom instruction. Before the program got underway, a number of points were established by staff and parents. These included:

(*1*) The district staff expressed a desire for the development of extended day programs to supplement Chapter 1 funded activities.

(*2*) The site administrator vowed to support any activity that helped gain visibility and credibility for the school, and that enhanced the regular instructional program.

(*3*) Teaching staff verbalized their frustration with students who had little or no success in the regular classroom.

(*4*) Instructional aides wanted to learn how to better assist minority students in the regular classroom.

(*5*) Parents indicated through informal conferences, parent teacher meetings and family nights, that they wanted their children to succeed academically, and to develop basic study skills that help to achieve success.

(*6*) The resource teacher requested permission to develop and conduct a test program that might serve as a model and potentially be adopted by other sites.

(*7*) Test scores for Chapter 1 identified students were consistently low at this school site; the site administrator was concerned about this problem.

The administrator must determine what change situations and resultant problems are most prominent in his/her organization.

The administrative staff includes the district staff, the site administrator and the resource teacher, who, with a project partner from the outside, play the most active role in implementing this change.

After all the surveys were made and the data gathered, the administration decided which changes needed to be made. They were: provide extended day activities as a supplement to core curricula in regular classroom instruction, so as to enhance academic achievement in a language and culturally enriched environment at grade levels four through six. This change will take place at the school site level. If successful, this intervention will be viewed as a pilot program for implementation at the district level.

The most prominent problems were determined to be:

(1) In assessing current resources and on-site constraints, it was determined that physical space was limited, and therefore only a small group of students could be accommodated by the extended day program in the first year.

(2) The site administrator was committed to supporting participation in an extended day program by the resource teacher, teaching staff, instructional aides, students and parents.

(3) Teachers expressed frustration with students who were not performing well academically, and who were experiencing language difficulties in the classroom, and requested assistance from the resource teacher.

(4) Parents were informally and formally polled about the study habits of their children to determine areas of need.

(5) Identified Chapter 1 students were given a homework assessment survey, the results of which were used to target thirty to thirty-five program participants.

The administrator must accurately assess the status of the system which is her/his responsibility to administer.

A number of factors were uncovered which indicated the program could be successful. They included:

(1) District staff would support the program due to pressure for new program development. There were currently no other extended day programs of this type established for these grade levels within the district. The district needed a model of success that could be applied to other sites at little cost.

(*2*) The site administrator would support programs that addressed low academic achievement and low student self-esteem, and would allow for parent participation.

(*3*) Teaching staff would or would not support the program depending upon the level of their input, and the time and effort required to assess students and to target them. In addition, some teachers were fundamentally opposed to Chapter 1 programs, and did not want to participate or cooperate with the resource teacher.

(*4*) Instructional aides would support the program because they wanted to have a more direct role with the students, especially working with children with learning and language difficulties.

(*5*) Parents would support the program because they wanted their children to succeed academically, to like school and to develop good study habits. In addition, many parents liked the idea of extended day activities because it relieved the latchkey kid syndrome by providing after-school care under adult supervision at no cost to the parents.

The administrator sorts out multiple pressures, for and against change, from the various constituencies of the organizational environment.

On the district level, a number of factors were identified that were pressures in favor of change. They included:

(*1*) District staff wanted a cost-effective pilot program with extended day activities for adoption at other school sites.

(*2*) Site administrators within the district wanted a program with proven results that was easy to adapt to their school sites.

(*3*) Families of potential program participants took time to fill out the homework survey, and wanted their children to develop good basic study skills, increase self-esteem, gain positive attitudes toward school and be allowed an opportunity for participation in a language and culturally enriched learning environment.

(*4*) Teachers wanted assistance with students who were not succeeding academically, in a way that would not disrupt regular classroom activity.

(*5*) Students wanted to participate in a language and culturally enriched environment in which they could identify, relate and succeed.

Pressure factors also came from within Glenelder Elementary. These included:

(*1*) The site administrator wanted a model program to be initiated at the school site.

(*2*) The resource teacher wanted to target and assist the most needy students who could benefit from the extended day activities.

(*3*) Most teaching staff were in favor of any program to assist students in performing at higher levels. Other teaching staff were not open to anything which was part of the Chapter 1 program, and which required additional time or effort on their part.

(*4*) Instructional aides wanted to have a more direct role in helping language and culturally disadvantaged students.

(*5*) Most families (thirty-eight of sixty) had taken direct initiatives to be involved in a program that enhanced the child-parent relationship, and gave them the opportunity to have direct input and a direct role in the process. The other families did not state a preference.

(*6*) Students in the program wanted an opportunity to learn new and different things in a structured environment after school.

(*7*) Other school staff, including custodians, librarians and office clerks, were happy to help students, in any way, to succeed.

Concept—Organizational members may perform various roles related to change. Selecting the most appropriate role is often determined by personal values and goals and/or organizational values and goals. The administrator may perform a variety of roles related to change.

Various people played various roles in getting the Glenelder homework club under way. They included:

(*1*) Initiator—The resource teacher and her partner proposed the program after learning of the district's need for a model.

(*2*) Stimulator—District staff envisioned all school sites with some type of extended day activity utilizing categorical funds.

(*3*) Reactor—The site administrator approved the project and encouraged staff to support it.

(*4*) Implementor—The resource teacher, her partner, other teachers and other site staff conducted the surveys, assessed results, set up parent education training and developed curricula for the program. Further, they provided ongoing input and direct instructional support.

(5) Conduit—The resource teacher was in the best strategic position to serve as conduit between administrative and teaching staff, as well as aides, parents and students, especially with information on objectives, parameters, needs and progress. To a lesser degree, the site administrator relayed information to district staff.

(6) Orchestrator/mediator—The site administrator and resource teacher shared the responsibility for ensuring that all parties fulfilled their designated responsibilities.

(7) Persuader or dissuader—The resource teacher and the site administrator were key persuaders in promoting the advantages of such a program to others. Some teaching staff served as dissuaders by not wanting to philosophically support Chapter 1 programs, and by not wanting to take on additional responsibility to assist with targeting students and monitoring effects over time.

(8) Advocate—The resource teacher, site administrator and parents served as primary advocates for the program.

(9) Ombudsman—Clerical and instructional aide staff were ombudsmen, serving as a barometer for feedback from all parties involved, especially the students who participated in the program.

(10) Nonactor—Some teaching staff were nonactors, simply noting the changes that occurred in student behavior and performance, attendance, parent involvement and academic test scores.

Concept—The organization seeks and responds to adequate data concerning its own functioning. Kinds of data, feedback processes, measurement and follow-up need to be incorporated in the administrator's planning. Some useful measurement tools are the student homework assessment (Figure 15.1), a support matrix (Figure 15.2) and a student homework survey (Figure 15.3).

Concept—The organization possesses adequate mechanisms for the establishment of change. This includes effective action strategies, effective efforts for establishing change climate and appropriate evaluation devices to measure the effectiveness of change. The administrator must be skillful in the use of strategies for establishing a change climate.

A number of strategies, including the following, can be used to implement a plan like the homework club.

Persons to Support the Intervention

Options	District Staff (1)	Site Admin. (1)	Resource Teachers	Teachers (14)	Instruction Aides (8)	Families (60)	Total
1. Initiate and implement program	1 × 10 = 10	1 × 8 = 8	1 × 6 = 6	12 × 4 = 48	7 × 2 = 14	38 × 2 = 76	162
2. Do not initiate and implement				1 × 4 = 4 1 × 4 = 4	1 × 2 = 2	22 × 2 = 44	4 50
3. No stated preference Power factor (on a scale from 1 to 10)	10	8	6	4	2	2	

Figure 15.2 Support Matrix Used to Indicate Levels of Support from Constituents, and Whether or Not to Proceed with the Pilot Program.

224

Student Homework Survey

Student Name _____

Evaluator/Tutor _____

Age _____ Grade _____ School _____

Teacher _____

Telephone _____

Parent Name _____

1. Do you like school?   Yes   No

2. Is it hard for you to get your homework done?   Yes   No

3. Do you often feel the need for further explanation regarding your homework?   Yes   No

4. Do you feel good when you have to perform in front of a group? Yes   No

5. What subject areas are most difficult to you? _____
_____

6. What are some of your interests (circle 1 or more)?
   Math   Reading for Leisure   Current Events   Fine Arts   Sports
   Crafts Church Activities Boy Scouts/Brownies Computer Activities
   Other _____

7. Who helps you with your homework at home? _____

8. Do you visit the public library?   Yes   No

9. Do you visit museums?   Yes   No

10. Do you have enough materials to work with at home?   Yes   No

Figure 15.3 Student Homework Survey.

11. What activities make you feel happiest at school? _____

_____

12. Does your school provide enough after-school activities?
    Yes   No

13. If you could design an after-school program what would it include?

_____

_____

_____

14. Prioritize the following from 1 to 3 to show which is the most important
    to your school success (1 is the most important).
    _____ My attitude _____ My effort _____ How I manage my time

15. Draw how you see yourself when you are an adult.

Figure 15.3 (continued) Student Homework Survey.

(*1*) Discuss intervention and assessment tools with mentor, and obtain approval.

(*2*) Share intervention outline with staff, parents and site administrator. Obtain input and make adjustments accordingly.

(*3*) Initiate process to complete student homework assessment tool. Allow for time opportunities to assist parents with draft format.

(*4*) Target and select a group of thirty to thirty-five identified Chapter 1 students from information obtained from assessment tool.

(*5*) Plan parent education training sessions with community liaison and site administrator.

(*6*) Plan family night activities with assigned staff members, site administrator and other community resource persons.

(*7*) Meet with staff to align homework policies and assignments with extended day activities.

(*8*) Schedule student orientation for homework club, Junior Achievement program and "Be a Better Student" seminar.

(*9*) Analyze student homework assessment tools to align other curricula to extended day activities.

(*10*) Schedule meetings/conferences with teachers and other staff in regard to student progress.

(*11*) Compare pre/post student homework assessment tool scores.

(*12*) Assess intervention program results.

CONCLUSION

Primary intervention objectives at Glenelder were to build study skills, increase academic performance and self-esteem of the students who participated and increase parent participation in the school and in the home. This intervention program was successful.

The program proved to be an effective method to empower those directly involved in the educational process at this site and, in addition, provided parents with an opportunity to be involved in a new and different way as adult mentors to their own children. For each parent this included treating the child with respect, setting an example for improvement, monitoring and helping with homework, reading with the child and keeping the school informed about the child's progress via the student homework assessment tool and family nights. The parents served as the primary link between the school and home. The program provided the framework, guidelines and curriculum that help to supplement and enhance the work of the school.

Attendance by parents of program participants reflected an average increase of 40 percent at school meetings, family nights and other interactions with the school. Parents expressed increased satisfaction with the teaching taking place through the extended day activities. In addition, children and parents spent more time together, and children were more inclined to complete their homework assignments. Teaching staff attested to this through both quantitative and qualitative means.

In regard to academic achievement, preliminary data at midyear indicate student performance on standardized achievement tests will increase, with 20 percent of the program participants scoring above the thirty-fifth percentile in math and reading, as compared to 5 percent of the remaining Chapter 1 students who did not participate in the extended day activities.

As a result of the program, students were less reluctant to join in other school activities, both academic and social. They appeared to take on more leadership roles with ease. Many of them served as a catalyst within their homes to increase family participation at school functions. Students were less intimidated by homework assignments, and the school structure and bureaucracy. They developed more personal relationships with various school staff, such as the resource teacher, librarian, and instructional aides.

Student commitment to academics improved as attendance records for the first semester reflected a 90 percent attendance rate in the extended day program.

The program helped to build a broader network of site staff and the family community in support of education. It encouraged parents to use existing school services and resources, and identified new ways for them to support their children. Parents took a role in sharing the school vision, participated in implementing the school plan and evaluated the progress of meeting the objectives in the school plan. Parent observations were used in decision making.

Ultimately, this intervention program recognized the important link between meaningful parent education, parent involvement, culturally and language enriched extended day activities and improved academic achievement. The school served as a bridge to the district and the community by serving as a resource to the families, students and other school sites within the district with similar Chapter 1 populations.

Chapter 16

A PLANNING MODEL
FOR REDUCTION OF DROPOUT

The following model is a series of steps which we recommend for school districts to utilize in establishing a model for assisting students at risk.

- Adopt a school-wide philosophy to promote a positive learning environment that ensures the success of every student.
- Assess needs by analyzing dropout statistics and by identifying major reasons why students drop out.
- Implement a preventive dropout program that provides early identification of high-risk students.
- Train teachers and counselors in intervention strategies that are effective with high-risk students (see Chapter 6).

Schools often use the following specific approaches.

- adopting and enforcing attendance and truancy policies (see Chapter 4)
- providing make-up and tutorial assistance
- fostering a school climate that promotes humanistic relationships
- providing early identification and remediation of academic failures (see Chapter 5)
- expanding special services by linking to community agencies (see Chapter 7)
- offering vocational and work-study programs (see Chapters 8, 10, 11 and 12)
- providing homebound tutoring for pregnant students
- providing reading improvement labs and individualized and computer-assisted instruction (see Chapter 21)

Prior to detailed planning, most districts will want to identify several interventions that are now working for their students at risk, so they can build on what is already working in some schools. This chapter includes the results of an at-risk-program survey which was filled out by staff at each school in the Orange Unified School District, Orange, California. The survey was designed to give the principal and district staff information about interventions currently operating in each school. In the SAR model, seen in Chapter 5, these data would be programmed into the Comprehensive Risk Assessment (CRA) software, and students would be scheduled into the interventions by the software.

The National Association of Secondary Schools and the National Association of Elementary Schools have recently published an important new resource titled the hm*Study Skills Program* (Burkle, 1986), which provides a rich array of interventions for students identified as being at risk through CRA software or other means.

Most districts will want to combine efforts to work with both potential dropouts and substance abusers since two-thirds of students at high risk for abuse are also at high risk for dropping out, and because substance abuse funds can then be used to support a combined effort.

The following guide contains suggestions for initiating a district-wide effort to identify and work with potential dropouts and substance abusers.

(*1*) *Develop a district-wide plan*—Meet with key district and school site staff to begin the process of developing a district-wide plan for identification of students at risk (see Chapter 5, "Identifying and Placing Students at Risk"). Focus on the essential information needed for identification which is seen in the Students-at-Risk, Inc. Combined Risk Assessment software, also in Chapter 5.

(*2*) *Identify present means for identification*—Meet with key school site staff to identify present means for identification of potential dropouts, including informal remarks by classroom teachers. Look for forms and checklists already in use in your district. You may wish to use the teacher at risk referral form (see Figure 16.1) to develop a list of students to fill out the Comprehensive Risk Assessment software.

(*3*) *Combine identification of abusers and dropouts*—Meet with staff who work with potential abusers, as well as those who work with likely dropouts. Discuss the possibility of both groups working

This form is a communication aid designed to call attention to any student who may need help right away. It is sometimes difficult to separate "typical" adolescent behavior from what may be called "red flag" behavior, yet it is important not to ignore warning signs which may indicate that a student is experiencing special problems. When a student demonstrates several of the behaviors listed below, swift intervention may be the key.

After completion, please return this form to the school counselor.

Student _____ Date _____

Grade _____ Person Referring (name optional) _____

Look for unusual or sudden changes in the observable behaviors listed below. Please check appropriate boxes.

Grades and Attitude

Sudden drop in grades/achievement ☐

Decline in homework completion ☐

Citizen deterioration ☐

Other observed behavior (explain)

Attendance

Increase in absenteeism ☐

Tardiness ☐

Frequently needs to leave classroom ☐

Truancy

Other observed behavior (explain)

Extracurricular Activities

Loss of eligibility ☐

Sudden noninvolvement ☐

Dropping out ☐

Other observed behavior (explain)

Figure 16.1 Teacher at Risk Referral Form.

Physical Behavior

Smells of tobacco ☐

Smells of beer or stronger alcoholic beverages ☐

Glassy, bloodshot eyes ☐

Frequently wearing sunglasses ☐

Poor personal hygiene ☐

Neglecting physical appearance ☐

Sleeping in class ☐

Weight loss ☐

Weight gain ☐

Frequent physical injuries ☐

Other observed behavior (explain)

Disruptive Behavior

Sudden defiance of classroom rules ☐

Irresponsibility (blaming/denying) ☐

Fighting ☐

Cheating ☐

Obscene/abusive language ☐

Temper tantrums ☐

Hyperactivity/nervousness ☐

Dramatic attention getting ☐

Other observed behavior (explain)

Figure 16.1 (continued) *Teacher at Risk Referral Form.*

Social Behavior

Talks openly about drugs and alcohol □

Change of friends □

Depression □

Sudden mood swings □

Defensiveness □

Withdrawn □

Deceptiveness/deceitfulness □

Other observed behavior (explain)

Other Comments

Figure 16.1 (continued) *Teacher at Risk Referral Form.*

together to use a combined set of predictor variables for identification of students at risk, as well as many of the same interventions.

(4) *Develop a list of interventions* —To begin the planning process, one can carry out a survey of principals and others who provide service to at-risk students to find out what programs are currently operating to serve these students. To get an idea of what your results might look like, see the outline developed in Orange Unified School District, in the next section. In order to save time and expense you may wish to use your school's approach to the suggested interventions listed in Chapter 6.

(5) *Develop a site utilization and intervention plan* —Meet with selected site-level pilot school staff from at least one elementary, junior and senior high school, to talk about utilization of district data on students at risk. Plan to link district data on student needs to appropriate interventions at various school sites. List present interventions that would not require new budgetary support.

(6) *Develop a district-wide evaluation plan* —Meet with key cabinet members to develop a district-wide plan for evaluation of services for students at risk. The completion of interventions form in Chapter 6 can serve as a pre/post evaluation of the effectiveness of the

software and related efforts. Using these data, which create item-by-item analyses of student progress, decision makers are provided with information to use in judging the success of the various interventions. If discrepancies are not reduced, the intervention needs serious revision. For example, if we compare the pre/post scores on an item such as anger control and find there is not a pre/post improvement, decision makers should consider changing the interventions used for teaching anger control.

The following planning outline is being used in the Orange Unified School District, Orange, California. It was written by Roger Duthoy, former Assistant Superintendent for Secondary Schools.

OUTLINE OF A DROPOUT REPORT
TO THE BOARD OF EDUCATION

1.0 HISTORICAL DATA

    1.1   Definition of a dropout:
        A student in grades ten, eleven or twelve who stops attending school prior to graduation for forty-five days or more, and has not requested that his/her transcript (academic record) be sent to another school or institution.

    1.2   Three-year statistics

$$\text{Three-year dropout rate} = \frac{(D1 + D2 + D3) \times 100}{E1}$$

$D1$ = Tenth grade dropouts (class of 1990)
$D2$ = Eleventh grade dropouts (same class)
$D3$ = Twelfth grade dropouts (same class)
$E1$ = Total tenth grade enrollment

    1.3   For Orange Unified, the 1988 three-year dropout rate is 21.3 percent (statistics are generated by the CBEDS report).

$$\frac{(110 + 177 + 218) \times 100}{2370} = 21.3$$

1.4   One-year statistics (class of 1989)

$$\text{One-year dropout rate} = \frac{(D1 + D2 + D3) \times 100}{E1 + E2 + E3}$$

D1 = Tenth grade dropouts (class of 1991)
D2 = Eleventh grade dropouts (class of 1990)
D3 = Twelfth grade dropouts (class of 1989)
E1 = Total tenth grade enrollment
E2 = Total eleventh grade enrollment
E3 = Total twelfth grade enrollment

1.5   For Orange Unified, the 1989 one-year dropout rate is 8.7 percent (statistics are generated by the CBEDS report).

$$\frac{(105 + 197 + 218) \times 100}{1892 + 2500 + 1612} = 8.7$$

2.0 CHARACTERISTICS OF A POTENTIAL DROPOUT
2.1   Frequently absent, truant from school
2.2   From low-income home (AFDC)
2.3   Transient family
2.4   Poor grades (retained or failed secondary courses)
2.5   Low basic skills ability (reading and mathematics)
2.6   Behind in credits earned
2.7   At-risk behaviors (poor citizenship, gangs, smoking, alcohol, drugs, sexually active, on probation, discipline problem at school, etc.)
2.8   Low self-esteem (dress, friends, goals, lack of participation in school activities, etc.)
2.9   Lack of attachment to school (no one at school knows them or, in their opinion, cares about them)
2.10 Nonsupportive family (lack of supervision, discipline, communication, models at home)

3.0 CURRENT INTERVENTION STRATEGIES IN ORANGE UNIFIED
Elementary Programs
3.1   DARE (drug abuse resistance education)

3.2 BABES

3.3 Project Self-Esteem

3.4 Developmental kindergarten

3.5 Saturday school

K–12 Programs

3.6 CASA (very active drug and alcohol effort by parents, students and staff)

3.7 PRIDE (parent to parent networking)

3.8 Red Ribbon Week, awareness weeks

3.9 Categorical programs (Chapter 1, GATE, ESL, etc.)

3.10 Summer school program

3.11 Successful Parents for Successful Kids conference

3.12 Migrant education program

3.13 School study teams

3.14 Special education programs, I.E.P. teams

3.15 Gang information workshops

3.16 Good working relationship with the Orange Police Department

3.17 SARB (school attendance review board)

3.18 Quest International (skills programs)

3.19 Home and hospital

3.20 Independent study program

3.21 Cocurricular programs (clubs, students government, etc.)

Secondary Programs

3.22 PAL (peer assistance leadership)

3.23 Athletic programs

3.24 Choices program

3.25 Pregnant minor program

3.26 Child development program

3.27 Continuation high school program

3.28 Middle school philosophy (homeroom, interdisciplinary teams, child centered, etc.)

3.29 Regional Occupation Program (ROP)

3.30 Opportunity class (grades seven through nine)

3.31 Work experience programs

3.32 Decision-making skills class

3.33 Summer recreation program

3.34 Rancho Santiago evening programs

3.35 Hispanic youth, leadership conference

3.36 Career day, college and university nights
3.37 Academy program (El Modena High School)
3.38 Olivecrest program

During the 1990–1991 academic year, the at-risk task force created an overall strategy for involving board members, school staff, students, parents, community members and a consultant, in the creation of a district plan for identifying and serving students at risk.

LONG RANGE PROSPECTS

Planning efforts, such as this one in Orange Unified, need to be supported at their present level of sophistication and commitment, whatever that may be. In time, they can be encouraged to consider appropriate new technologies and approaches. Some of those approaches follow.

Community Networking/Outreach

- Establish cooperative networks with schools, law enforcement agencies and juvenile courts, as well as mental health, substance abuse and other community agencies to provide effective referrals and services.
- Galvanize the support of community organizations, such as churches, businesses and community members, in the war against alcohol/other drug abuse.
- Conduct vigorous outreach efforts through culturally appropriate media materials, statewide conferences, community presentations, rallies and other visible events.
- Provide alcohol and other drug education to raise awareness and knowledge of youth, parents, teachers, other family members and the community.
- Train teachers, health-care professionals, community service agency counselors, day-care providers and others on issues related to alcohol/other drug abuse, and on how to identify and help young children of chemically dependent parents or adolescent gateway drug users.

Ethnic/Cultural Approaches

- Recruit, train and support the involvement of respected community members, such as businessmen and tribal elders, as positive adult role models for high-risk youth.
- Demonstrate staff sensitivity to the culture of the target population through recruitment of minority staff at all levels of prevention programs.
- Encourage cultural revitalization activities to eliminate cultural alienation among minorities, such as celebrating cultural festivals, and teaching the traditional language, values and rituals.

Parenting Help/Support

- Reach out actively to involve parents whose support is critical for improving the life chances of their children.
- Provide individual, group and family therapy for youth and families.
- Offer parents help through parenting and other skill-building courses, support groups and aid in accessing social services.
- Provide pregnant teenagers with prenatal and postnatal care, education about the effects of drugs on unborn babies and treatment to help them stop their substance use.
- Offer day-care services for parents of preschool children.

Youth Help/Support

- Provide life skills training (includes decision making, effective problem solving, coping with stressful situations, forming nurturing relationships, developing social skills and refusal skills for resisting negative peer pressure) to build self-esteem and social competence in young people, and to enable them to make healthy life choices.
- Involve youth in community volunteer work or community development schemes, reintegrating them into their communities and reducing their social alienation.
- Organize drug-free activities, such as recreation and

challenging wilderness trips, that build self-confidence and teamwork among participants.

- Provide help with education, vocational counseling, job training and job placement services.
- Provide health education, including courses on sexuality, birth control and AIDS prevention.

MENTORING AT-RISK YOUTH

One of the least expensive and most promising strategies for serving students at risk is the use of other students who have been trained as mentors. The Glasgow Intermediate School in Fairfax County, Virginia, has developed a successful model program described by Aiello and Gatewood (1989).

The Glasgow mentoring program had been in operation for four years at the time of the Aiello-Gatewood report. It was designed to provide personal support for at-risk students. Each year, the school's guidance department first identifies and trains mentors, who are teachers and other staff members, who volunteer to work closely and personally with from one to three students. For instance, fifty-seven mentors volunteered for the program one school year. Together, the mentor and the student develop a warm, caring and positive working relationship. The mentor also develops communication among parents, teachers and counselors to provide support in both personal and academic growth. Improved academic performance, motivation and self-esteem are primary goals of this interaction.

Each year certain students are offered an opportunity to participate in the mentor program, based upon teacher recommendations and/or low first-quarter grades. Student protégés must then volunteer, and their parents must approve their participation in the program. Out of a total school population of 850, eighty protégés participated in the 1987–1988 program.

After an orientation meeting with protégés and their parents early in the school year, each protégé is matched with a mentor and placed in the mentor's homeroom. Aside from daily homeroom interactions, mentor and protégé meet at least once a week after school for academic remediation and personal guidance. Monthly group guidance sessions on study skills and self-concept are held. Once a month, all of the mentors and protégés have an after-school get-together for social activities such as games and informal discussions, as well as for assistance in homework and test preparation. The program concludes each year in June with a mentor-protégé softball game and awards ceremony.

Mentors receive four in-service training sessions a year on topics such as program goals and objectives, adolescent development and research-based strategies to raise academic interest and achievement. In addition, monthly evening information and support sessions are held with parents.

The Glasgow guidance department is responsible for managing and assuring smooth operation of all aspects of the program. Counselors help prepare the "Mentor Program Guide" (previously reviewed by a staff mentor committee), coordinate in-service and study skills planning, oversee data collection and dissemination and provide overall support for both mentors and protégés.

Some Results

Formative and summative evaluation of the program is conducted each year with a variety of forms and assessment instruments. For example, teachers complete monthly logs indicating the number of meetings they held with protégés. Students complete both a self-assessment survey on study skills and a self-concept/motivation inventory. Teachers who have protégés in academic classes complete an assessment of their classroom performance.

In a recent academic year, the following major improvements of grades were reported: a 37 percent increase in grades of A, a 29 percent increase in grades B+ through A, and a 7 percent increase in grades C through A. Protégés decreased the number of D+ through F grades by 12 percent. In the three years of the program's existence for which there are data, the overall failure rate of program students has declined from 28 percent to 12 percent. In addition, the school-wide failure rate declined from 7.2 percent in 1984–1985, to 5.8 percent in 1985–1986; 5.0 percent in 1986–1987, 4.4 percent in 1987–1988.

As you consider new strategies, you may find these developed by William Gray helpful (Gray, 1991).

Essential Components of a Mentoring Program

Since 1978, researchers have identified certain generic components related to mentoring success. More than 800 researchers, practitioners and writers have documented the importance of these components to varying degrees. These generic components must be carefully adapted to fit the contextual aspects of each situation, or success is not likely.

(*1*) Planned mentoring must be supported from the top as well as at the grass roots level so that voluntary participation occurs. Imposed programs seldom work as well as those in which people want to buy in as volunteers because they see the benefits for themselves and the organization, and they can meet program expectations. To attract volunteers, the program's structure, organizational expectations and anticipated benefits must be communicated to potential participants. Focus groups comprised of prospective participants and needed supporters provide useful input for improving the program's design. Having such input increases the support for the program.

(*2*) Each program should be designed around the specific goals (or intended outcomes/benefits) to be promoted. These goals relate to the needs of participants, determining mentor and protégé selection and what type of training to provide.

(*3*) Begin small. Carefully plan a short (six to twelve months) pilot program for a few participants (ten to forty), so that inevitable start-up bugs can be rectified. Employ a research and development approach to ensure that the pilot program is working as desired before expanding it to a larger audience.

(*4*) Prospective participants should receive an orientation to clearly outline items such as the organization's expectations related to intended goals, duration of mentoring, time requirements, etc. This orientation provides one means for enabling prospective participants to buy in and become committed volunteers.

(*5*) Carefully select mentors and protégés from among volunteers, and match them without forcing this. Match so that intended goals can be achieved. One strategy for matching would be for protégés to nominate mentors and vice versa, with the nominated person being given right of refusal. Another approach would be for the program coordinator to suggest possible matches, with candidates being given the right to refuse, etc. Still, another useful strategy is to use a test instrument.

(6) Mounting research indicates that not training participants is the primary cause of unsuccessful mentoring in planned programs. Training must be provided for mentors and protégés so they know what is expected and how to fulfill those mentor-protégé roles and functions requisite to achieving goals. This can be done a number of ways. It is a mistake to assume that just because mentors have greater experience and practical wisdom, they automatically know how to fulfill essential mentor roles.

(7) Primarily, mentoring is a close personal relationship and a process of working together to achieve agreed-upon goals. This relationship and process must be carefully monitored on a regular basis to resolve emerging conflicts and problems before crises develop. It is a mistake to assume that a training program, no matter how well designed and delivered, will automatically result in mentors and protégés correctly applying those skills taught in the training session. With this in mind, a key person within the organization is needed to provide ongoing monitoring and additional training when needed. This monitor is usually the program coordinator or a human resources development staff member.

(8) At some set point in time, program goals should be evaluated to determine benefits for mentors, protégés and the organization. Quantitative data from questionnaires can be collected as a means of measuring perceived group gains/benefits. Qualitative data from interviews is a means of obtaining in-depth information about worst- and best-case situations. Both types of data are then used to improve the pilot program until it is ready for expanded use with more mentors and protégés. It is important to note that since mentoring is such a personal experience, and matching of mentors and protégés is so crucial to success, it does not make sense to randomly match mentors to protégés as required when using a rigorous control group research design. This means that relationships between program interventions (e.g., training, mentoring style, etc.) and other program outcomes must be determined in other, more appropriate ways.

POLICY RECOMMENDATION

Prior to detailed planning, most districts will want to identify several interventions that are now working for their students at risk, so they can build on what is already working in some schools. They can then include the results of an at-risk program survey, which is filled out by staff at each school, in their planning document to give the principal and district staff information about successful interventions. Students could then be scheduled into them manually or with the help of a software program.

Chapter 17

CASE RECORD ANALYSIS

Of special interest are the case record analyses, which describe a student whose identifying characteristics have been changed, and the interventions that were delivered for him. These case records are data that come from the Comprehensive Risk Assessment software or any other means you have for identifying students at risk of dropping out. These data are combined with other student information utilized by your school and district, and placed in forms which automatically create a data base as the student data is entered. The resultant records are of great interest to teachers, and help to motivate them to deliver interventions in their schools. They are designed for use by student study teams or the equivalent group that works with students who need special help. A series of life skills and wellness skills are included to suggest possible strategies for student study teams to consider in designing interventions for students.

In order to implement case record analyses, you begin with the student study team forms you now use, plus any new items you wish to add to your newly created data base. Then you need to purchase a form designer program. We use a pair of integrated programs titled Informed Designer and Informed Manager, both from Shana Corporation for Macintosh users.

Our sample forms were developed for a small, mainly Hispanic district in southern California, and are used to integrate school services with those of the many county agencies that provide assistance to needy families. In California this type of effort is funded by the state and called Healthy Start.

Healthy Start projects address the needs of the student, his family, the school and the community, in a comprehensive approach, through the following strategies.

(*1*) Student
- Provide appropriate health care.
- Identify and reduce behavioral and academic deficits.
- Increase social skills, decision-making skills and self-esteem.
- Increase bonding to home and school.
- Increase academic performance and confidence in interacting with peers at school and at home.
- Decrease antisocial behaviors.

(*2*) School
- Increase teachers', counselors' and administrators' prevention knowledge, skills and curriculum.
- Sensitize staff to student problems.
- Provide a comprehensive program to address cognitive, social and health concerns.
- Address family needs for parenting skills.

(*3*) Community
- Coordinating committee, from schools, parents, police and health agencies, meets regularly to guide policy and streamline delivery of services.
- Facilitate meeting the data requirements of SRI by designing forms that fit the service delivery style of school and agency staff.
- Through the collection of data, inform school and agency staff as to whether or not their goals and objectives are being accomplished.

(*4*) Family
- Families benefit from agency collaboration to deliver services in a timely fashion.
- Parents gain knowledge about what services are available to them and how to obtain these services.
- The need for better family management techniques and parenting skills is addressed by school and agency staff.
- Parents who need resources are given help and support in order to obtain these resources.

Figures 17.1, 17.2 and 17.3 are computer screens created with Informed Designer and Informed Manager. These forms are used in Duarte Unified School District, Duarte, California.

"HEALTHY KIDS ~ HEALTHY DUARTE"
INDIVIDUAL INTERVENTION PLAN
CONFIDENTIAL

Name			Birthday
JONES, ANDREW			6/20/78
PRINT	Last	First	

Address	Telephone
1234 EAGLE VIEW DUARTE, CA 91010	714 773-3366

Parents Name
JONES, ROBERT & SANDRA

Language	Home Language
ENGLISH	ENGLISH

Spec Prog: Spec Ed	Spec Prog: GATE	Spec Prog: Other
		Health: Epilepsy

School	Teacher	Grade
Washington High	Mr. Brown	9

School Status: Enrolled	School Status: Moved	School Status: Re-entered
9/1/92		

Interviewer	Date
Ms. Flower	2/3/93

Assessment Survey Questions: (Circle) 1 2 3 4 5 6 7 8 9 10 11 12 13 14
1,3,4,11,13

Assessment Survey Questions: (Check)

Substance Abuse: Low Risk: ___Pre ___Post   Medium Risk: ___Pre ___Post   High Risk: ___Pre ___Post
Dropout: Low Risk: ___Pre ___Post   Medium Risk: ___Pre ___Post   High Risk: ___Pre ___Post

Level 1 Interview (After topics are discussed, summarize student responses)
Andrew, age 14, was referred to the at-risk program by his counselor, primarily because of failing grades. Andrew attended school every day but could not complete his work. His behavior seemed strange to other students. He did not fit in with his peers. He had witnessed his mothers death from a blood clot on the brain. He was alone with her when she died. His father was not capable of taking care of Andrew by himself because of his own emotional problems and a drug habit. Andrew was sent to live with his father's sister and mother. While in their care he was emotionally and physically abused. Once he was taken out of their care he went to live with his mothers sister and her husband. They have two children and the home was loving and stable. His aunt, however, is concerned that Andrew is still failing his classes.

Recommendation: ___
___No Further Intervention ___Level II ___Level III

Study Team Recommendation:
___No Further Intervention ___Level II ___Level III

Figure 17.1 Screen One.

249

Level II Interventions

Date	Parent Conference	Date	Positive Activities Assigned to:
10/2/92	Mrs Green & Mrs Went (the aunt)	10/5/92	Increased teacher-student interaction
Date	Interest Analyzer	Date	1.
		10/7/92	Mr. Stern, Social Studies Teacher
Date	SST (Site) Attach Plan	Date	2.
		10/19/92	Ms. Webster, Alternative Classroom
Date	SIT District	Date	3.
Date	Student-Parent-School Contract	Date	4.
10/5/92	Andrew, Mrs. Went & Ms. Webster		
Date	Academic Assistance (Tutor)	Date	DCP Parent Classes
			SCH. ___ ENG. ___ SP. ___
	Days and Time	Date	Operation School Bell
Date	Program/Class/School Change	Date	Psychological Testing
Date	Being Useful Project	Date	School Nurse
		10/8/92	Arranged medication for epilepsy
Date	Other	Date	Monrovia Health Clinic
Date	Community Council Services	Date	Outside Health Provider (Agency)

Quarterly Progress Report: (Include dates of Parent Teacher contacts)

Date	Progress Report I
9/30/92	Andrew had several problems that were causing him to fail. One problem was his hostility toward his father's sister and mother. This was reflected in various forms of negative behavior. A second problem was Andrew's idealized view of his mother who died. No woman could stand comparison with his perfect mother. His third problem was his epilepsy. Ms. Webster is working to help him talk about his hostility and the Nurse has arranged for medication.
Date	Progress Report II
12/20/92	We have asked Andrew to see his at-risk counselor, Ms. Webster, and an outside counselor once a week for four months. He is doing this fairly regularly. He is improving in his understanding of his resentment of women.
Date	Progress Report III
3/12/93	Andrew has been focusing upon developing consistency and his best area of performance is water polo. He is bringing his grades up to a C slowly. He has been taking his epilepsy medication regularly.
Date	Progress Report IV
6/20/93	Much improvement this past three months in making friends. Andrew's grades are up to a B average and he is not acting strangely anymore. We are going to recommend that Andrew go back into the regular school program. The alternative classroom has really worked for him.

Figure 17.2 Screen Two.

250

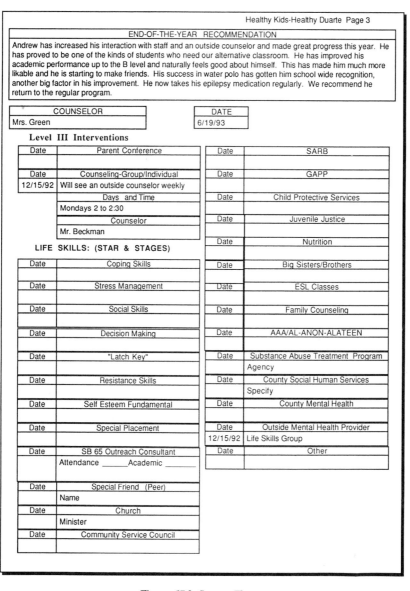

END-OF-THE-YEAR RECOMMENDATION

Andrew has increased his interaction with staff and an outside counselor and made great progress this year. He has proved to be one of the kinds of students who need our alternative classroom. He has improved his academic performance up to the B level and naturally feels good about himself. This has made him much more likable and he is starting to make friends. His success in water polo has gotten him school wide recognition, another big factor in his improvement. He now takes his epilepsy medication regularly. We recommend he return to the regular program.

COUNSELOR	DATE
Mrs. Green	6/19/93

Level III Interventions

Date	Parent Conference	Date	SARB

Date	Counseling-Group/Individual	Date	GAPP
12/15/92	Will see an outside counselor weekly		
	Days and Time	Date	Child Protective Services
	Mondays 2 to 2:30		
	Counselor	Date	Juvenile Justice
	Mr. Beckman		

LIFE SKILLS: (STAR & STAGES)

Date		Date	Nutrition
Date	Coping Skills	Date	Big Sisters/Brothers
Date	Stress Management	Date	ESL Classes
Date	Social Skills	Date	Family Counseling
Date	Decision Making	Date	AAA/AL-ANON-ALATEEN
Date	"Latch Key"	Date	Substance Abuse Treatment Program
			Agency
Date	Resistance Skills	Date	County Social Human Services
			Specify
Date	Self Esteem Fundamental	Date	County Mental Health
Date	Special Placement	Date	Outside Mental Health Provider
		12/15/92	Life Skills Group
Date	SB 65 Outreach Consultant	Date	Other
	Attendance _____Academic _____		

Date	Special Friend (Peer)
	Name
Date	Church
	Minister
Date	Community Service Council

Figure 17.3 Screen Three.

251

Grade	Life Skills	Wellness Skills
K	SELF-ESTEEM AND SCHOOL ADJUSTMENT THROUGH LITERATURE (STAGES) Developing "who I am" and positive self-esteem Identifying and understanding feelings Learning how people react to change Learning about different types of families Respecting self and others	POSITIVE LIVING SKILLS Learning how we feel DECISIONS FOR SAFE LIVING Exploring feelings in disasters Learning about safety and medicine
1	FEELINGS AND SOCIAL BEHAVIOR (GOAL) Developing the concept of "being myself" Reinforcing concept of "It's OK to be me" Introducing passive, aggressive, assertive behaviors Introducing skill of making assertive "I" statements Using assertive requests Understanding effects of positive/negative communications Developing ability to give and receive compliments Developing ability to identify and express feelings Decision making based on feelings Integrating and reviewing lessons on feelings	HEALTHY HABITS Learning about physical growth and nutrition Learning how doctors promote health and well-being POSITIVE LIVING SKILLS Learning to recognize how we feel Learning how people differ Learning how families differ Learning how families grow and change Developing awareness of dangerous situations

Figure 17.4 Life Skills and Wellness Skills Guidelines.

Grade	Life Skills	Wellness Skills
2	INTRODUCTION TO THE REACTIONS TO CHANGE (STAGES) Learning how people and families differ Learning how changes produce stress Discovering the six stages of change Developing awareness of the stage of denial Developing awareness of the stage of anger Developing awareness of the stage of bargaining Developing awareness of the stage of depression Developing awareness of the stage of acceptance Developing awareness of the stage of hope Developing ability to identify the stages in review lesson	HEALTHY HABITS Developing awareness of healthy eating and nutrition Discovering how senses work POSITIVE LIVING SKILLS Recognizing family structures Reviewing types of families Learning about others' feelings Learning about positive and negative feelings
3	RESPONSIBILITY AND GOAL SETTING (GOAL) Establishing concept of agreements Establishing concept of consequences Using puppets to understand agreements Making agreements at home Relaxing through proper breathing Building awareness of positive and negative consequences Identifying habits and how they relate to agreements Identifying behaviors that hinder keeping agreements Identifying helpful habits Reviewing the accountability skills concepts	HEALTHY HABITS Learning about body structure and functions POSITIVE LIVING SKILLS Learning how emotions affect the body Learning about individual uniqueness Understanding ways to prevent accidents Discovering skills to make friends DECISIONS FOR SAFE LIVING Discovering safety procedures for emergencies and earthquake preparedness

Figure 17.4 (continued) Life Skills and Wellness Skills Guidelines.

Grade	Life Skills	Wellness Skills
4	MANAGING STRESSFUL CHANGES (STAGES) Introducing awareness of stressful changes Understanding the six stages of change Developing an understanding of denial Developing an understanding of anger Using art to handle stress Developing an understanding of bargaining Developing an understanding of depression Developing an understanding of acceptance Developing an understanding of hope Reviewing ways to identify and manage change	POSITIVE LIVING SKILLS Finding ways of reducing stress DECISIONS FOR SAFE LIVING Risk taking: safe and dangerous risks Learning characteristics of substances Proper and improper use of drugs Discovering effects of tobacco and secondhand smoke
5	PROBLEM SOLVING AND DECISION MAKING (GOAL) Recognizing a need for problem solving Introducing "think aloud," step one Introducing "think aloud," step two Introducing "think aloud," step three Introducing "think aloud," step four Remembering the "think aloud" technique Applying "think aloud" to academic problems Applying four steps to interpersonal problems Applying four steps to personal problems Applying "think aloud" to goal setting	POSITIVE LIVING SKILLS Understanding personality Learning abilities and differences DECISIONS FOR SAFE LIVING Learning why people take risks Discovering the risks that families take Seeing how we take risks with friends Making decisions involving risks Recognizing laws that affect decisions Discovering the persuasive role of advertising Building decision-making skills for times of disaster

Figure 17.4 (continued) Life Skills and Wellness Skills Guidelines.

Grade	Life Skills	Wellness Skills
6	INTERPERSONAL COMMUNICATION AND PEER PRESSURE (STAR) Introducing concept of legal and personal rights Recognizing passive behavior Understanding consequences of passive behavior Recognizing aggressive behavior Understanding consequences of aggressive behavior Recognizing assertive behavior Introducing ways to manage stress Communicating assertively through "I" statements Communicating assertively through compliments Communicating assertively through requests Communicating assertively through assertive refusal SAFETY, SELF-ESTEEM AND DRUG PREVENTION (DARE) Practice for personal safety Drug use and misuse consequences Resistance techniques—ways to say "NO" Building self-esteem Managing stress without taking drugs Media influences on drug use Decision making and risk taking Forming a support system (making friends) "DARE to be a STAR" culmination	POSITIVE LIVING SKILLS Choosing healthy personal habits Understanding the concept of fitness Learning to live a safe drug-free life DECISIONS FOR SAFE LIVING Understanding the major influences in risk taking Recognizing effects of smoking on the body and on others Learning how advertising influences our decision to use or not use drugs Understanding the impact of alcohol on the body Deciding to not use alcohol Recognizing dangers of inhalants Identifying health effects of marijuana Learning stimulants' effects on the body Choosing ways to refuse substances Role playing to resist using drugs Reviewing the major concerns of substance use and abuse

Figure 17.4 (continued) Life Skills and Wellness Skills Guidelines.

255

Grade	Life Skills	Wellness Skills
7	PEER-RESISTANCE SKILLS AND UNDERSTANDING OTHERS (STAR) Reviewing passive, aggressive, assertive skills Reviewing assertive refusal technique Practicing skill of broken record Managing stress using broken record technique Practicing use of open-ended questions Developing awareness of criticism Using negative assertion effectively Practicing the skill of fogging Practicing the skill of negative inquiry Reviewing skills to handle criticism Practicing stress-management skills Introducing personality skills Recognizing extroversive/introversive traits Recognizing sensing and intuitive personalities Recognizing thinking and feeling personalities Recognizing judging and perceiving traits Recognizing the responsible personality Recognizing the spontaneous personality Understanding the feeling type personality Understanding the thinking type personality	FAMILY LIFE EDUCATION Making choices that promote wellness Decision making and well-being USE/MISUSE OF SUBSTANCES Understanding legal and illegal drugs Relating drug use and the spread of communicable disease Differentiating kinds of dependencies Identifying effects of substances on body/mind Discovering danger of smokeless tobacco Learning smoking reasons and ways to stop Discovering alternatives to drugs Finding community resources for giving support and rehabilitating

Figure 17.4 (continued) Life Skills and Wellness Skills Guidelines.

Grade	Life Skills	Wellness Skills
8	MANAGING STRESSFUL CHANGES IN ADOLESCENCE (STAGES II)	
	Understanding stages of adolescent changes	
	Understanding stress in adolescence	
	Discovering resources available	
	Finding personal resources for stress	
	Coping with denial stage during adolescence	
	Dealing with denial through relaxation	
	Using assertiveness to deal with anger	
	Expressing anger in behavior	
	Coping with anger using relaxation	
	Using assertive refusal for bargaining	
	Managing bargaining stage with relaxation	
	Understanding adolescent depression	
	Managing depression stage	
	Using problem solving with acceptance	
	Managing acceptance stage in adolescence	
	Understanding stage of hope in adolescence	
	Setting goals, relaxing to manage hope	

Figure 17.4 (continued) Life Skills and Wellness Skills Guidelines.

257

Grade	Life Skills	Wellness Skills
10	COPING FOR ANGER AND DEPRESSION (STAGES II) Integrating six stages and reactions of change Applying knowledge of reactions to change Integrating knowledge of resources Integrating skills to cope with denial Integrating the effects of anger Utilizing assertion skills to deal with anger Integrating the effects of bargaining Utilizing assertive refusal to cope with bargaining Integrating the understanding of depression Accepting and integrating reactions to STAGES Integrating skills to understand hope	USE AND MISUSE OF SUBSTANCES Recognizing alcohol dependency Recognizing effects of marijuana use Understanding alcohol and marijuana Physical and mental effects of alcohol Learning about effects of other substances on self and others Differentiating between prescription and nonprescription drugs Learning about misconceptions and myths of alcohol and alcoholism Examining factors that influence decision not to use Analyzing the influence of advertising Developing resistance, peer and media benefits of giving up tobacco and other substances

Figure 17.4 (continued) *Life Skills and Wellness Skills Guidelines.*

258

Grade	Life Skills	Wellness Skills
10	DEVELOPING EFFECTIVE PROBLEM-SOLVING SKILLS (PLUS)	FAMILY HEALTH
	Developing effective problem-solving skills	Recognizing family influences and differences
	Understanding of difference between fact and belief	Learning how the family meets basic needs
	Developing awareness of rational/irrational beliefs	Locating community resources and family assistance
	Differentiating between rational/irrational beliefs	Developing awareness of individual rights and responsibilities in relationships
	Developing the skill of problem solving	Recognizing dysfunctions within families
	Developing understanding of self talk	Identifying, preventing abuse
	Developing the skill of brainstorming	Identifying proper steps in solving family problems
	Developing skills of alternative solution	
	Understanding the consequences of brainstorming	PERSONAL HEALTH
	Recognizing skill of listing alternatives	Achieving and maintaining health
	Recognizing consequences in problem solving	Understanding how health choices affect quality of life
	Practicing implementing plan	Understanding when health changes require professional assistance

Figure 17.4 (continued) Life Skills and Wellness Skills Guidelines.

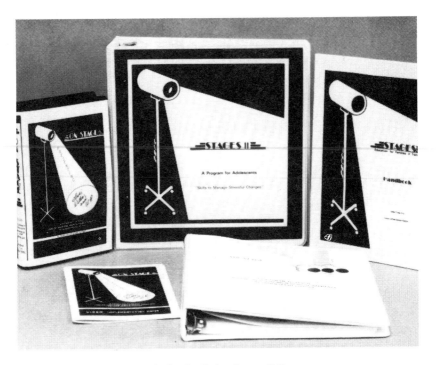

Manuals for the Irvine Stages II Program.

THE NEW BEGINNINGS PROJECT

The New Beginnings project in San Diego, California, develops pilot approaches which demonstrate how school districts and community agencies can learn to share information about students and their families who are in serious need of public and private support. Participating agencies in the New Beginnings project include San Diego Unified School District, Hamilton Elementary School and staff from AFDC, Foster Children, Child Protective Services, GAIN, probation and public housing. Some of the data which the project gathered on Hamilton Elementary students includes:

(*1*) Number of households from Hamilton that have family members who are receiving services from the agencies listed

(*2*) Percentage of households from Hamilton that have family members who are receiving services from the agencies listed

(*3*) Caseload percentage of households from Hamilton served by each agency, compared to county-wide average served by each agency

(*4*) Number of households from Hamilton that are served by more than one of the agencies

(*5*) Number of at-risk students from Hamilton served by each agency

This is a sample of the types of data that will be gathered, analyzed and reported through the management information system and the evaluation system.

LIFE SKILLS AND WELLNESS SKILLS

Student study teams may find it useful to examine a series of life skills and wellness skills guidelines developed in Irvine Unified School District, Irvine, California (see Figure 17.4). The guidelines can be used to help staff design interventions for their at-risk students.

Chapter 18

EVALUATION OF
SYSTEM EFFECTIVENESS

Development of the students at risk comprehensive model for dropout program evaluation was based on two sources of data. The first source comes from the completion of interventions form (see Figure 5.2), from the Comprehensive Risk Assessment system. A level of intervention completion for each item is filled in by the school staff member responsible. When a pre/post comparison of scores is made at the end of the testing period, the staff member can check the level of intervention completion on the forms to see if areas of no improvement resulted from staff not completing the interventions they agreed to implement.

The second approach is from the conceptual work of Novak and Dougherty (1980). Categories upon which a system evaluation is based include centers on the student, serves all students, offers a comprehensive scope of services, coordinates resources and personnel and incorporates feedback and evaluation into the system.

THE NOVAK AND DOUGHERTY APPROACH

One way to use the Novak and Dougherty model is to give each evaluation item two ratings on a one (low) to ten (high) basis. The first rating is the extent to which the item is presently implemented; the second is the extent to which the rater believes it should be implemented. This provides the administrator in charge with a sense of the changes needed to improve the program, with those items with the highest discrepancy receiving priority.

Centers on the Student

The broad goal of any dropout prevention effort is to help students stay in school, while recovery activities seek to get students to return

263

to a structured program of education and, often, work. An effective evaluation could focus on formal assessment of the student utilizing grades, test data and staff entries in the student's permanent record. Informal assessment might be developed from observation of student behavior, school record analysis and teacher interviews.

Grades

Grades are a convenient way to identify students in academic difficulty. In particular, you can use the dropout prediction model in Chapter 4 to create a list of potential dropouts, and then use that list to build a dropout prevention program. Grades are also a convenient way to measure student improvement, individually and for the program as a whole.

Grades

- _____ presently implemented
- _____ should be implemented

Test Scores

Test scores serve the same function as grades in that we can readily see which students are in difficulty (using district proficiency scores) and, at the same time, record pre/post scores to find out if they are improving. These data can be used to analyze individual students and the program as a whole.

Test scores

- _____ presently implemented
- _____ should be implemented

Staff Entries in Permanent Record

The written notes that teachers and other staff members make in the student's cumulative record are a fine indicator of the student's progress and, especially, difficulties. The dropout prevention staff member can build a student case history from information in the cumulative folder.

Staff entries in permanent record

- _____ presently implemented
- _____ should be implemented

Student Behavior

There are four categories of student behavior of special interest that one could record in the case history folder. These include:

- student behavior on assigned tasks
- student behavior when free time is provided
- student interpersonal behavior
- key incidents and other information of interest

Student behavior

- _____ presently implemented
- _____ should be implemented

School Record Analysis

The records we consider are the cumulative folder and the case history folder. The emphasis here in on *analysis.* After a careful reading of both folders, the staff member attempts to see patterns. For example, at one urban high school we visited, many of the predicted dropouts attended only one class each day, a computer lab that was not boring and was run by an aide they liked. A study of attendance data in cumulative folders could help find students who respond well to the computer lab in this school. Just as importantly, it would help determine which students predicted to drop out do not like the computer lab. Those students (usually 40 percent don't like computers) could be steered towards group work and other approaches that don't utilize computers.

School record analysis

- _____ presently implemented
- _____ should be implemented

Teacher Interviews

The teacher interview schedule should yield specific information unobtainable any other way. For instance is the student

- reporting for special help as assigned
- using care in doing homework and getting it in on time
- completing make-up work on time
- bringing required materials to class
- taking accurate and useful notes
- using class time well
- taking an active and positive role in class discussions
- learning to work independently
- respecting the rights of others

If there are negative responses in this list, the student can be given special help as needed.

Teacher interviews

- _____ presently implemented
- _____ should be implemented

Serves All Students

Identification of each student's needs is the key concept, and, to the extent possible, programs are inclusive. At the same time, some groups of students may need additional attention to bring them to a satisfactory level in reading or social skills, for example. We can typically build more support from teachers and parents for programs that serve all students, such as proficiency testing and analysis, than we can for services designed for a narrow group such as predicted dropouts. The key is to set a minimal standard, such as the fortieth percentile in reading, and work to bring every student up to that level. Many of the difficulties faced by potential dropouts are problems to a lesser degree for other students. This approach builds in assistance for students who need it. Here are some examples and techniques that may help.

Hyperactivity

The student is unable to sit still in class and pay attention. Give the student medication as prescribed, extra gym time, extra shop time and permission to leave class and go to study hall, gym or shop when class is too "talky."

Disorganized Behavior

There is a tendency to move from one activity to another without purpose or thought. Try to focus on topics of special interest to the student, such as photography or automobiles. See if the student can finish one very brief activity. Construct activities in a step-by-step fashion so they can be started in the middle, even after a break.

Poor Written Expression

The student hates to write reports, letters, anything that will show him/her to be "stupid." See if you can teach the student to write by writing down her/his own words from tape-recorded answers she/he makes to questions she/he doesn't mind answering about a friend or a hobby.

The Novak handbook offers many suggestions of this type in the chapter titled "Dropout Prevention Approaches" (Novak and Dougherty, 1980).

Serves all students

• _____ presently implemented
• _____ should be implemented

Offers a Comprehensive Scope of Services

The range of services must be as broad as the varied problems students have. These services might include instruction in basic and social skills, tutoring in areas of individual need, counseling to help work on personal problems, testing to identify areas of competence and interest, as well as developing a supportive learning environment. Here are several examples for each category of service.

Instruction in Basic and Social Skills

- special offerings of basic/social skills in summer school
- flexible curriculum offering basic/social skills
- individualized courses with basic skills options
- resource teachers who offer basic/social skills

Instruction in basic and social skills

- _____ presently implemented
- _____ should be implemented

Peer Tutoring in Areas of Individual Need

- listening to the student read
- providing individualized content help
- playing instructional games
- working through programmed materials
- drilling on a specific academic skill
- assisting with development of a motor skill

Peer tutoring

- _____ presently implemented
- _____ should be implemented

Counseling on Personal Problems

- involving the student's parents
- providing a relaxed atmosphere
- being a responsive listener
- discussing strengths as well as weaknesses
- starting and ending conferences with a positive comment

Counseling on personal problems

- _____ presently implemented
- _____ should be implemented

Testing to Identify Areas of Competence and Interest

- achievement tests – norm-referenced (where the student's score

can be compared with a national mean score) and criterion-referenced (where the student's score can be looked at with reference to a specific instructional objective)
- questionnaires – to measure attitudes, opinions or judgments
- observation instruments – to measure involvement or process behaviors
- logs, records and checklists – to record informal, but key, information

Testing
- _____ presently implemented
- _____ should be implemented

Supportive Learning Environment

- academic tutoring by referral
- flexible placement in regular school, school-within-a-school or some other appropriate setting
- variable time/day scheduling
- opportunity classes that move at a slower pace
- fifth year of four-year high school option
- pregnant teenager and child care option
- small group instruction option
- big brother/sister connection

Supportive environment
- _____ presently implemented
- _____ should be implemented

Coordinates Resources and Personnel

The comprehensive services suggested in the previous section may all be available through a school district, but a potential dropout often would not know about them or how to get them. Hence, there is need for a staff member to coordinate the efforts of teachers, librarians, counselors, health staff and business contact persons who can provide training and employment opportunities.

Administrators

- to support and participate in in-service efforts pertaining to the dropout program
- to visit program activities frequently
- to allow program staff access in a timely manner

Administrators

- _____ presently implemented
- _____ should be implemented

Special Education Coordinator

- to discuss students of mutual interest on a regular basis
- to develop educational plans for students of mutual interest
- to develop in-service materials on special education topics for dropout staff
- to share administrative and instructional materials of interest
- to exchange information about students of mutual interest on a timely basis
- to jointly select materials that would be of use to both programs

Special education coordinator

- _____ presently implemented
- _____ should be implemented

Resource Staff

The resource staff includes the reading specialist, speech therapist, social worker, language/math specialist, bilingual specialist, job placement coordinator, work experience coordinator and vocational education coordinator.

- to discuss students of mutual interest on a regular basis
- to develop educational plans for students of mutual interest
- to develop in-service materials on relevant topics for dropout staff
- to share administrative and instructional materials of interest

- to exchange information about students of mutual interest on a timely basis
- to jointly select materials that would be of use to both programs

Resource staff

- _____ presently implemented
- _____ should be implemented

Out-of-School Resources

Out-of-school resources include parents, advisory committees, citizens' organizations, business-industry-labor, social agencies and other education providers. They can help dropout programs in many ways, including:

- improving the school's public image
- providing services to help meet the needs of dropouts and potential dropouts
- providing feedback to increase the quality of the program

Out-of-school resources

- _____ presently implemented
- _____ should be implemented

Incorporates Feedback and Evaluation into the System

The evaluation aspect of a dropout plan is critical in that so much of the effort is one-on-one. It is very difficult to keep staff informed about what is and is not working unless a strong evaluation effort is implemented. One way to organize the effort is a case study system where each student with special needs is dealt with by a team of professionals who diagnose needs and suggest treatment and/or remediation as appropriate. All of these efforts are recorded in a permanent folder or computer record. The following documents could be included.

Skill Expectations

Rate the following using one (poor), two (adequate) or three (good).

- _____ bringing and using an assignment notebook
- _____ keeping and organizing all papers in a subject folder
- _____ handing in legible and presentable assignments
- _____ budgeting time to meet the increasing homework demands
- _____ arriving at class on time
- _____ bringing the text and necessary supplies to class
- _____ completing assignments on time and turning them in
- _____ showing respect for staff, peers and property
- _____ working cooperatively with the teachers to meet course expectations

Areas for Improvement

Rate the following using one (poor), two (adequate) or three (good).

- _____ reporting to the teacher for special help because the student is weak in basic skills
- _____ being more careful about neatness and accuracy of homework
- _____ turning in assigned homework on time
- _____ completing make-up work on time
- _____ bringing required materials to class
- _____ taking accurate notes
- _____ learning to use class time to the fullest extent
- _____ taking a more active and positive role in discussions
- _____ learning to develop initiative and work independently
- _____ being prompt and regular in attendance
- _____ respecting the rights of others

Student Records

The following materials can be taken from the student's permanent record or gathered separately if needed.

- basic personal data
- home background
- school background and progress
- attendance record
- entrance and withdrawal information

- health and physical development reports
- academic record
- test results
- data explaining the differences between test results and classroom achievement
- social and personality characteristics
- interests and activities (in-school and out-of-school)
- vocational interests and plans
- educational interests and plans
- work experiences
- comments, observations and summarizations
- guidance notes
- follow-up data (Novak and Hammerstrom, 1976)

Incorporates feedback and evaluation

- _____ presently implemented
- _____ should be implemented

POLICY RECOMMENDATION

Each district should consider providing a dropout program evaluation developed from the conceptual work of Novak and Dougherty. Categories include: centers on the student, serves all students, offers a comprehensive scope of services, coordinates resources and personnel and incorporates feedback and evaluation into the system. The centers on the student category should include formal assessment of the student, using grades, test data and staff entries on the student's permanent record. Also included could be informal assessments based on observation of student behavior, school record analysis and teacher interviews.

Chapter 19

INSTRUCTIONAL STRATEGIES FOR STUDENTS AT RISK

Activities that offer extrinsic rewards to students at risk, who may place limited value on education, are discussed in this chapter. They include strategies such as creation of an active and thoughtful learning setting, visible recognition of various types, creation of curricula that interest these students, setting clear goals, using positive reinforcement, encouraging cooperative learning, inducing a readiness to learn, encouraging student responses in class, teacher efficacy, self-concept development, tutorial services, flexible scheduling and alternative schooling options (Allen et al., 1987).

CHARACTERISTICS OF SCHOOLS

In a presentation describing schools that were outstanding in delivering services to Hispanic students, Eugene Garcia, of the University of California at Santa Cruz, made the following observations. Of seventeen schools in the Phoenix, Arizona area, three were judged outstanding. Although each school had its own atmosphere, they shared many common features. They included:

- The teachers in each school emphasized communication between teacher and students, and between students and other students.
- Classrooms were organized to use heterogenous groups rather than homogenous groups.
- Teachers used integrated curricula where reading, science and social studies were blended together, as were art and mathematics.

- Instruction was given most often to small groups, and rarely to the whole class. Hetergenous groups were constantly reformed into new ones.
- Teachers working with at-risk students began instruction by asking lower-order questions such as, "What color is this?" and later moved to higher-order questions.
- Classes seemed like families—teachers treated students like sons and daughters.
- Writing was going on constantly, with prompts such as "how they felt," "what they thought."
- In the early grades, all writing was in Spanish; in the third and fourth grades there was a transition to English.
- Teachers were advocates for students, and demanding of students.
- Teachers worked autonomously, and were clear about why they did everything; they would argue strenuously with the principals to get to do what they wanted.
- Schools had 90 plus percent parent involvement.
- Teachers refused to refer students to remedial classes or special education; all problems were handled in class, often with the help of older students.

CREATE AN ACTIVE LEARNING SETTING

Students at risk need to be challenged by active learning opportunities and many different instructional strategies. They are easily bored, which makes them difficult to teach. It is therefore worth extra effort on the part of the teacher to set up an active learning environment. Kierstead (1986) suggests teachers focus on sharing responsibility for creating an active learning setting with students.

> While allowing students to operate independently through planning the use of their own time, and by making decisions regarding pace, sequence and content of the projects, the teacher never fully relinquishes control. Instead, the teacher establishes a set of rules, routines and consequences which make it possible to monitor and guide what students are doing. For example, students are taught to follow a procedure which looks like the following:

(*1*) Gather materials and equipment. They begin by gathering what they need to carry out their work. These resources are usually kept in a preestablished location, within easy reach of the students, so that they do not waste time searching for them, or waiting for them to be handed out.

(*2*) Carry out the task. Students know what is expected of them as they work. They understand the rules for general behavior such as where they may sit, how much talking and walking about is acceptable and whether they may work with other students. Standards for the quality, quantity and complexity of work have been established. They know where and how to get help. Peer tutors or a student buddy system encourages students to share information and ideas with fellow students.

(*3*) Have work checked and signed off. Students are responsible for asking the teacher to check and sign off on their work upon completion of all or a predetermined portion of a project. At this point, they receive specific feedback, and may be required to make a correction or expand the work and then return for another check before the teacher completely signs off on it.

(*4*) Record that work is complete. Once the teacher has made the final check, the student indicates by a visual signal (usually by checking off on a class chart) that his or her task is complete. This allows the teacher to see, at a glance, how far each student has progressed during the project period.

(*5*) Turn in completed work. Students usually place completed work in a central location so the teacher can look through it outside class time. This allows the teacher to assess student work, and plan which students should receive special attention during the next project period.

(*6*) Return materials and equipment. Students know how to care for and return materials and equipment to storage areas so that they remain in good condition.

(*7*) Begin another activity. The student knows what to do once the first portion of a project is complete.

In addition to creation of an active learning environment, teachers should consider questioning strategies which encourage a thoughtful classroom. This is especially important for students with poor self-images who have not been quick enough to play an active role in most classes in the past.

When teachers rely on questions with short, correct answers, and call on students with their hands raised, they are encouraging recall in some students and ignoring others entirely. Instead, teachers should

Teachers' Discussion.

- Ask questions which have a range of appropriate responses, all of which require some explanation of the student's thinking.
- Wait five to ten seconds for all students to think.
- Call on students without anyone raising hands.

This approach accomplishes several important goals.

- All students know they are expected to think.
- They are given the time and silence to think.
- All students must be ready to communicate their thoughts (Middle Grade Task Force, 1987).

Visible Recognition

The following activities offer extrinsic rewards to the potential dropout who may place little or no intrinsic value on education. These activities may have a positive effect by encouraging students to attend school.

(*1*) Award the most improved attenders a certificate of recognition.

(*2*) Provide special field trips for improved attenders.

(*3*) Reward improved attenders with paperback books.

(*4*) Hold a drawing for special prizes donated from local businesses open to students with the greatest improvement in attendance. Ask businesses to provide reduced-price coupons for products and services that students like.

(*5*) Send letters of commendation home to parents of students with excellent improvement in attendance.

(*6*) Provide special lunch-time and end-of-school parties for students with improved attendance.

(*7*) Allow students with the greatest improvement in attendance to opt out of some examinations; base grades on classwork.

(*8*) Publicize attendance awards in your local newspaper. Seek television coverage for attractive attendance-oriented events. Reward and publicize schools with the greatest improvement in attendance and related issues, like reduction in tardiness.

(*9*) Schedule special assemblies and other attractive events on Mondays and Fridays when students are often absent.

Getting students to come to school and to stay in school are critical steps in improving attendance and instruction. Many schools are using computerized attendance programs that help administrators routinize parent contact by automating the personalized letters that are mailed to students' homes. Some programs offer period-by-period attendance record keeping as well. More expensive programs help administrators set up their attendance records so they link to the main student records. Making student records easy to access and use takes time and money, but improved attendance can easily pay for these efforts.

Building an Interesting Curriculum

Students are motivated in school when their studies relate to topics that are of real interest to them. There are many ways to find out what those interests are. They include:

(*1*) Use questionnaires to identify general and specific interests of students.

(2) Observe what students do in their free time to guide you to their real interests. Plan surprise activities and events. Use instructional games, especially those involving the computer.

(3) Consider how student interests can be integrated into the curriculum as starting points of lessons, examples of concepts and applications of skills they have learned.

(4) Individualize by providing choices, so students have more opportunity to select assignments, activities or projects that are interesting to them.

Set Clear Goals

Students will move toward goals when they know what the goals are. The goals need to be specific and challenging, and communicated as expectations for the results of learning. Some ways to do this are

(1) Involve students in some of the goal setting for the class and for themselves individually.

(2) State objectives in behavioral terms so you can measure students' progress and find out which of your approaches works best.

(3) Communicate your goals and objectives to students before each lesson, orally or in writing.

(4) Design new lessons that take advantage of your most effective approaches.

Use Positive Reinforcement

Positive reinforcement can be used as a powerful extrinsic motivator. Effective employment of reinforcement strategies requires careful reading of the models, skill and understanding in establishing them and patience and practice to finally refine them so they work for you. Some ways to get started are

(1) List the specific things students do that you want to reinforce, so you can work consistently and systematically toward rewarding them for the appropriate behaviors.

(2) Use verbal and nonverbal reinforcers immediately when students move toward your target behaviors.

(3) Remind students of specific academic objectives or social be-

haviors that you will be looking for, and then acknowledge them and show your appreciation for the examples you see.

(*4*) Give specific praise for what you can find that is correct and successful in students' work.

Cooperative Learning

Motivation can be enhanced by actively teaching students how to cooperate in achieving academic goals. Cooperation can build supportive relationships and group morale as well as increasing student motivation. Some ways to build cooperation are

(*1*) Assign learning tasks to students in heterogenous pairs, triads or small groups. Group as well as individual grades and recognition may be given.

(*2*) Develop a skill bank of student experts where, to the extent possible, every student is expert at something and is asked to help other students.

(*3*) Teach small-group skills directly. Let effective groups discuss how they work, so they can serve as models to the other groups.

(*4*) Have students evaluate their own group processes and effectiveness; discuss these results in class when it is appropriate.

Induce Readiness to Learn

Effective teachers/motivators plan specific instructional activities that create interest in a topic about to be taught. Inducing readiness to learn requires planning and imagination. Try to build on the natural power of student anticipation with some of these tools.

(*1*) Ask thought-provoking questions that can only be answered in an activity that follows.

(*2*) Start with an event in school or community life, and work back to the topic of the lesson.

(*3*) Use cartoons, pictures, newspaper headlines, taped excerpts from television programs, records, computer activities and other strategies to liven up class and get students' attention.

(*4*) Design specific activities to introduce lessons, and then check to see if students' progress is greater than it is for lessons where you have not done this.

Encourage Student Responses

Students need to be encouraged to respond to questions, and to interact with each other during most lessons. Dropout-prone students are often quiet, and special effort needs to made continuously to draw them out in class. If you as a teacher do not feel you are effective with these students, work with the administrators to put fewer of them in your classes until you have improved your skills in working with them. Some ways to encourage students include:

(*1*) Ask students questions to find out what they know and do not know. Avoid questions that tend to trap, trick or punish students. Allow students to demonstrate what they know, believe and value.

(*2*) Give more wait time (time the teacher waits for slower students to react) to questions you ask. You may be pleased at the responses of students who never get recognized if you don't consciously wait for them.

(*3*) Ask questions that you do not know how to answer. About one in four dropout-prone students is gifted (and very bored) and this gives students an opportunity to explain things they know about to you and the class.

(*4*) Suspend judgment when students respond to queries. Instead of saying "right" or "not quite," move on and gather several responses before commenting.

These principles of motivation, when used by a competent teacher, can help you turn routine instruction into exciting teaching. The thrill of catching the interest of a formerly apathetic student is a sweet memory for years to come.

Teacher Efficacy

Ashton and Webb have reported some research that can significantly help administrators who are working to assist students at risk. High-efficacy teachers create a more positive classroom climate than do low-efficacy teachers. They are less likely to punish students or scold them, and more likely to accept student feelings and ideas than is true for low-efficacy peers. High-efficacy teachers also are more likely to include all students in their class in instruction and seatwork activities than is true for their counterparts (Ashton and Webb, 1986). Some ways to promote teacher efficacy are

(*1*) Administrators might seek to schedule, to the extent possible, dropout-prone students into the classes of high-efficacy teachers.

(*2*) In order to be fair to high-efficacy teachers receiving difficult students, the low-efficacy teachers could be asked to participate in training activities that help them improve classroom climate, strengthen human relations skills, increase their interest in motivating weak students and strengthen their instructional skills through clinical supervision and similar strategies.

(*3*) Administrators could improve the organization of schools and teacher effectiveness by encouraging collaborative planning between teachers who instruct the same dropout-prone students, by involving these teachers in key decisions that affect their problem students, and by seeking special funding which allows the teachers release time and needed resources to meet the special needs of students they have identified in their collaborative planning.

Alternative Instructional Strategies

Some students are not successful in a regular classroom setting, but they can work effectively in less formal environments. Students often need to be involved in transactional analysis or a similar program to improve their self-awareness and self-esteem in order to develop a positive attitude about pursuing their education. Emphasis may be given to building a feeling of self-worth through the arts, for example, or wherever a sympathetic teacher is willing to give this effort their special attention. Some alternate instructional strategies are

(*1*) Tutorial strategies can use other students to help those likely to drop out.

(*2*) Similarly, peer counseling efforts have been organized in scores of districts to help students learn how to work with substance abusing students.

(*3*) Use of retired persons as volunteers in classrooms and as tutors has been a successful strategy in some districts.

(*4*) College students who are not as active socially as they would like to be make excellent candidates for cross-age tutoring of secondary students. We operated an informal program of this type from the admissions office at Occidental College in Los Angeles some years ago.

(*5*) Retired teachers are another fine group to approach when a school is looking for tutors for students with special needs.

THE ALLENDALE SCHOOL

Harris has described the very successful tutoring program at Allendale School in Oakland, California.

Student tutors are recommended by their teachers on the basis of responsibility, conscientiousness and reliability. During four training sessions, tutors learn their responsibilities, positive tutor behavior and the content of their skill-based reading and math tutoring units. Tutors and tutees are matched on a one-to-one basis for the entire year. Tutoring sessions range from thirty minutes twice a week to thirty or forty minutes five times a week. Tutors meet once per month to share insights and problems. At least twice per month, the trainer meets individually with each tutor to discuss the progress of the tutee. A network of referrals among tutor, teacher and trainer kept everyone working together. Thorough written evaluations take place at the end of the year. The program changes, grows and improves each year. (Middle Grade Task Force, 1987)

Flexible scheduling may be a critical strategy to consider as you consider the findings of Wehlage and Rutter cited in Chapter 1. They call for students at risk to be divided into groups of 100–125, where they can have informal relations with their five or six teachers. In other situations, late afternoon and evening classes may make it possible for some students to work earlier in the day and go to school later in the day.

PEDAGOGY OF POVERTY

Martin Haberman (1991) has written that there is a *pedagogy of poverty* so powerful that an urban teacher who did not follow it would be regarded as deviant. It is probably more true for high school than junior high teachers. The pedagogy consists of the following core functions of urban teaching.

- giving information
- asking questions
- giving directions
- making assignments
- monitoring seatwork
- reviewing assignments
- giving tests
- reviewing tests
- assigning homework
- reviewing homework
- settling disputes
- punishing noncompliance
- marking papers
- giving grades

The problem with this sensible looking list is that it does not lead to successful performance for most urban students. Teachers become enforcers of rules to minimally control student behavior, not successful educators. Research indicates that successful teachers have quite a different agenda.

- involving students with issues they see as vital
- spending time discussing human differences
- teaching major concepts and general principles
- involving students in planning what they will be doing
- applying ideals such as fairness, equity and justice
- involving students in real-life experiences.

Many of us would have no problem agreeing with this approach. The difficulty with implementing it is that students in urban schools have learned to control teachers by complying with the activities on the first list, and by resisting the more complex activities that are used to implement the second list. If control is the name of the game, urban students have learned that for them to succeed in controlling, the activities need to be simple. Haberman cites the example of the experienced teacher who has learned one way to have a quiet, orderly classroom: "Take out your dictionaries and start to copy the words that begin with *h*."

We believe urban teachers can move in the direction of control of their classrooms by a political strategy that comes from the work of Gamson (1968). If students are divided into positives, neutrals and negatives, give verbal praise and recognition to the positives, tangible rewards (certificates of recognition, field trips, paperback books) to neutrals and no recognition to the negatives.

Alternative schooling of many types appears attractive to students at risk. Some of the options include work experience, independent study of various designs, continuation schools, opportunity classes aimed at special interests and a variety of nontraditional experiences that allow teachers and students to operate in a casual environment. Teachers need to be interested in the personal lives of these students and their families, and willing to work on the myriad personal problems that fill them, in order to move toward success in their academic efforts.

POLICY RECOMMENDATION

Each district should consider developing activities that offer extrinsic rewards to students at risk who may place limited value on education. They include strategies such as creation of an active and thoughtful learning setting, visible recognition of various types, creation of curricula that interest these students, setting clear goals, using positive reinforcement, encouraging cooperative learning, inducing a readiness to learn, encouraging student responses in class, teacher efficacy, self-concept development, tutorial services, flexible scheduling and alternative schooling options.

Chapter 20

LINKING SCHOOLS TO COMMUNITY AGENCIES

It has become increasingly clear that we serve students and their families best if we use schools to link families with other services from community agencies. Agencies need to share information about services provided in order to reduce costs and prevent misunderstandings that arise from contradictory expectations on the part of agency staff. In this chapter we present a school-based model from Duarte Unified School District, Duarte, California, for utilizing a variety of agencies to provide services to students and their families. An evaluation form is utilized which allows us to integrate data from community agencies with school-based information.

COMPREHENSIVE COMMUNITY SERVICES

The concept of Comprehensive Community Services can be implemented in five steps.

(*1*) Establish linkages to all relevant community agencies that serve the students and families from your school. These might include health services, social programs, church programs, health promotion programs and mental health services.

(*2*) Carry out a needs assessment to categorize and, later, prioritize the services offered by community agencies that can help your students and their families.

(*3*) Develop contracts/agreements for health services including access to care, access to emergency care, health screening, student-initiated care and problem identification and access to chronic care.

(*4*) Develop and improve your existing school district health care by including the following.

287

- instructional objectives consistent with major health objectives for each age group
- instruction integrated into other school curricula, especially dropout prevention aspects
- instruction about self-care, medical decision making, nutrition and diet improvement
- instruction to include parents and family and to involve them in key areas

(5) Develop and improve your school environment to focus upon: safety and cleanliness, with special attention to old construction and hazardous materials; school nutrition and healthier food options; school-wide physical activity programs; development of a smoke-free environment, with special emphasis upon teachers and school staff; development of a philosophy that supports reaching into the family and community to provide assistance.

DUARTE UNIFIED SCHOOL DISTRICT—1990–1992[27]

The Duarte Unified School District (DUSD) project is a two-year substance abuse/dropout prevention effort funded by the U.S. Department of Education. At the time of this report, we were concluding our second year and preparing for our final data analysis by piloting two new forms and the accompanying statistical analysis for the intervention completion form.

This evaluation was designed by Dr. Callison and he is implementing it. It indicates how a model from Irvine Unified School District (IUSD) can be adapted to a small, mostly Hispanic district, and be successful in obtaining funding. This project is of interest because it uses materials developed in Irvine Unified School District. Many of the interventions from IUSD were used and several new forms piloted. Of interest is the intervention completion form, designed by Dr. Callison, which allows a project director to ascertain the extent to which there is a reduction in likelihood of abuse or dropout, and to further see how many interventions were completed. Interventions are analyzed item-by-item, and by level.

[27]This report was written by Alberta Schroeder, Special Projects' Coordinator, Duarte Unified School District, Duarte, California.

A second evaluation tool being piloted is the use of a new piece of software, created using the InFORMed Designer and Manager programs, both for the Macintosh. This software allows a project director to create new forms that are compatible with a school's present forms, and that then utilize a common data base. Forms can also be designed for participating agencies so they can be on a central data base with the schools. The forms are seen in Chapter 17.

Project Aims

The aims of the district at-risk management project are to develop a computer management system

- to identify potential substance abusers and potential dropouts
- to use an expert system to connect identified students at risk with appropriate interventions to reduce student risk levels
- to use the intervention completion form to ascertain the extent to which there is a reduction in the likelihood of abuse or dropout, and to further see how many interventions were completed
- to create new forms that are compatible among the various agencies, and that use a common data base for reporting information about students and their families to agency staff

The objectives of the DUSD project are

- to decrease antisocial, aggressive behaviors and develop prosocial behaviors
- to decrease the tendency to associate with drug using peers due to passive behavior and lack of alternative activities
- to improve parental drug-free information, attitudes and skills, related to family management, value systems, modeling and communication of no-use message
- to increase student achievement and interest in school activities
- to improve health and attitudes toward health
- to increase awareness of personality needs and develop healthy alternatives and resources for high-risk students who may be sensation seekers, cognitively impulsive, isolated, highly tolerant of deviance and/or low self-esteem, etc.

- to improve attitudes, skills and use of resources to achieve individual goals

Formative and Summative Evaluation

We utilized the teacher referral system in Chapter 16 (see Figure 16.1), which identifies students likely to need special attention. Self-report data, from students with special needs, were then placed on our Scantron forms and automatically input into the Comprehensive Risk Assessment software, which uses research-based formulas to identify students. For this task we used Macintosh computers. We then identified students and placed them in interventions as described in Chapter 6.

This at-risk management system makes a significant impact on reducing student drug use and dropout by creating a research-based system for prioritizing student need. In our experience, programs that do not prioritize student need, and admit all students who need service, typically fail. There are not enough staff and teacher hours available to offer the help the students must have to succeed. The teachers who are involved begin to realize they are not making the kind of difference required, and they withdraw from the program, first unofficially, by not working hard, and eventually formally. At this point they tell the principal that the program does not work and it is cancelled for the coming year.

Since the primary effort in the project is the introduction of the identification and placement procedure, we rely on measures of success in this area as critical indicators of project implementation. The intervention completion forms are completed by the project director. They indicate what interventions have been completed for each student, and the level of completion. This in turn allows the staff to understand why a student's predicted score for dropout and substance abuse may not be improving.

In the proposal we committed ourselves to a context evaluation. In it we assess whether we are developing a computer management system

- to identify potential substance abusers and potential dropouts using our Scantron data gathering approach
- to use an expert system to connect identified students at risk with appropriate interventions which will reduce student risk levels

Working in Pairs.

- to evaluate the effectiveness of the interventions by assigning new risk levels to participating students

We are meeting these objectives successfully as we enter the last half of year two of the project.

Objectives, Tasks and Quantitative Measures

Objectives unique to this project include:

(*1*) Install an expert system, the Comprehensive Risk Assessment software, in the five elementary schools, which allows them to connect identified students at risk with appropriate substance abuse and dropout prevention interventions. Dr. Callison supervised the in-

stallation of the CRA software on a Macintosh in the district office
and taught the project assistant how to use it.

(2) Input data from the Scantron forms into the Comprehensive Risk
Assessment (CRA) software. Dr. Callison worked with staff to see
that risk data from the Scantron forms was scanned into the software at his university office. We had expected to do this at the district office, but decided to use the funds allocated for the purchase
of the scanner, to hire aides at each site instead.

(3) Provide training and educational resources to facilitate the implementation of the proposed at-risk management system. Dr. Callison supervised the implementation of the training, and worked
with site staff to see that the training was appropriate and timely.
This work was carried out on schedule in months one to three.

(4) Increase the accuracy and speed of placement of at-risk students
into appropriate interventions. This was to include the development of a version of the CRA software that staff can use which does
not have to be scanned, thus reducing delays when there is no immediate access to the scanner. This keyboard entry version of the
software can be used to enter data on a few students who were not
present when the original data gathering took place.

*TABLE 20.1 Statistical analysis (items and student raw data averaged
by item for fifteen students).*

ITEMS	CRA PRETEST	CRA POSTTEST	IMPLEMENTATION
1. Anger*	3	2	2
2. Friends' use*	3	2	3
3. Adult users*	3	2	3
4. High/drunk*	3	2	3
5. Family against drugs*	3	2	3
6. Parents know	2	2	2
7. Try marijuana	2	2	2
8. Times arrested	1	1	2
9. Expelled	1	1	3
10. D's and F's	3	2	3
11. Been arrested	1	1	2
12. Juvenile record	1	1	3
13. Disability	0	0	0
14. Moved/changed school	1	1	2

*Items are the top predictors of substance abuse.

TABLE 20.2 Comprehensive risk analysis.

PRETEST RESULTS					
X₁: CRA PRETEST					
Mean	Std. Dev.	Std. Error	Variance	Coef. Var.	Count
3.2	5.031	1.299	25.314	157.229	15
Minimum	Maximum	Range	Sum	Sum Squared	# Missing
0	21	21	48	508	0
POSTTEST RESULTS					
X₂: CRA POSTTEST					
Mean	Std. Dev.	Std. Error	Variance	Coef. Var.	Count
1.533	.64	.165	.41	41.735	15
Minimum	Maximum	Range	Sum	Sum Squared	# Missing
0	2	2	23	41	0
ONE SAMPLE *t*-TEST X₁: CRA POSTTEST					
DF	Sample Mean	Pop. Mean	*t* Value	Prob. (2-tail)	
14	1.533	1	3.228	.0061	

This version of the software was completed on schedule and turned out to be the most important aspect of the project. We discovered that in a tight economy, no one was willing to spend project funds for the purchase of a scanner. The development of the keyboard entry version of the CRA software has made it possible for dozens of other schools to use this system without purchase of a scanner. In our experience it is typical of a funded project. The most important aspect of the project turns out to be something no one could have predicted.

Student data are taken from the intervention completion forms, as seen in Chapter 5, and completed by the project director, working with staff at each school. These data are then analyzed as shown in Tables 20.1, 20.2 and 20.3.

The data are estimates, since actual data were not yet available at press time. They do allow the reader to see the kind of analyses that will be used.

TABLE 20.3 Contingency table analysis.

OBSERVED FREQUENCY TABLE			
	COLUMN 1	COLUMN 2	COLUMN 3	TOTALS
Row 1	3	2	2	7
Row 2	3	2	3	8
Row 3	3	2	3	8
Row 4	3	2	3	8
Row 5	3	2	3	8
Row 6	2	2	2	6
Row 7	2	2	2	6
Row 8	1	1	2	4
Row 9	1	1	3	5
Row 10	3	2	3	8
Row 11	1	1	2	4
Row 12	1	1	3	5
Row 13	0	0	0	0
Row 14	21	2	0	23
Row 15	1	1	2	4
Totals	48	23	33	104

Sample data in Table 20.2 indicate that the project showed a strong improvement with a reduction in the mean from 3.2 on the pretest to 1.5 on the posttest which gives us a t value significant at the level of $p < .006$.

Table 20.3 helps one to see at a glance the average pretest in column 1, the average posttest in column 2 and the level of implementation by the teachers in column 3.

Chapter 21

USING TECHNOLOGY IN INSTRUCTION

One of the critical tasks in preparing a district to move forward with an effective dropout prevention effort is locating appropriate instructional materials. Many of these materials will have an emphasis on basic skills, and hence will be found under headings like reading, language arts and mathematics (or, more accurately, arithmetic). It is also likely that some computer-assisted instruction materials are appropriate for students at risk. It is important to know that as many as 25 percent of dropouts are gifted, and that problem-solving and higher-order thinking skills materials will be of special interest to them. Materials may include computer-based options where a complete curriculum is offered, computer-assisted instruction which uses microcomputers to supplement the efforts of individual teachers and print and media packages which do not use computers.

The use of technology is increasing in U.S. schools. It may be having its most rapid expansion in schools where dropout or predicted dropout is a major problem, because computer-assisted or -managed instruction is more interesting to many troubled students than routine classroom lectures. Administrators are finding technology can help them keep track of these students and their records, and that software programs for doing this are better every year. Dropouts and predicted dropouts need to be treated like special education students with individual educational plans, and there are programs available to do this, including the Comprehensive Risk Assessment software.

A special feature of this chapter is a detailed description of two dropout prevention programs using WICAT computer-managed instruction. The Duarte program has been recognized by the California State Department of Education as a model, and the Azusa program is

295

under review for national recognition as an Anderson Medal contender.

SOME AVAILABLE TECHNOLOGICAL TOOLS

Computer-Assisted Instruction

Computer-assisted instruction, or CAI, is widely used and appears in many forms. As the name implies, CAI supplements the teacher. In fact, most commercial firms that sell CAI to schools have designed the software to accompany the most widely used texts in each subject area. The texts are designed to accompany state-approved curricula. Texts and CAI are a powerful instructional assistance package. One firm, that may have sold the most CAI units nationally, Computer Curriculum Corporation (CCC), now owned by Paramount Publishing in Sunnyvale, California, even has the capability to test a student in mathematics, say, and then predict how many hours on the program it will take to bring the student up to a performance level specified in advance. If the level was grade equivalent 5.0 for example, and the student was at 3.8, the program might predict it would take thirty-three hours to bring him/her up to 5.0. The prediction is accurate to within plus or minus three minutes according to CCC's data (Staff, 1986b). In four months on the CCC system, participants in a study averaged more than a ten-month gain in reading, and a twenty-three-month gain in mathematics. This occurred where regular classroom instruction of twenty hours in a content area in four months was used to complement the computer-assisted instruction on CCC of sixteen hours in four months (Staff, 1985).

Computer-Managed Instruction

Computer-managed instruction, or CMI, comes in two basic forms. At the simplest level, CMI is a program designed to test student performance and identify what competency domains need more work. Managed at this level means that the program uses information from student test results to indicate to the teacher what additional assignments would be appropriate.

At a more advanced level, CMI means that the entire course in Alge-

Teachers Using CAI.

bra I, for example, is taught using the software. PLATO, the most complex and extensive of all educational software programs, has more than 10,000 hours of instructional material available. The PLATO learning management system guides the student through an entire course, which typically includes a variety of media such as CAI, texts, videotapes and perhaps slides. Thus, CAI is part of a total system which is managed by the computer software for a true CMI system. An updated version of PLATO is called NOVANET, and is aligned with the new curriculum frameworks in California.

Listed next are descriptions of four elementary and six secondary technological interventions that are successful, or show great promise, in helping at-risk students acquire necessary skills. These interventions are all operating in the Corona-Norco Unified School District in southern California (Wilson, 1989). All students can learn, and effective applications of educational technology provide much of the at-risk student's motivation for attending school and improving academic achievement.

Writing to Read

The Writing to Read program uses an IBM computer with a digitized voice which enables the computer to "talk." This creates a computer-based instructional program providing multisensory instruction which is both self-paced and interactive.

Designed to develop writing and reading skills of students in kindergarten and first grade, IBM's Writing to Read teaches children how to write anything they can say, and read anything they can write. In the Writing to Read center, children use a variety of equipment and language arts materials organized as learning stations. Equipped with a digitized voice, the computer introduces the individual phonemic sounds of the alphabet.

Educational Systems Corporation (Jostens)

An integrated learning system in reading, mathematics and science, from Education Systems Corporation, includes a networked laboratory, CD-ROM technology and a trained attendant to manage the lab. In addition to the emphasis on essential concepts and skills for students in grades one through eight, there is an even stronger program commitment to the development of higher-order thinking skills. The multisensory, interactive curriculum with voice uses IBM, Tandy or Apple computers, and CD-ROM technology, to deliver instruction and manage student records.

Computer Checkout Program

Elementary students and their parents can be trained in the use of computer hardware and software through an elementary school computer checkout program. Tandy color computers and software programs are used as a regular part of the classroom instructional program. However, parents of students in grades four through six are permitted to check out the computer equipment and appropriate programs to use at home in acquiring basic skills in math and language arts.

The primary program objectives are to reinforce basic skills through the use of computer-assisted instruction, increase interactive use of leisure time, motivate learning, increase instructional time and improve the learning environment at home.

Elementary Science Videodisc Instruction

National Geographic's videodisc is an instructional tool that interactively combines still and motion pictures, informative narration, follow-up activities, remediation, positive reinforcement and on-screen text. Characteristics of whales, kinds of whales, behavior of whales and whales and people are the four major areas addressed by the program.

EduTech Courseware's Courseactive science videodisc application is used by students in grades four through six. The three-disc program is self-paced, and has the capability of immediate review of material and records management. The course covers: weather instruments that measure air temperature and pressure; air circulation, wind direction and wind speed; air masses; evaporation, condensation and precipitation elements of the water cycle; and cloud types and storms.

A level two laserdisc player, with its own microprocessor, is needed for both these science programs, and is interfaced with a television set or monitor for group or individual instruction.

PALS

The Principle of the Alphabet Literacy System (PALS) is an interactive instructional program that combines the IBM personal computer and InfoWindow software with a videodisc to teach functionally illiterate adolescents and adults to read and write. PALS also uses an IBM typewriter for touch typing training, and for word and sentence composition; the IBM computer for the same purposes, as well as word processing; and a work journal that reinforces the audio and visual information on the videodiscs.

The PALS classroom is a learning environment in which students use all the components in a planned program. These components include videodisc players and computers, videodiscs, IBM computers and typewriters, work journals and typing manuals.

Accounting and Word Processing Computer Programs

High schools should provide at-risk students with automated accounting and word processing classroom programs, within a simulated office computer environment, to develop vocational skills.

South-Western Publishing Company's automated accounting programs can be used. Students use the computer in applying accounting concepts and procedures they have worked with manually. They prepare financial records for businesses. The areas covered include general ledger/financial reporting, accounts receivable, accounts payable, inventory and payroll.

Word processing programs and concepts should be taught to students. Along with accurate, increasing production rates, students learn about input media, automated office systems, distribution and communication and the storage and retrieval essentials of records management.

Computerized Science Balance

The Computer-Assisted Science Lab (CASL) system is a new dimension in the teaching of chemistry and general science. With the interactive software, a single Apple microcomputer can be used effectively by all students in a science classroom. The menu-driven program links a central computer to a top-loading electronic balance from OHAUS Scale Corporation. The program exposes students to the standard quantitative topics covered in chemistry courses. Students develop critical thinking skills as they perform labs involving determination of density, heat of chemical reaction, conservation of mass, molecular mass, stoichiometry, molarity, solubility constant and many more lab experiments.

Technology in Art Instruction

Technology can be effectively used in the secondary art curriculum.

An art lab provides instructional and production capabilities in videodisc technology, computer graphics, video production and desktop publishing, as well as the ability to integrate any or all of the technologies. Laserdisc instruction, group or individual, includes the National Gallery of Art and Vincent van Gogh disc programs. Desktop publishing, utilizing Macintosh computers, for example, is included in art as it relates to the design and development of textual and graphic layouts by students for campus publications. Graphics development software is also used with computers and printers to design and develop computer art incorporating line, color, form and shape, texture, value and space elements of art instruction. Camcorders and a professional editing system make up the video production segment of the class.

Industrial Technology

An industrial technology curriculum has been expanded by integrating drafting and metals into a course entitled Design-Manufacturing Technology. This course is taught by high school instructors. The course concept includes components of design drafting, CAD (computer-aided drafting), computer programming, CNC (computer numerically controlled) machining and technical writing. The goal for the student is to design and manufacture a high-quality, marketable product in a simulated industrial setting, utilizing technological equipment. This program has been recognized as a California State Model program, with academic learning stressed in these vocational and pre-engineering experiences.

Video Microscopy Teaching Station

Mideo Systems, Inc., a subsidiary of Southland Instruments, markets the Video Microscopy Teaching Station for science instruction. The station can be custom designed, but typically consists of two high-quality optical microscopes, a fiber optic illuminator, an attachable solid-state color camera and a color video display monitor.

This innovative instructional system allows classroom instructors to use the microscope as a tool for whole-group instruction. Students can receive necessary basic information before they view the material on their own. Microscopic images and action sequences, with sound-over narration, can also be videotaped for future home or school use.

THE DUARTE PROGRAM

The Duarte Dropout Recovery program in Duarte Unified School District, Duarte, California, operates with a group of 100 students. Recovery efforts with these students brought an average daily attendance funding (ADA) increase, after program implementation in 1986–1987, of sixty-four student full-time equivalent attendees, an improvement of approximately 11 percent with no increase in the local community population. At $3,000 per student, that gives the district $192,000 to work with in expanding their efforts at the junior high and elementary levels.

Once students have been identified and placed into the outreach program they are enrolled in the outreach lab. The lab is the focal point for the student's individualized educational program. Each student in the lab is placed in an independent study program. The program is based on each student's basic needs, career and employment plans, life situation and goals for educational improvement.

The academic portion of their program consists of three basic ingredients, which include:

(1) Computer-assisted instruction using PLATO-WICAT in the student's course and basic skills requirements

(2) A series of readings, research and study activities that are consonant with the state model curriculum standards

(3) The input of appropriate compensatory educational programs that meet the needs of the student, such as the regional occupational program, work experience, special education, limited English program, English as a second language program, tenth grade counseling, vocational education and migrant education

The student has a minimum of twenty hours of instructional experience per week. The basic approach of these three ingredients is to construct a program that meets students' needs in academic, career and social/personal areas.

The lab is directed by the outreach consultant. Two paraprofessionals assist him, a lab manager and an outreach aide. The lab manager operates the computer-assisted instruction system and monitors the progress on outside-the-lab learning tasks. The bilingual aide monitors students in a guidance lab station, provides individualized tutoring and instruction to students and assists the outreach consultant in clerical and procedural matters.

The outreach consultant's job is

(*1*) To work with the student and his/her parents during the input process

(*2*) To serve as chair of the student study team

(*3*) To counsel the student, with the help of the school guidance counselor, to an appropriate academic placement that meets her/his ability level

(*4*) To monitor the progress of the student through the course curriculum

(*5*) To consult with parent, student and counselor regarding the student's progress, both in terms of academic achievement and personal/social development

(*6*) To relate to the special needs of any student in the program

(*7*) To assist in the career planning, job search and hiring needs of students

The outreach consultant also develops an early warning network to identify students exhibiting the preliminary signs of dropout, such as low grades, poor attendance, tardiness, retention in grade and poor test scores. These students are assigned to the guidance lab for the first stage of the intervention. In addition, the outreach consultant works closely with all other faculty and staff to develop appropriate in-service experiences, to articulate the needs of at-risk students to the personnel in both the core and compensatory programs and to coordinate the return of students from the outreach lab to the traditional academic program, or the placement of students in other educational opportunities, such as those provided by the military, colleges or trade/vocational schools.

THE AZUSA PROPOSAL

The following proposal was submitted by Dr. Duane Stiff, Superintendent, Azusa Unified School District, Azusa, California, to the Anderson Foundation in a national competition. The words in italics denote information which the foundation asks grant applicants to provide.

Scope of Program

Program goals — identify the problem in your community, or the perceived national problem, that your program seeks to solve, and state your objective(s).
The goal of the program is to increase the number of students receiving high school diplomas, and to insure that those students are prepared to enter the job market, continue their education and contribute to community life as productive citizens. The problem is that 50 percent of the entering ninth grade students at Azusa and Gladstone High Schools do not complete their education in Azusa. The objectives of the program are to improve retention rates, attendance rates and academic achievement of at-risk target students as measured by district attendance records and norm-referenced tests.
Program strategy — list the steps that will lead to the attainment of your goals.

* Design a unique program plan and delivery system for high-risk target students.
* Create a school-within-a-school family environment at both comprehensive high schools.
* Select and train staff in the use of technology and program philosophy. Develop student selection and exit criteria.
* Identify areas in which students need remediation.
* Align district curricula with the needs of students and the available resources (computer software, printed materials, guidance).
* Maintain target student progress reports on computer-assisted instruction usage. Review and refine the program quarterly with teachers, site administrators, site counselors, district office administrators including the superintendent and business partners.
* Emphasize self-esteem, success-paced curricula and mainstream participation of students in one or two electives.
* Hand schedule tenth, eleventh and twelfth grade target students.

Program structure — how many students, classrooms and schools does your program reach?

- It includes two high schools, Azusa and Gladstone, each with a two-room center.
- There are thirty-two student computer stations in each center.
- There is a new target group of forty greatest at-risk incoming ninth grade students at each high school each year.
- It supports target students in grades nine to twelve.
- The anticipated total population for September 1990 is 200 ninth, tenth and eleventh grade project students.

Describe the points and methods of interaction between your program and the students' parent(s) or guardian(s).

- An initial invitation is sent by mail for incoming ninth grade project students.
- A follow-up phone call or family conference is scheduled for each incoming project student.
- Each project center is equipped with a phone for regular contact with students' homes during the school year.
- Individual student/parent conferences occur as needed during the school year.
- Invitations are sent to parents to attend student recognition receptions.

When did implementation begin (term and year)?
Implementation began in the fall semester of the 1988 school year.
What is the planned duration of the program? Explain your reason(s) for this.
The initial partnership duration was planned as a minimum of four years. However, the program will continue as long as it is successful and needed.
What are your plans for evaluation, redesign and replication? If you have already evaluated your program, state your findings and how you have made use of them.
The evaluation design for target students included:

- Gather attrition rate of greatest at-risk ninth graders for five previous years before start of project.
- Maintain retention rate data.
- Maintain attendance rate data.

- Collect academic achievement data including credits completed versus credits attempted, grade point average (GPA), district proficiency test pass rate and growth on norm-referenced test scores (CTBS).
- Solicit student opinions.

Evaluations of the data for the first two years of the program are reported in the section entitled "Evidence of Student Progress." These program progress reports have been used to:

- Refine and modify the program after quarterly meetings.
- Make reports to the Azusa Board of Education.
- Expand the program to the elementary school level in the Azusa Unified School District.
- Share with many other school district visitors.
- Conduct workshops with other school district personnel.
- Establish similar programs in other school districts.

Evidence of Student Progress

Sample indicators—these can include improved student attendance, reduced dropout rates, college/university attendance rates, improved job placement or other indicators appropriate to your program. The more quantified evidence you provide the better. Progress should not be described in terms of percentages unless absolute totals are also given. State the time frame for which your data apply.

The evidence of student progress is tabulated in Tables 21.1, 21.2 and 21.3.

Quality of Commitment

Sample indicators of business and college/university commitment can include employee leave to work in schools and donations of money, equipment or facilities.

Business-WICAT Systems

- two thirty-two student workstation integrated learning systems
- appropriate courseware/testware in language arts and math
- full-service maintenance program
- ongoing staff in-service

TABLE 21.1 Retention and attendance rates.

	1987	1988	1989	1990
Retention Rates:				
# of GOAL students	0	72	140	
1988 target students still in school as of 9/89			69 (95.8% retention rate)	
1988 and 1989 target students still in school as of 6/90				139 (99.3% retention rate)
Attendance Rates:				
1988 target students	108 days out of 180 (60%)	167 days out of 180 (93.1%)		
1988 and 1989 target students			172 days out of 180 (96.1%)	

TABLE 21.2 Academic growth of 1988 target students.

	READING	MATH	LANGUAGE ARTS
Eighth grade percentile scores on CTBS	24.	25.0	26.1
Ninth grade percentile scores on CTBS	32.2	28.7	30.8
Relative gain above normal grade level growth	30.4%	14.8%	18.0%
Average relative gain in all three areas		21.1%	
Grade point average		1.73	

TABLE 21.3 Academic growth of 1988 and 1989 target students.

Credits attempted/completed   6,201/4,877 (78.6%)

District reading, math and language proficiency pass rate:
 Fall 1989   50 tests passed, out of 420 required
 Spring 1990 269 tests passed, out of 420 required

- ongoing educational consulting (WICAT account manager and educational consultant assigned to program)
- cooperative data gathering and evaluation development
- four-year (1988–1992) cost for two locations as WICAT's partnership risk—approximately $190,000

University

The Azusa Unified School District participates in a partnership with California State University at Fullerton and ten other districts to look at the needs of high-risk students, and to determine a profile for advising these students and providing assistance. Our committee consists of local police, business representatives, community agency representatives, administrators and teachers, who meet monthly. The purpose of the committee is to work in a collaborative manner to resolve the dropout problem. The charges of the committee are as follows.

- Work at a local level to set up a drug task force.
- Identify relative objectives for our agencies.
- Be a training component for the partnership.
- Identify high-risk characteristics (for which we are developing a data base) in an effort to develop a profile and offer assistance.
- Develop a list of trainers and specialists for districts for parent training work sessions.

For training, our committee has met with John Mills, FBI special agent in charge of narcotics, who discussed drugs and the role they play in students dropping out of school. We also met with Bill Beecham, representing Public Health, who discussed a student assistance program. Mr. Beecham is the executive director for the Center of Drug Free Communities. We also attended a PRIDE parent training session which made parents aware of the effect they can have in curbing the dropout problem.

Public School's Commitment

Sample indicators of the public school's commitment can include development of new curricula, innovative teaching and testing methods, fresh approaches for meeting the academic and vocational needs of students and the presence of a champion (the superintendent) for the program.

In Azusa, here's what we did to involve the school in the program.

- Maintain a teacher/student ratio of one to twenty in classes for at-risk students.
- Provide two air-conditioned rooms, with access to each other, for a lab center on each high school campus.
- Provide instructional aides for each campus GOAL program.
- Formalize recognition of improved student attendance and achievement at special receptions.
- Clearly identify at-risk students as those with poor attendance, poor grades and relatively high test scores.
- Protect GOAL program from becoming a catchall by servicing special education and limited-English-speaking students in programs specifically designed for them.
- Coordinate communication between district office, business partner, Cal State at Fullerton and site personnel.
- Provide start-up costs (shipping, installing and first-year maintainance) as vested interest in program, $11,500 for two high schools and $8,000 for elementary schools.
- Share a portion of ADA for students who remain in school with business partner to help repay costs to business partnership for hardware and software.

In what way have these contributions made possible the implementation of an education-reform program? Explain how your alliance spurred change.

The uniqueness of this school district/business partnership is that both take the risk. It is either a win/win or lose/lose situation. Students receive an education, and therefore greatly enhance the odds of being contributors to society. The school district gains increased ADA, and from that increase generates resources to buy the labs and pay for all services. Business shares a portion of increased ADA revenue to offset costs of running the program. This is a one-of-a-kind program in the state of California.

In addition, educational experiences, expertise, time and monetary resources, are shared. The district contributes knowledge of students' needs, staff facilities and a cooperative desire to succeed. The university offers research and expertise in the field of students-at-risk strategies for schools. Business provides successful models in working with students at risk, and the technology resources to make individualized instruction programs possible.

USING MULTIMEDIA

One of the new developments in technology is the use of a combination of media to deliver instruction, which is often referred to as multimedia instruction. At-risk students are especially motivated by the fast moving pace of multimedia, together with the lively music and pictures that are frequently used. The matrix in Table 21.4 provides the reader with an overview of the various media that are commonly used. We have provided a brief explanation of how to start a multimedia program in a school.

Multimedia—A Personal History[28]

The use of technology in the classroom is an area that is ever advancing. Trying to keep up with the changes can occupy more time than the average teacher has available. Teachers must experiment with different areas to find what works for them.

I (the author) was fortunate when I started teaching. My school had many resources, and they had made the commitment to use technology in the instructional process. There were several teachers who regularly used the school's equipment in their teaching. Each teacher had a classroom computer which students could use. The school also had a computer lab with twenty-nine Apple IIGS computers. The computers were used for skill practice, computer-aided instruction, word processing, graphics, etc. The school also had eight VCRs and monitors mounted on carts. We had a small amount of school-owned videos that augmented the reading program, and were available to be checked out.

The school had access, through a checkout system, to films and videos owned by the county superintendent of schools. Topics included fine arts, geography, history, English literature, mathematics and science. Additionally, the school district was a member of a regional educational television advisory council that made copies of original broadcasts of educational television programs. The district was

[28]This report was written by Albert Williams, seventh grade teacher, Chino Unified School District, Chino, California.

TABLE 21.4 Model to conceptualize multimedia.

COMPONENTS	HARDWARE	SOFTWARE	TEACHER KNOWLEDGE			TEACHING MODALITIES		
			LOW	MEDIUM	HIGH	VISUAL	AUDIO	TACTILE
Television	•		•			•	•	
Microcomputer with a 30 MB RAM*	•		•	•	•	•	•	•
VGA/EGA monitor*	•		•			•		
Videocassette players	•		•			•		
Laser disc players	•		•			•		
Recorded laser videodisc		•	•			•		
CD-ROM drives*	•			•	•	•	•	•
CD-I players	•			•	•	•	•	•
Multifunction players	•			•	•	•	•	•
Video/data projectors	•			•		•		
LCD panels	•			•		•		
Large-screen monitors	•		•			•		
Still video cameras	•			•		•		
Camcorders	•			•		•	•	•
Scanners	•				•	•		
Video digitizers	•				•	•	•	•

(continued)

TABLE 21.4 (continued).

COMPONENTS	HARDWARE	SOFTWARE	TEACHER KNOWLEDGE			TEACHING MODALITIES		
			LOW	MEDIUM	HIGH	VISUAL	AUDIO	TACTILE
Compact disc players	•		•				•	
Stereo systems with speakers	•		•				•	
Printer, b and w*	•		•	•		•	•	•
Printer, color	•		•	•		•	•	•
Video printer	•		•	•		•	•	•
Sound cards	•		•	•			•	
Video cards	•		•	•		•		
Multifunction cards	•		•	•		•	•	
Quick Time for Macintosh		•	•		•	•	•	•
Amiga-Vision		•	•		•	•	•	•
IBM Ultimedia		•	•		•	•	•	•
HyperCard for Macintosh		•	•		•	•	•	•
Networks	•	•	•	•	•		•	•
Satellite dishes	•	•	•	•	•		•	•
Modems	•	•	•		•		•	•

*These components are used to make up a basic multimedia system with matching system software.

licensed to make copies from these original cassettes, to be used in instruction.

Several teachers knew there was even more that could be done with technology in the instructional process, if we but had the equipment. The decision was made to apply for a technology grant from the county. After many discussions, it was decided that the area that most needed enrichment, and was most likely to help the students understand better, was science. After researching the available media and equipment, we decided that our focus would be on laser disc technology. It should be noted that there are two types of laser discs on the market. One is just like a videocassette, in that you play it and it gives information; there is no interaction with the information presented. The second type is an interactive disc that allows the teacher, with the use of a remote control, to program the laser disc player to show just a portion of the information on the disc. The teacher can move to another portion of the disc, either forward or backward, instantly without lost interest or teaching time. The disc also can be paused between segments to allow for classroom discussion of the information just presented.

We received the grant and, with additional support from our school site council funds and from the principal's budget, were able to purchase the following.

- two Pioneer laser disc players with remote control
- a Sharp LCD projector that allows for projection of VCR or laser images on a screen or wall with up to a twelve-foot picture
- three Apple Macintosh Classic computers
- an Apple Macintosh SE computer
- two Apple LC computers with CD-ROM players
- an Apple I Scanner
- an Apple LaserPrinter II
- four Apple ImageWriter IIs
- training on how to use these items

We also included consultants, release time and substitute teachers, to allow in-servicing of the entire school staff in the use of the equipment.

Additionally, we purchased several laser discs on science, art and history, topics taught by most teachers at the school. Specifically, we purchased the complete set of Windows on Science laser discs dealing with life, earth and physical sciences. Each disc comes with a teachers' instruction manual that provides a complete guide to the disc, and lessons with worksheets, a test and a script for the teacher on each topic. We also purchased ten CDs from Discis, with books for our reading program, to be used primarily in the lower grades and with our resource and special day classes.

With the new equipment, teaching took on more challenges. Applying what we had to what we needed took trial and error. Multimedia sometimes meant multiproblem. Getting the right cables hooked up to the right connectors, scheduling around other teachers who needed the equipment, making sure that there were blank videotapes for the video camera, were just some of the problems. However, I would rather focus on the successes we had.

When I was teaching cell theory to my sixth grade class, the textbook only had pictures or drawings of cells undergoing the process of mitosis, or cell division. The Windows on Science disc has a short clip on mitosis. We were able to see the process from start to finish, like watching a movie, and compare it to what we thought went on. Then we were able to replay the clip for a frame-by-frame review, and were able to see all of the four phases. It was from these frame-by-frame advances that I had the students draw and write their understanding of the process. I used both the book information, and the script provided with the disc, to explain what was taking place. I also showed a video to provide additional information and to reinforce what they had learned earlier. I used worksheets provided by Windows on Science, as well as outside sources, to give the students a place to check their grasp of the subject. I feel that the students had a much better understanding of the process when we were finished than they would have had with only one of the sources. The same was true when I taught about protist and protozoans. The students were actually able to see an amoeba put a pseudopod out. They were able to see a paramecium and a euglena swim. It made my explanations much easier and much clearer when the students could actually see what it looked like. I could go on to say the same for teaching about fungi, animal classification, biomes or ecosystems. The use of more than one medium enhances the learning process.

I can also say that getting the students involved in the process is exciting and challenging. I used the video camera while teaching language arts, social studies and science. In one instance, I had the students put on a late-night talk show with different kings, queens and pharaohs of ancient Egypt as guests. They had to do all the research, script writing, props and set design. They also had to produce commercials that might have been aired during that period, such as the "Econo Mummy Wrapping Service" or the "Nile Boat Tour Service."

I also used my computer to produce a hypercard stack relating to Egypt. I would write text into the hypercard stack using two or three cards as necessary to convey the information I wanted them to know. This would be followed by one card that would have a question on it. The students would answer the question by clicking on the button by the answer they chose. If they answered correctly, the button sent them forward to read more text and answer more questions. If they answered incorrectly the button sent them backward to review the text. For some questions I would use the scanner to input pictures into the computer and then, to save memory space, reduce them to one inch by two inches, and then cut and paste them onto a card. The question then would be about the text and/or the picture.

I really enjoyed teaching with what we had then. However, things change. I have moved on from teaching sixth grade into teaching seventh grade prealgebra, science and two electives—computers and an educational technology lab. The technology lab really has the students and me excited. The lab is currently divided into eight modules, with plans to expand to sixteen when we move into our new school in two years. The eight modules are:

- computer-aided drafting
- drafting
- robotics
- aeronautics
- engineering
- research and design
- electronics
- audio-visual

The lab is equipped with six computers and monitors, one hooked up for a CAD system and plotter, one used for the robotic arm and the rest in general use in the lab. There are also five VCRs and televisions for general use with each of the modules, and a satellite dish with its own VCR and television set. The lab is used between two and four periods a day depending on the number of tracks on at the time. Students who are in the ed tech lab rotate through the modules on a two-week cycle.

There have already been some plans to integrate the resources into the aspects of teaching. The audio-visual module is planning with the physical education department to tape instructional videos of sports skills such as bumping and serving in volleyball, or hitting and fielding in softball. They are also planning to D.J. one of the school dances. Other teachers have asked to use the lab for their classes, and for the ed tech lab students to come to their classes to tape speeches or plays put on by the students.

As I stated earlier, I am lucky to be employed in a district that has embraced technology. However, until individual teachers are committed to implementing the use of technology in the classroom, just having the resources is of no use to the educational process. Again I will say that it takes time and effort to discover what works for you and what is available. It also takes more time in some of your lesson planning to implement these resources. I didn't say it would be easy, I just said it would be worth it.

POLICY RECOMMENDATION

Each district should, in its efforts to move forward with effective dropout and substance abuse prevention programs, locate appropriate materials for prevention use within the present curriculum. Since at-risk students frequently respond well to computers and other technologies, a special effort to develop a variety of modes of instruction, including technology, should be a priority.

Chapter 22

WRITING PROPOSALS FOR OUTSIDE FUNDING[29]

A guide to successful proposal writing for funding dropout and drug prevention activities is presented in this chapter. Topics addressed include assessment of need, identification of project aims, background and significance of the new effort, objectives and activities for the project, project design and methods for carrying it out, identification and description of target population, formative and summative evaluation and capacity and commitment.

Certainly one of the more enjoyable ways to develop identification and intervention services for at-risk students is to apply for and receive additional funds from government or private sources. Although grant writing is labor intensive and not guaranteed, receiving a grant, like childbirth, makes up for a lot of pain. The key to successful grant writing is to first clearly think through your idea, get excited about it and then describe it clearly in writing.

The second important key to grant writing is to carefully follow the directions given by the funding agency, and to respond clearly to each grant section. Typical grant headings include an assessment of need and identification of the target group, identification of project aims, background and significance of the new effort, description of objectives and activities for the project, project design and methods, formative and summative evaluation, plan of operation, budget and cost effectiveness and commitment and capacity.

---

[29]This chapter was written by Dr. Nancy Richards-Colocino of the Irvine Unified School District, Irvine, California, and Dr. William L. Callison.

GRANT WRITING SUGGESTIONS

Here we have included brief starter sentences from proposals to illustrate the various sections. These sections would typically be reordered and renamed to fit the suggestions of the request for proposal from the funding agency. Appendix B, "Dropout and Substance Abuse Prevention Proposal," contains a complete proposal.

Need/Target Population

A winning proposal typically includes a strong presentation of need for the activities that are listed in the proposed project. Take time to gather information from staff and other research sources about the special need for your new effort. This is often a good section to define the target population with lots of descriptive words and numbers to present the need. Try to show how some promising things have been accomplished, but that more resources will really make all the difference in building the new approach.

> The magnitude of alcohol and other drug abuse problems has caused increasing nationwide concern among educators, policy makers and the community at large. Although the rates of drug use have declined recently (NIDA, 1988), smoking and drinking are still very prevalent teenage activities. In fact, high school students in the U.S. are more involved with illicit drugs than youth in any other industrialized nation (Johnson et al., 1989). A recent survey of drug use and dropouts in California and Irvine found. . . .

Project Aims

Present the purpose of the project clearly, demonstrating an understanding of what research indicates is effective.

> The aims of the district at-risk management project are to develop a computer management system that will identify potential substance abusers and potential dropouts, and use an expert system to connect identified students at risk with appropriate interventions to reduce student risk levels.

Background and Significance

Logically describe the background steps leading to the current proposal.

Project activities were developed during the past eight years from needs assessments with staff and students, and a review of the current literature on high-risk and substance-abusing students. Components respond to the research findings, particularly the research on high-risk factors for adolescents.

Objectives and Activities of Project

Present a plan for accomplishing the aim of the project, describing the objectives to be accomplished and the activities that will lead to the completion of these objectives.

The proposed program offers a comprehensive holistic approach for preventing alcohol and other drug use by 500 high-risk middle school students. The project addresses the needs of the student, his family, the school and the community, in a comprehensive approach to prevention through the following.

(*1*) Student objective: decrease the use of alcohol and other drugs in participating students at a .05 level of significance.

(*2*) Student activity: provide individual and small group counseling to identified students. Assign and monitor progress of identified students in interventions.

(*3*) School objective: increase knowledge and skill levels of educators to implement interventions to reduce risk factors, as measured by pre/post assessment.

(*4*) School activity: train staff in the use of a computer management system to identify and intervene with at-risk students.

(*5*) Family objective: increase parent knowledge of risk and protective factors and improve family management skills, as measured by pre/post assessment.

(*6*) Family activity: provide education, support and referral services for parents of identified high-risk students.

Project Design and Methods

Describe the process of program services as part of the overall design, and describe individual program components more completely if necessary.

A data-gathering system, involving students, parents, school personnel and community resources to identify students who need help, is being developed. It will include:

(*1*) A data base of all students in the district, identifying the lower quadrant based on academics, low test scores and students exhibiting at-risk behaviors

(2) A referral form for teachers who have identified a problem with a student, and a procedure for handling referrals and tracking disposition of each referral

(3) An information system to let referring teachers know the disposition of the referral

(4) A plan for sharing information with parents of students

Formative and Summative Evaluation

Describe your evaluation plan, linking it to the measurement of objectives you describe. Try to think of an accurate and easily gathered measure of your success in each area. The evaluation ought to focus upon two areas, process, "Are the steps to achieve outcomes conducive to program success?" and product, "How well is the program accomplishing its specified objectives?"

Teacher knowledge and skills in implementing the computer management system will be measured by locally developed pre/post tests and observation checklists. Outcome evaluation will be based on significant changes (improvement at the .05 level) in baseline data gathered from participant surveys on drug use against which future drug use and parenting practices of high-risk students' parents will be compared.

Plan of Operation/Budget and Cost Effectiveness

List general information describing your organization, including the line of authority and role definitions for project staff. Generally describe and support the budget requested.

The board of education is responsible for the project and management operations. The project director will coordinate all program activities and supervise project staff. The budget is adequate to complete project activities and is cost effective in that. . . .

Accomplishments/Capacity and Commitment

List any related accomplishments of your program and how they relate to the present effort. Show commitment to continue activities beyond the funding period.

The district has a history of commitment to addressing the needs of at-risk students and has developed a number of innovative prevention programs, e.g., STAGES program, which help at-risk students to be successful in school despite stressful changes in their lives. This proposal develops an at-risk management system, which complements the prevention and identification strategies now in place. This at-risk management system will make a significant impact on reducing student drug use by creating a computerized delivery system for drug abuse prevention and intervention. The system uses the latest research to predict potential abusers and dropouts with an identification system that links to some of the most effective interventions in the country. The identification and intervention services will continue after initial funding through. . . .

We wish you every success in your pursuit of external support for your students and teachers.

Chapter 23

THE USE OF VOLUNTEERS AND FOUNDATIONS

The two sources of support that may be most available to staff in a local school district for dropout prevention, job training and job placement, are funds from a local or area foundation, and the use of volunteers. These sources are related in that you may use one to gain access to the other. Typically, the use of volunteers increases your credibility, and this makes you a candidate for foundation support. The use of volunteers will also increase your chances for state and federal funds for substance abuse and gang prevention efforts.

ENLISTING VOLUNTEER SUPPORT

The primary sources for volunteers may be churches and local service clubs. One process that can help you reach them is:

(*1*) Find out which administrators in your district are members of Rotary, Kiwanis, Optimists and so forth.

(*2*) Ask those administrators to give you the names and telephone numbers of the club members who are most sympathetic to dropouts and similar causes.

(*3*) Write up one page about your project, make copies of it and give several to the sympathetic club member.

(*4*) Ask the club member to help you contact the program chair so you can make a presentation at the club to ask for volunteers. Make up a second one-page description of what types of volunteer jobs there are, how much time they take ánd whom to contact.

(*5*) Ask the program chair what the priority areas are for all the local

323

service clubs. You may find another club that is your best bet for help.

Go through the same process for enlisting help from local churches. Retired people are a good bet, and be sure to ask who else they can suggest.

ENLISTING FOUNDATION SUPPORT

Once you have volunteers working, write up what they are doing for you in about two pages, and then seek the names of local or area foundations. Probably the best way to do this is to contact the fund-raising office of your nearest university, and get names and telephone numbers from them.

When you get the contact names, call them and ask if they are interested in your type of project. Usually the answer is no, for any number of reasons. Tell them a bit about your project and ask them to tell you which area foundations might support you.

Send the candidate foundation a letter indicating who recommended that you contact them, together with your two-page project description. Tell them you are using volunteers and doing everything you can to be efficient. Ask to meet with them personally. Once you have met with them, ask if you can write a brief proposal and get them to help you follow their procedures.

POLICY RECOMMENDATION

Districts should consider using two support services that may be available for assisting at-risk students to obtain job training and job placement. These are local service clubs and businesses. In order to have credibility with them, administrators should become members of the service clubs and participate in their activities.

SUMMARY

We have presented a variety of strategies for identifying students at risk and offering them improved instruction and services. Our aim has been to identify the most promising efforts now operating throughout the country, and to describe them for you. We have developed a step-by-step process for implementing these strategies, and each step is a chapter in this book. In order to make the entire effort feasible, we have designed and implemented software to identify students who need help, place them in effective interventions and, finally, evaluate the interventions to see if they are working. We trust you will find personal satisfaction and renewal in your efforts to help our nation's young people in need of assistance.

A DROPOUT RESOURCE GUIDE

As you begin a proposal you should have access to key facts and definitions that are relevant to your topic. For example, if you were writing a dropout prevention proposal and wished to describe a typical set of district-wide prevention strategies, you could turn to this resource guide for quick help in formulating your thoughts and language.

THE MEANINGS OF TERMS

Centers on the Student

The broad goal of any dropout prevention effort is to help students stay in school. Recovery activities seek to get students to return to a structured program of education and, often, to work. The student may need help in improving the skill areas, dealing with a personal or family problem, self-understanding or learning new job skills. We work to help dropout-prone students one by one.

Serves All Students

Identification of each student's needs is the key concept, and, to the extent possible, programs are inclusive. At the same time, some groups of students may need additional attention to bring them to a satisfactory level in reading, social skills or other areas.

Offers a Comprehensive Scope of Services

The range of services must be as broad as the varied range of student problems. These services might include instruction in basic and social skills, tutoring in areas of individual need, counseling on personal problems and testing to identify areas of competence and interest.

Coordinates Resources and Personnel

A potential dropout may not know about available resources or how to get to them. Hence, there is need for a staff member to coordinate the efforts of teachers, librarians, counselors, health staff and business contact persons who can provide training and employment opportunities.

Incorporates Feedback and Evaluation into the System

The evolution aspect of a dropout plan is critical in that so much of the effort is one-on-one. It is very difficult to keep staff informed about what is working and what isn't unless a strong effort to evaluate is implemented. A case system is one way to organize the effort, where each student with special needs is dealt with by a team of professionals who diagnose needs and suggest treatment and/or remediation as appropriate. All of these efforts are recorded in a permanent folder or computer record.

With these characteristics of a comprehensive strategy in mind, and written up in a brief handout, an administrator can approach the school board for support to begin work on a specific district plan for dropout prevention and recovery. Once approval is gained, contact with key staff can be initiated, and the elements of a strategy and plan can be developed.

At-Risk Management Project

The at-risk management project is designed to assist staff in the identification of students at risk for substance abuse and dropping out. An expert software system (Comprehensive Risk Assessment) is used to connect the identification of at-risk students with one or more of the many interventions available.

When the expert system is fully in place, it can be used by teachers and other school personnel to identify early problem behaviors connected to potential for drug and alcohol use/abuse, to refer students for intervention, to process referrals and to track the disposition of each referral. An information/communication system will be developed to apprise referring teachers of the disposition of their referrals. Finally, a procedure for sharing information with parents of high-risk students, while guarding confidentiality, will also be developed.

Defining Risk in Students

Research has found that there are many paths to drug abuse, therefore interventions must also address many specific areas. A student's risk factors may be related to problems with school, family, peers or personality, and may be a combination of these areas. Students must also be identified by the degree of risk, as strategies that work with at-risk students may not work with high-risk students.

At-risk youth have a limited number of risk factors. They may be students with low self-esteem; passive or aggressive students, who are experiencing peer pressure problems; children who lack realistic information on destructive aspects of drugs; children experiencing failure in school; children with behavioral or antisocial problems. They may be children of substance abusers and genetically at risk, representing the 25 percent of children affected by alcohol risk characteristics.

High-risk youth experience multiple risk factors. These students have multiple problems with attendance, discipline, family, self-esteem or academic matters; they may have alcohol and other drug use problems at school or in the community.

High-risk students' school problems may be academic, behavioral, social or personal. Family problems may be due to living in dysfunctional or abusive family environments, such as homes where alcohol and/or drug abuse occurs or has occurred. Other indications of high risk are: child of a substance abuser; victim of physical, sexual or psychological abuse; dropping out of school; becoming pregnant; being economically disadvantaged; committing a violent or delinquent act; experiencing mental health problems; attempting suicide; experiencing long-term physical pain due to injury; experiencing chronic failure in school.

Preparing a Prevention and Recovery Strategy and Plan

One of the key strategies in developing a prevention and recovery strategy typically involves the creation of a (or utilization of an existing) task force where the members are selected for their interest in helping students at risk (see Table A.1). This is often done after an incident has focused attention on some aspect of the at-risk issue. For example, a large K–12 district we served as a consultant used the publication of unsatisfactory test scores as a lever to generate interest in improving services for potential substance abusers and dropouts. The main tasks are identification of types of participants, selecting strategies which will bring key members of each group onto the task force and choosing tasks for each group that they feel are appropriate to their status and skill levels.

TABLE A.1 *A conceptual model for developing an at-risk task force.*

PARTICIPANTS	STRATEGIES	TASKS
Parents	Obtain representation from key organizations	Recruit parents who will be able to influence board members
School Administrators	Select representatives who will be positive and who can influence their colleagues at other schools	Justification of budget for at-risk programs (some successful experience with an at-risk program)
Minorities	Representation of primary constituent groups is key, especially those that are likely to speak out at meetings	Speak from experience about an at-risk program that has helped them
Teachers	A critical group which needs to include teachers who have been successful in working with at-risk students	Utilize their knowledge and experience with at-risk programs in planning and in lobbying for budget support for programs
Students	Representation of groups that will receive much of the program help	Use experience to help task force members feel these programs will work
Consultants	Select one or two that have already built reputations in the district, or who are immediately credible	Ability to share program information which stresses good programs already operating; a vision for future programs that has support of key staff

PREVENTION AND RECOVERY STRATEGIES

The plan should be student centered so the unique needs of each individual are considered. It should offer a variety of services in education, guidance and support services. All school levels from elementary through high school should be included. Activities and services from both the schools and the community should be included in the plan. The plan should include both prevention and treatment efforts so that students who are predicted to drop out, and those who already have, are served well. See Chapter 12 for a planning model.

Creation of a Dropout Prevention and Recovery Delivery System

Step One—Gaining School Staff and Community Commitment

Once the appropriate district administrators become aware of the need for a district-wide dropout plan, they can schedule a school board meeting and make a presentation using materials from this book, as well as other data describing the local situation. Some of the key considerations in developing support for the program are:

- The new effort must be perceived as better than what we now have, or there is no advantage in adopting it.
- It must be compatible with present values, and fit with existing operating procedures.
- It should be simple enough to learn to use so that staff feel the effort to learn to use it is worth the time it takes.
- It should be tried out on a small scale so that any problems can be worked out before many staff are involved.

Step Two—Assignment of Responsibility for Dropout Prevention and Recovery Strategy

The board will assign a district staff member responsibility to design a strategy for reducing and recovering dropouts. The strategy should:

- Identify the target population to be served, perhaps by using a dropout prediction model such as the one seen in Chapter 4. Goals, staffing, method of operation and budget should be described. For recovery, advertising in the community—especially on popular radio stations—has proven effective. School and community agency staff may be able to offer suggestions for contacting dropouts.
- Goal statements should be written based on an assessment of need.
- Specific objectives that will implement the goals should be written, and staffing to implement the objectives should be assigned.
- Training for staff should be planned.
- Method(s) of operation should be described. To state the obvious, the same old approaches that have caused dropout in the first place should not be used. As we have indicated in the review of the literature on program size, small, relatively autonomous efforts should be considered where perhaps four to six teachers work with about 125 students.
- A budget adequate enough to make a difference should be provided. After all, these students are predicted to drop out if nothing special is done to interest them. If predicted dropouts do drop out, this will in turn cost the district $3,000 per student (or whatever your average daily attendance rate is), and hence it is worth a serious effort. If dropouts are recovered there will, in turn, be a financial advantage to the district. If this is not true, your state should be asked to change its legislation to provide such an incentive.

Step Three—School/Community Resource Assessment

School and community resources need to be identified, written down and put in a format, such as a computerized data base program, so they can easily be updated.

- Probably the most important resource within the school is the staff that will be involved. If they aren't interested, how serious can the effort be? In particular, each school should consider the appointment of an outreach coordinator or some equivalent title. This person will have demonstrated that they like your students at risk as well as their families. The job includes the coordination of the myriad tasks (as mentioned in this book) to be carried out at the school level, as well as the planning and implementation skills to bring the ideas to reality over a period of years. In California, the person playing this role is funded by the state in schools with a high dropout rate.
- Support staff within the school could include counselors, department chairs, librarians, reading and learning disabilities specialists as well as clerical staff.
- In a large district, a list of community agency staff and facilities could include over a hundred entries.
- Business and industry training and job placement opportunities may exist in your district. One way to start a list of these resources is to contact your state's liaison in the governor's office for the Department of Labor to identify your local private industry council.

Present students who should be served can be identified through a dropout prediction model such as the one described in Chapter 4. Identification of students who have dropped out is difficult, but teachers can often recall them if they have a list of students from previous years to jog their memories.

An advisory committee should include people who can serve as consultants, as well as linking agents from key industries and community service agencies that provide important connections to the district.

DROPOUT AND SUBSTANCE ABUSE PREVENTION PROPOSAL

In this appendix we have a complete proposal, written by Nancy Richards-Colocino, Irvine Unified School District, for use as an example.

SPECIFIC AIMS

The aims of project SAFE (Student/Staff and Family Education) are to develop a program model to: identify risk factors for Hispanic students and families; identify potential substance abusers, dropouts and gang affiliates; use an expert system to connect identified students with appropriate interventions which will reduce student risk levels.

The project goals are

- Increase resiliency and protective factors for high-risk youth ages twelve to fourteen, their families and the community, to reduce the use of alcohol, drugs and tobacco.
- Reduce the risk factors of using alcohol, drugs and tobacco, for high-risk youth ages twelve to fourteen, their families and the community.
- Increase community agency involvement in establishing a drug-free community.
- Provide and field test alternative activities to the use of alcohol, drugs and tobacco for high-risk youth ages twelve to fourteen.
- Develop a model for assisting inner city Hispanic students and their parents, in a community with strong gang involvement, to resist drugs, alcohol and tobacco.
- Implement, evaluate and disseminate the SAFE project to create an adoptable/adaptable model to prevent abuse of alcohol, drugs and

333

tobacco, in predominantly Hispanic communities, for students ages twelve to fourteen.

The objectives of this project are

(*1*) By September 1996 project participants will report a decrease in alcohol, tobacco and drug usage, and gang affiliation.

(*2*) By September 1996 students will report positive behavior responses to risk factors for using alcohol and other drugs as they impact on individual high-risk youth, and on the environments in which high-risk youth and their families function.

(*3*) By September 1996 the majority of project students and parents will report an increase in the frequency of behaviors (such as effectiveness in work, play and relationships; healthy expectations and a positive outlook; self-esteem and internal locus of control; self-discipline; problem solving; critical thinking) that reflect resiliency and protective factors for drug and alcohol usage.

(*4*) By September 1996 there will be a significant statistical reduction among SAFE participants in these school risk factors — academic failure, poor attendance, discipline referrals and low commitment to school.

(*5*) Annually, all project participants will be screened, identified and placed in the SAFE program.

(*6*) Annually, an individual profile will be developed for project participants.

(*7*) By September 1996 an individual profile will be perfected for clients ages twelve to fourteen who are at risk for alcohol, drug and/or tobacco use or distribution.

(*8*) Annually, 90 percent of project participants will attend supervised school/community after-school activities that promote alternative activities to alcohol, drug and tobacco use.

(*9*) By September 1996 successful after-school activities for high-risk students will be written in a publication based upon evaluation reports in the project, and the publication will be disseminated.

(*10*) By September 1996 project participants will report a reduction in: alienation and rebelliousness; use of gateway drugs such as tobacco; peer associates who use drugs, alcohol or tobacco; as well as an understanding of the health risks associated with usage.

(*11*) By September 1996 participants will report improved family management, clear parental expectations, high expectations for personal success and the benefits of healthy life-styles.

(*12*) Annually, teachers will receive training in self-esteem enhancement and the prevention, detection and treatment of substance abuse.

(*13*) By September 1992 linkages will be improved with the YMCA and Girl's Club to provide alternative activities for high-risk youth involved in the SAFE program.

(*14*) By September 1992 a community network will be developed with assistance of United Way agencies and the board of directors to promote community involvement by increasing agency collaboration with schools, providing volunteers and mentors for school sites and assisting in publicizing a no-use message.

(*15*) By September 1992 a written plan will be developed with the sheriff's department and school district to coordinate project activities in drug prevention education and drug use intervention.

(*16*) By September 1994 a pamphlet will be developed and distributed in English and Spanish to explain signs and symptoms of alcohol and drug use, and listing local agencies for treatment and assistance.

(*17*) By September 1995 a project dissemination/replication manual for the SAFE program will be available for distribution.

(*18*) By September 1995 the SAFE project will begin disseminating information to interested LEAs through project SAFE manuals, conference presentations and site visitations.

Population to Be Served and Time Frame

This project will reach over 800 high-risk youth and their families over the five years of operation.

Rationale for Project Success

This project is based on sound research, theory and experience. It is based on the research and models developed by Perry and Jessor (Health Promotion); Hawkins, Lishner and Catalano (Developmental Perspective), on attachment and bonding; Botvin and Perry (Pro-Social Instruction) and others. The experience of Sunshine, in working with high-risk youth in the areas of academics and school adjustment programs, has been extensive.

Needs Assessment Process

Sunshine School District's Substance Abuse Prevention Advisory was formed three years ago to determine the need for refinement and expansion of the existing substance abuse prevention program. The advisory is now composed of the following: ten teachers and administrators representing all district schools; two law enforcement personnel; three parents; two representatives from local businesses; three representatives from community counseling. The committee regularly reviews data from local and state agencies (Los Angeles County Sheriff, Office of Criminal Justice, California State Attorney General) on the frequency and severity of substance abuse among youth. The following highlights of that research indicate the tragic proportions of the drug abuse problem: by age eleven, 11.7 percent of students report being intoxicated at least once; by age sixteen, 52 percent report being intoxicated at least once; 40 percent of the students, by age eight, report experimenting with drugs; 7.4 percent of eleventh graders report daily use of marijuana; 39.3 percent of eleventh graders report engaging in the extremely dangerous practice of using two or more drugs at the same time during the last six months. The advisory also looks at those behaviors and factors that place students at risk for substance abuse. Results on a review of records and needs assessment surveys completed by staff and parents showed that over 37 percent of K–12 students showed problems with chronic school failure, discipline and attendance; were children of alcoholics; and/or were educationally disadvantaged among other things. Also, over 60 percent of the students had no skills to cope with peer pressure for substance abuse.

Immigrant parents do not understand the criminal justice and educational systems. Parents, when confronted with the legal system, lack trust in, and an understanding of how the system works. They often come from a country where law enforcement and government institutions are corrupt. They need education about the legal system, the juvenile justice system, law enforcement and the expectations of American institutions in general. In a telephone survey conducted by the district, 97 percent of parents support curriculum instructing students on the dangers of drugs and alcohol, 50 percent were unaware of counseling programs, 61 percent were unaware of gang prevention programs, 45 percent were unaware of parenting classes, 40 percent were unaware of the drug education program, 80 percent were unaware of the dropout prevention program, 72 percent were not involved in community groups and 54 percent were aware of district committees, but only 2 percent participated. Ninety-two percent of the parents surveyed approved of district programs. This gives evidence that parents need assistance in getting more involved in their children's education, but frequently do not know how because of cultural and linguistic differences.

As a result of this needs assessment, the Sunshine School District is implementing a highly successful, curriculum-based, K–12 substance abuse prevention program, funded from the district's general fund and from the Drug-Free Schools and Communities program. While this program has been successful in reducing substance abuse—especially at school—local needs assessment and research indicate there is a significant need for prevention programs focusing on high-risk youth, parent education and a community-based campaign.

BACKGROUND AND SIGNIFICANCE

Objectives Are Based on Research

Research substantiates that 30 percent of all children experience school adjustment difficulties, stress and behavior problems, which are predictors of future maladjustment and drug use. Therefore, the project is utilizing successful intervention strategies that have addressed these and other high-risk factors.

Steinberg, Blinde and Chan reported that being Spanish-speaking and being Hispanic resulted in significantly greater likelihood of educational difficulty. They report that there is a special disadvantage associated with speaking Spanish that is not simply attributable to not speaking English or to being of Hispanic origin. Veltman reports that traditional approaches to education do not work effectively for Hispanics, particularly Spanish-speaking Hispanics. The project addresses specific risk factors that pertain to the Hispanic- and/or Spanish-speaking community.

Social and communication skills, cognitive health lessons and group activities with a prevention specialist will be used to provide prosocial options. These approaches are based on vast research by Botvin (1986), finding that personal social skills training, when combined with cognitive and behavioral coping strategies (problem solving and stress reduction), provides the most successful approach to prevention.

Association with Drug Using and Gang Affiliated Peers

Association with drug using and/or gang affiliated peers has been among the strongest predictors of adolescent drug use and gang involvement. Drug experimentation and gang association may be viewed as a peer-supported phenomenon, reflecting the importance of peers during adolescence. Therefore, the positive utilization of peer groups can be highly effective in promoting a drug-free, healthy life-style. The project includes support groups led by trained prevention specialists, and utilizes teamwork in sharing information about drug-free and gang-free activities (i.e., hikes, sports, group projects and programs). Healthy role models are being invited to speak and encourage drug- and gang-free living.

Family Role and Socialization Deficits

The family role in preventing drug use and gang affiliation among adolescent youth has been well documented. The importance of family socialization includes the adult role as a model for the youth of the family. Kandel (1982) found that three factors help predict youth initiation into drugs—parent drug use, parent attitudes about drugs and parent and child interactions. Parental use seems to act as an impetus to experimentation according to most findings (Rachal et al., 1980; 1982). Arias found that parent support of gang lifestyles and sibling membership are the most potent reasons for gang affiliation. Parents are quietly molding the child's behavior and in this project are carefully trained to provide positive models.

Lack of School Interest and Achievement

Poor school performance, though not always leading to drug use, is a common antecedent of drug initiation (Kandel et al., 1978). Robins (1980) noted that drug users are noticeably "underachievers." Spivak (1983) further concluded that academic failure in late elementary grades does exacerbate the effects of early antisocial behavior. Hawkins and coworkers found that such factors as how much students like school, time spent on homework and perception of the relevance of coursework, are also related to levels of drug use, confirming a negative relationship between commitment to education and drug use, at least for adolescents in junior or senior high. Ochoa and Espinoza found that 80 percent of all Hispanics were underachieving by the third grade, and achievement progressively declined as students moved up the grades. Consequently, the district is utilizing the core and support staff at the school sites to screen and assist students who seem to be academically weak or failing.

Description of the Complete Delivery System

The Sunshine SAFE program offers a comprehensive holistic approach for preventing alcohol and other drug use by students, in particular high-risk students, and is being evaluated over a period of five years. The project addresses the needs of the student, his family, the school and the community in a comprehensive approach to prevention. The program's goals vis-à-vis its focal groups are as follows.

Student

- Identify behavioral and academic deficits, and provide for peer tutoring, support group and social skills and health curriculum.
- Increase social skills, peer-resistant strategies, decision-making skills and self-esteem.
- Increase bonding to home and school, and with positive role models.
- Increase academic performance and confidence in interacting with peers at school and home.
- Decrease antisocial behaviors.

School

- Increase teachers', counselors' and administrators' prevention knowledge, skills and curriculum.
- Sensitize staff to student problems.
- Provide a new dimension of health, allowing extracurricular activities and more challenging physical fitness programs for risk-taking youth.
- Provide a comprehensive program to address cognitive, social, health and personality concerns, as well as providing curriculum and materials.
- Address family needs for parenting skills and drug prevention education.
- Provide prevention specialists who interact with high-risk students, parents and community.

Community

- A prevention committee representing schools, parents, police and health agencies meets quarterly to reinforce an anti–drug use message for students.
- A concerted effort is made to strengthen a spirit of unity and responsibility to prevent youth from experimenting with substances.
- Businesses offer time, jobs and services.

Family

- The need for better family management techniques and parenting skills is met through Neighborhood Watch and Active Parenting classes.
- Parents gain an increased knowledge of drug use and ways to cope with children who have problems or are using drugs.
- Circle of Warmth meetings are provided for at-risk parents.
- Parents in need of resources gain help and support.

Software Used

Students-at-Risk, Inc. will work with the school district to match interventions with a computerized profile of high-risk students using Comprehensive Risk Assessment software. This software is designed to use the many dropout and drug prevention interventions developed for potential substance abusing students. A variety of media, including laser discs, films, videotapes and interactive computer-managed instruction, are used to deliver the instruction.

The technical aspect will be low in operating costs, and will focus on an area—substance abuse prevention—that is in great demand in school districts throughout the nation.

It is apparent that a large number of school districts would be interested in a delivery system that addresses two of their most critical problems—students who use drugs and alcohol, and students who are likely to drop out of school. That we will have products which can do this seems likely, in that much of this work is already accomplished. What will be difficult to achieve, however, is effective implementation of the delivery system. We will work diligently to accomplish this during the funding period. The identification software will not only serve to predict potential abusers and dropouts, it will serve as a means for evaluation of the effectiveness of prevention programs.

Dropout, Drug and Gang Prevention Curricula

The Sunshine Unified School District is committed to combating the ongoing problem of dropout, alcohol and other drug abuse on campuses and in the community at large. In addition, the district is a leader in the reduction of gang activity in schools. Many district administrators are called upon to make presentations throughout the region and state, to faculties and professional organizations in the areas of at-risk students, drug and alcohol use and gang affiliation. These presentations have been made at the Superintendent's Academies, the Association of California School Administrators, the Los Angeles County Office of Education, and for numerous other professional organizations.

The district has an adopted self-esteem program that is used in preschool through twelfth grade. The programs, Magic Circle (PK–6) and Yo Puedo [I Can (7–12)] are delivered to every student daily in Spanish and English. A companion program, Circle of Warmth/Circulo de Carino, is provided for parents. In addition to wellness lessons daily, each student participates in twenty hours of drug prevention each year, through a partnership with the Los Angeles County Sheriff's Office, in grades four through six. Other grade levels receive instruction with the Here's Looking at You 2000 program in English and Spanish. This instruction includes social skills training using an assertive communication model, and health concepts that promote health-enhancing behavior.

In the *Journal of School Health,* Dr. Pentz (1986) commented that the "drug resistance" approach (social/assertion skills training and a cognitive approach to health) has been successful in preventing drug use in large population samples of youth. Botvin of Cornell University (1986), after twenty studies, verifies that combined, a cognitive appeal to health and social skills training are the best prevention strategies.

Sunshine—A Leader in Working with High-Risk Youth

Sunshine School District has been recognized for its efforts in meeting the needs of high-risk youth. The school district has initiated and maintained a storefront program for dropout students called Youth Connection. Outreach counseling programs are available in Spanish and English for families of students preschool through high school. The district operates a pregnant minors program called GENESIS that serves the needs of young parents, their children and pregnant minors. Groupings for school success are provided to students at every level. Teachers have been specially trained to meet the needs of students of all ages. The district superintendent, board members and administrators have met and established an action plan for gang and drug reduction efforts. An outdoor adventure course is available and used to teach noncompetitive problem solving. At the center of every program is the goal of working with the whole family. With the addition of this grant, programs will be expanded to include the home and community, using interventions based on health promotion, transformations and social development models.

Using lottery funds, extra resources are provided to help the school staff create a dynamic and innovative center in an area of curriculum instruction. The program focuses staff energies on a specific area of special interest, promotes risk taking and research, rewards collaboration rather than competition and produces many sources of internal expertise throughout the district.

The Sunshine School District is committed to the implementation and continuation of this holistic substance abuse prevention program. During the 1987–1988 school year, Sunshine implemented a comprehensive, curriculum-based, K–12 drug prevention program with district general funds and Drug-Free Schools and Community program funds. While this program has been successful in reducing substance abuse—especially at school—local needs assessment and research indicate there is a significant need to focus most heavily on linguistically and ethnically divergent students.

Sunshine has an exemplary record of working with special-needs youth. It is recognized as a leader in servicing the needs of special education students. The district has pioneered consultative models of special education. Their multidisciplinary team approach to diagnosis and program planning will be used as a component of project SAFE.

Experience of Project Consultants

Dr. William L. Callison has extensive experience which will be helpful in the implementation of the at-risk management system. He is in the process of installing the identification system in eleven school districts, with support from the U.S. Department of Education, and has become sensitive to the issues—such as site-level autonomy—that can block a district effort such as this. He has written a book, *Students-at-Risk: Strategies for Schools (SAR)*, which describes in detail all aspects of the installation of a district plan for serving students at risk, including identification and placement in interventions.

Dr. Alberto Ochoa and Dr. Ruben Espinoza are known for their work in the development of the transformational model. In their "Empowerment Models: For Ethnic Divergent Students," conditions that create and foster at-risk conditions for high-risk ethnically divergent students are clearly documented. These at-risk conditions provide an environment for drug and substance abuse with gang affiliation.

The combination of these expertize, in an environment that currently is the "turf" of the substance abuser, and provide a backdrop for quality research and assistance, to an under-represented population, with the latest technological capability.

Integrating Three Models

The Sunshine School District's project SAFE will, for the first time, integrate the health promotion, sound development and transformational models, to determine which cultural/linguistic variables impact their success with minority students. All of these models have their basis in social learning theory, and complement each other. The reduction of additional risk factors and strengthening of resiliency factors will be greatly enhanced. The cultural/ linguistic component (transformational model) will dimensionalize services to under-represented groups. This program will be designed so that other school districts can easily adapt/adopt successful strategies into their own alcohol and other drug abuse and gang prevention programs.

TARGET POPULATION

The service area is generally a bedroom community with residents in the middle- to low-income groups. Employment is basically in the trades and general labor. Although the area lacks available land for development, the affordability of housing is generating some growth in the younger age groups. Population trends for the service area indicate increasing immigration of Spanish-speaking families.

Identification of Target Population

A coordinated intervention system that identifies high-risk juveniles or students from divergent ethnic/linguistic backgrounds, with chronic drug abuse problems and gang affiliation, and facilitates their referral to an established intervention system or drug abuse treatment program, will be developed.

An alcohol and drug abuse prevention program will be provided to a total of 1,200 middle school students. An estimated 800 students will be identified yearly as at high risk for developing problems of drug abuse and gang affiliation. Twenty-five percent of the student population will be based on family alcohol risk characteristics. These high-risk students may be children of substance abusers and genetically at risk; students with low self-esteem; passive or aggressive students experiencing peer pressure problems; children who lack realistic information on destructive aspects of drugs; children with behavioral or antisocial problems.

A high-risk student, or one with a chronic drug abuse and/or gang affiliation problem, is defined as

- a student having problems with attendance, discipline, family, self-esteem or academics
- A student with observed, reported and/or self-reported substance abuse problems at school or in the community

A data gathering system involving students, parents, school personnel and community resources, to identify students who need help, is being developed. The system will include:

- a data base of all students in the district, identifying the lower quadrant based on academics, low test scores and students exhibiting at-risk behaviors
- a data base of students with known gang affiliations and police records
- a list of students working with the juvenile justice system
- a referral form for teachers who have identified a problem with a student, and a procedure for handling referrals and tracking disposition of each referral
- an information system to let referring teachers know the disposition of the referral
- a plan for sharing information with parents of students

Description of Target Population

The target population to be served by the Sunshine SAFE project is comprised of the 1,200 middle school students in Sunshine Unified School District, including Mountains Middle School and Trees Middle School, which have drug and alcohol abuse problems similar to other urban schools. The onset of adolescence signals new challenges for alcohol and other drug prevention efforts. As students encounter the demands and increasing freedoms inherent in the middle school structure (multiple teachers for reduced periods of time, increased schoolwork loads), as well as increasing social opportunities (dances, parties) and peer pressures (fitting in socially), the opportunities and pressures to use drugs increase dramatically. Figures from the 1985 National Household Survey show that "smoking (45 percent) and drinking (56 percent) are the most prevalent activities in the early adolescent age group. However, nearly 30 percent had tried at least one illicit drug or controlled substance, without medical orders, during their lives."

Although there has been only a slight increase in use by students prior to seventh grade since the early 1970s, the increase in use for middle school students has been much more dramatic. For example, regular, daily cigarette smoking was begun by 11 percent of smokers prior to tenth grade, 55 percent who use alcohol initially used before high school and 26 percent smoked marijuana before high school. Because use is a necessary antecedent to abuse, this information has important implications about the seriousness of substance use in the middle school population. Similar but less serious types of drug use are good predictors of subsequent use of more serious drugs. Although involvement at one stage does not necessarily lead to involvement at the next stage of drug abuse, involvement at the next stage is unlikely without prior involvement in the previous stage. It is therefore essential to intervene with the population of at-risk middle school students during or before the earliest experimental phase of use.

In addition to the normal stresses undergone by students in middle school, the 93 percent of Sunshine's middle school students who are members of racial/ethnic minorities may experience even greater pressures to use/abuse drugs. Language barriers to success in school, and economic distress among immigrant and minority families, often set in motion the dynamics which lead to drug use.

The student ethnic distribution statistics graphed in Figure B.1 demonstrate the ethnic distribution of students in the school district.

Approximately 82 percent of Sunshine's population is of Hispanic origin, followed by Anglo (7 percent), Black (3 percent) and Asian (4 percent), with others comprising the remaining 6 percent of the students.

High-Risk Youth

Approximately 800 students identified as high risk for use/abuse will receive ongoing services through the SAFE project. High-risk students are those who

- experience problems in school (academic, behavioral, social or personal)

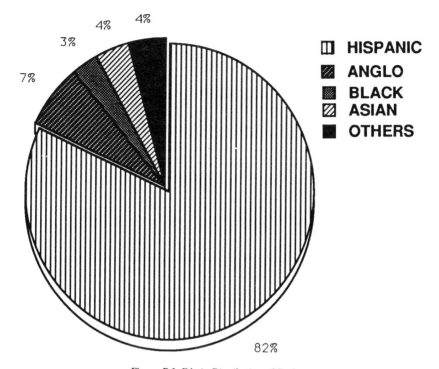

Figure B.1 *Ethnic Distribution of Students.*

- experience problems in their families (acting out, withdrawal, children in homes where alcohol and/or drug abuse occurs or has occurred, or otherwise dysfunctional and abusive family environments)
- are children of substance abusers
- are victims of physical, sexual or psychological abuse
- have dropped out of school
- are pregnant
- are economically disadvantaged
- have committed a violent or delinquent act
- have experienced mental health problems
- have attempted suicide
- have experienced long-term physical pain due to injury
- have experienced chronic failure in school

High-risk youth, those who experience multiple risk factors, will be identified through student self-report, parents, school personnel and community service agencies. A data base of all students in the district, identifying the lower quadrant based on academics, low test scores and students exhibiting at-risk behaviors, will be implemented. The dropout data base, for example, is designed to identify high-risk students in the areas of attendance, number of D's and F's, reading level, retention during school history, mobility of school/home and adjustment factors, which include juvenile delinquency, citizenship, special education and physical disabilities.

A procedure is being implemented to enable teachers and other school personnel to: identify early problem behaviors connected to potential drug and alcohol use/abuse; refer students for intervention; process referrals and track the disposition of each referral. An information/communication system will be developed to apprise referring teachers of the disposition of their referrals. A procedure for sharing information with parents of high-risk students, and which respects individual confidentiality issues, will also be developed.

This project will implement an at-risk management system for the identification of students at risk, and early intervention of school staff to assist youth who may become substance abusers and/or dropouts. Dr. Callison has extensive experience which will be helpful in the implementation of the at-risk management system. He has installed the personal computer version of the identification system in more than a dozen other school districts.

We have utilized the latest research on risk factors for both substance abusers and dropouts to develop software for identification. We would like to expand the program to identify cultural/linguistic variables. For example, many of the characteristics which we use for predicting which students are likely to be substance abusers are reported in an article entitled "Levels and Psychosocial Correlates of Adolescent Drug Use," by John A. Kovach and Nita W. Glickman.

Interventions Available for Linkage with Students

The interventions available for linkage with students include:

- individual and group counseling directed toward improved social skills, increased interest in and information about drug-free activities and group support of nonuse, and when indicated, referral to community counseling services
- family intervention, counseling and referral
- presentations on special topics of student concern and drug abuse, utilizing comprehensive health curriculum materials and visiting experts
- development of school-sponsored activities for high-risk students, such as adventure courses, field trips and after-school programs
- referral to, and support for, use of available community resources

A five-year follow-up procedure will track participants as they progress through middle and high school, providing important research information about the support needed for continued nonuse of drugs and alcohol, and no gang affiliation.

APPROACH

Sunshine's SAFE project, will demonstrate effective approaches to prevent high-risk youth from use and abuse of alcohol, drugs and tobacco, and gang affiliation. Sunshine's experience in working with high-risk youth, the focus on interventions for risk factors and the development of resiliency and protective factors, provide a research-based model for high-risk youth. To our knowledge, no one else has tailored risk-factor analysis and interventions to culturally and linguistically divergent student populations. The model will be easily transportable to other schools. Among the risk factors SAFE is designed to deal with, and the means it uses to deal with them, are

(*1*) Poor early identification of high-risk youth
- Establish screening, identification, follow-up and programming, including process and appropriate forms.
- Counselors and adult partners will reinforce healthy living and no–drug use beliefs using social learning methodology.
- High-risk youth will participate with parents in the Circle of Warmth home drug prevention and positive social interaction program.
- High-risk youth will participate in physical education programs stressing fitness and purposeful play.
- Risk factors that relate to culturally/linguistically divergent students will be identified.

(*2*) Antisocial behaviors (aggression, property destruction and discipline problems)
- High-risk youth will participate in a behavior management program operated by the counselor. The counselor will develop contracts and establish reinforcement schedules in collaboration with classroom teachers and the home.
- High-risk youth will participate in individual or group counseling that is developmentally based, and that will develop problem solving, assertive communication skills and adaptive functioning.
- High-risk youth will be referred to community mental health agencies when appropriate.
- High-risk youth will work with school officials, program staff and teachers to identify cultural conflicts that lead to antisocial behaviors.

- High-risk youth will work in groups to learn how cultural differences can be either assets or liabilities depending on the choice of the user.

(3) Poor bonding or attachment to school and peers (includes social withdrawal, inattentiveness in school and participation in peer groups lead by inappropriate models)

- High-risk youth and adult staff will be partners to establish one-to-one relationships. Each adult and high-risk youth will spend twenty minutes together each week in positive, nurturing activities (games, crafts, discussion). The adults will make themselves available for assistance with high-risk youths' concerns and questions.
- High-risk youth will voluntarily join formal groups (under the direction of responsible adults in the community or under the direction of city recreation personnel) which will operate schools as community centers. Participation in the formal groups will be encouraged through a community-wide media campaign aimed at enlisting the support of guidance assistants, adult partners, classroom teachers and parents. These formal groups will be centered on sports, hobbies, games and/or other interests.

Staff Training to Support Interventions

Staff will be trained during the first three years of the project. Training will be conducted by the project director, project specialist, project counselor and consultants.

The counselor will receive forty hours of training in

- expanded Magic Circle, Yo Puedo and Circle of Warmth
- human development theory
- intervention strategies with culturally divergent students
- evaluation
- interpersonal communication
- building rapport with high-risk youth, staff and parents in multicultural settings
- social learning reinforcement techniques
- cultural and ethnic community issues

By the end of three years, all staff from each school will be trained in Magic Circle, Yo Puedo and cultural index intervention strategies.

One hundred staff will be trained in the SAFE program. They will learn how to build rapport and provide a nurturing relationship in a multicultural context during their twenty minutes per week of interaction. Each staff member will be assigned three high-risk students.

Fifty teachers will be trained in the major academic thrust of this project, active learning and cooperative learning strategies.

Home/Family Interventions

Based on the successful pilot work of Hawkins and coworkers, using the social development model, Perry and Jessor's health promotion model and Ochoa's transformational model, the experience of SAFE will significantly reduce the impact of risk factors associated with home. These factors, and the way SAFE deals with them, include:

(*1*) Poor parenting practices (behavior management skills, communication skills and developing proper attachments to the family)
  - Community relations specialists will make home visits to develop rapport and assess family need. When appropriate, the guidance assistant will recommend parent participation in a school-based parent training program on behavior management and communication, led by the project counselor. For some parents, these behavior management and communication skills will be delivered in the home on an individual basis.
  - Families that need referral to other community resources for family therapy, further help assessment or other need, will be directed. The community relations specialist will act as a link to community resources that can assist the family.
  - A prime target will be to assist the family in strengthening the attachment and bonding of the high-risk youth to the parent/family and home cultural values.
(*2*) Beliefs and behaviors related to healthy living and abuse of alcohol and other drugs
  - The Sunshine SAFE project will build on the work of Ochoa and Espinoza, to develop training programs for parents and students where they work together to learn the principles of healthy living and the prevention of drug abuse and gang affiliation.
  - Parents will collaborate with school in the development of intervention plans, and in providing social reinforcement. Parents will provide reinforcement for targeted behavior changes, such as reduction of aggressive behavior, fitness and nutritional changes.

Community-Based Intervention and Networking

The Sunshine SAFE project will develop linkages with community agencies and groups that assist high-risk youth. The SAFE project will work with the recreation departments to increase the participation of high-risk youth in formal group activities. This will be conducted by opening up the schools in the evening hours to operate as community centers. Existing formal groups at parks will also be linked.

In addition, the Family YMCA will collaborate with the district in meeting the needs of high-risk youth. The Family YMCA presently operates programs in the district. They will integrate high-risk youth into their program.

Soroptimist International has collaborated by bringing prominent community leaders to work with the district on meeting the needs of high-risk youth. They will participate in the implementation of this program.

Sunshine School District has worked to improve drug education prevention programs for students. Deputies from the county sheriff's department, identified as school resource officers, provide twenty hours of drug prevention education to all fourth through sixth grade students. These school officers will operate as adjunct members to SAFE, and will participate in providing assistance to high-risk youth where appropriate.

City staff are on the Substance Abuse Prevention Advisory and will help coordinate a nine-month-long drug awareness campaign that will promote a no-use message. The city council will pass proclamations and provide support for this campaign.

Collaboration with the County of Los Angeles

The Sunshine SAFE project will link, and develop with, the county departments of mental health, education and alcohol and drug abuse. The Sunshine SAFE project will collaborate with these agencies to meet the needs of specific high-risk youth, and families who would benefit from their assistance. These agencies will participate in the implementation and development of the project. The project counselor will be the key liaison between the agencies.

The Sunshine district operates a school attendance review board (SARB). The SARB has membership from county probation and social services. This board reviews cases of students who present serious attendance, discipline or emotional disturbance problems. The board has legislative authority to make specific recommendations to schools and parents to meet the needs of high-risk youth.

Collaboration with the State

The Sunshine district has discussed this project with the California Department of Alcohol and Drug Abuse program. Norma Lee Jenning-Bradley of the department was supportive of the approaches being developed by the grant. The SAFE project will coordinate its activities with those of the state agency to insure that there will not be a duplication of effort. Resources provided through the state office will be integrated into the program where appropriate. The Multifunctional Resource Center, funded for linguistically divergent students in the southern California region, has agreed to collaborate with the project. The center adds the dimension necessary to address the cultural/ linguistic factors for high-risk students in the Sunshine district.

Mass Media Campaign

The Sunshine SAFE project will develop a campaign for a drug and gang awareness and healthy living month. The local newspaper, radio and television will participate. In addition, the SAFE project will develop regular features on community prevention.

Five-Year Plan

This project will reach over 800 high-risk youth and their families over the five years of operation. Table B.1 provides information on the plan and the number of students impacted.

Dissemination

This project will develop a transportable program that can be replicated in other school districts. Project consultants and staff will develop a dissemination manual on how to establish a community network including collaborative relations with police and local government, involving parents and staff in training, developing mass media campaigns and using schools as community centers. The project will design and implement a multicultural/multilingual parent training program and develop an awareness packet. A schedule for the completion of dissemination products will be developed by March 1994, and products will be field-tested from March to July. A validity study on products, with expert review of the program, will be conducted. Products will be disseminated to over 500 interested local education agencies (LEAs) and demonstration sites and visitations by LEAs will be established. Articles on the project will be prepared for publication, and five conference presentations will be scheduled.

Needs of Minority High-Risk Youth

The needs of the high-risk youth who are Hispanic, Black or Asian will be addressed by bilingual staff who represent these cultures and primary language groups. The project director has directed four large grant projects for

TABLE B.1 Five years of SAFE.

YEAR	MAJOR ACTIVITIES	NUMBER OF HIGH-RISK YOUTH AND FAMILIES
1	Staffing, planning, preservice training • baseline data collection • screening identification and recruitment of high-risk youth • pilot schools-based intervention	800 400
2	Expand programs • implement schools as community centers • initiate community-wide drug-free living campaign	400
3	Expand program at schools • expand Circle of Warmth program to all families • expand community-wide drug-free living campaign • adjust/modify program, based on evaluation results	800 800
4	Continue to refine program • work toward institutionalizing program • continue home/community programs • develop dissemination materials	800
5	Finalize institutionalization of the program • institutionalize home/community program • actively disseminate the program	800

minority language groups. She has worked with Hispanic youth in a multicultural setting for twenty years.

The project counselor is bilingual and experienced in working with minority groups. The bilingual staff are important for working effectively with high-risk minority youth and their families. Understanding the culture and speaking in the primary language is critical to assisting the youth and families to reduce risk factors. All materials sent home—referral forms, screening instruments and parent materials—will be translated into the four major primary languages of the project.

The district's extensive experience in bilingual education and multicultural education will help insure that all materials are free of cultural bias. In addition, all materials will be reviewed by an expert panel to insure freedom from cultural bias.

A primary goal of the project is to develop an appropriate linguistic/cultural delivery system to meet the needs of high-risk students of ethnically divergent backgrounds who speak languages other than English in their homes.

EVALUATION PLAN

Objective Attainment

An evaluation will determine the attainment of project objectives; each objective has been designed to be measurable. Two forms of evaluation will be conducted, product and process. The product evaluation will focus on the expected performance of the participants. The process evaluation will monitor the completion of activities which support each objective, and will facilitate replication if the approach proves promising. During the first year of the project, only baseline data will be collected from which to make annual comparisons.

Product Evaluation: A Comparison Group Design

The project proposes to use a GAP reduction design as described by Tallmadge, Lam and Camarena. This is a variation of the norm-referenced design, and measures growth from pre- to posttest. GAP reduction refers to the achievement or behavioral level of program participants getting closer to the test norm over time. In this project, high-risk youth will close the gap between their performance on project instruments when compared to a normative population. A formula to determine GAP reduction is shown in Figure B.2.

As the authors state, "In the absence of a 'live' comparison group, we might wish to measure GAP reduction with respect to some fixed standards such as the national norm on the program's exit criterion."

The project's impact is the observed post-treatment performance minus the expected no-treatment performance. The observed post-treatment performance is always the mean or median posttest score of the treatment group. Local normative data on attendance and discipline will be used for GAP reduction comparison analysis.

GAP reduction = (pretest gap) − (posttest gap)
              = X − X − Y + Y
              = (Y − X) − (Y − X)
              = (treatment group growth) − (comparison group growth)
C = comparison group
T = treatment group

Figure B.2 GAP Reduction Formula.

Test-Instruments and the Reasons for Their Selection

The CTBS (comprehensive test of basic skills) is a standardized and nationally normed test used by the Sunshine School District for assessment of student growth in English, reading, language and math. It is also coordinated with the district's basic skills program and diagnostic procedures. This test is published by McGraw-Hill. The technical manual reports appropriate reliability and validity studies.

The Teacher's Rating Form was developed by Achenbach and Edelbock. The items and format were refined through successive editions that were pilot tested with parents of children referred for mental health services. The Teacher's Rating Form will be administered annually to parents and teachers. These scales have been translated into twenty-four languages.

For identification and placement procedures, we will rely on an instrument developed by Hall at the University of Texas entitled Concepts Based Adaption Model: Levels of Use as our measurement tool.

The information and data which will be collected for the purpose of identifying the high-risk students will be derived from the data base program Comprehensive Risk Assessment, by Dr. William L. Callison. Table B.2 describes the instruments to be used, with the appropriate information.

Context Evaluation

The context evaluation will assess whether or not we are developing a computer management system that

- identifies potential substance abusers and potential dropouts

TABLE B.2 Test instruments.

DEPENDENT VARIABLE	INSTRUMENT/DATA SOURCE
Antisocial behaviors	Achenbach Teacher Rating Scale
Drug use and association	Social Influence Survey
Parent practices	FACES-III (a forty item questionnaire)
Behavioral/emotional	Achenbach Child Behavior Checklist
School achievement	California Test of Basic Skills
Attendance	Official records of attendance— mandated by state law and local school board
Health knowledge and attitudes	A criterion-referenced test designed by project staff and consultants
Personality factors	Achenbach Youth Self-Report
Self-esteem	The Piers Harris Self-Esteem Scale

- uses an expert system effectively to connect identified students at risk with appropriate interventions to reduce student risk
- evaluates the effectiveness of the interventions by assigning new risk levels to participating students

The context evaluation will focus upon the big picture. Is the community supportive? Is Sunshine offering leadership in key areas, such as planning and budgeting? Do parents understand the aims of the project? In this regard we are especially interested in parent support of data gathering from students pertaining to their use of alcohol and drugs. We will obtain parent permission for this data gathering. Once a year we will survey a random sample of parents to ascertain their level of support for the identification of at-risk students, and their placement in appropriate interventions.

Process Evaluation

The process evaluation will provide independent input to management decision making on a regularly scheduled basis. The process evaluation will consist of the following major qualitative and quantitative activities.

(*1*) Monthly staff meetings to review/modify project activities as necessary based on input from staff, participants, administrators and evaluator

(*2*) Questionnaires, opinionaires, checklists and observation (records, files, classrooms) as necessary to assess implementation according to plan, including the following instruments:
- parent questionnaire on parent involvement
- log of parent attendance/participation at parent education meetings
- log of participation in formal group
- log of counseling activities
- log of one-to-one partner activities
- log of parent visits to schools
- staff in-service meetings evaluation appraisal form
- classroom teacher assistant activity log
- log of participation of high-risk youth in fitness programs
- log of home visitations
- counselor log

(*3*) Classroom visitations and monitoring of program maintenance in the classroom

(*4*) Ongoing assessment of high-risk youth project students' status to determine project's progress toward objectives

(*5*) Periodic review of materials developed by project goals in the given topic areas

The process evaluation will provide the information that a grantee is required to collect. This information will be collected and reported in the annual evaluation report. The evaluation information to be collected will include:

- educational background of high-risk youth
- annual assessment of student needs
- intervention activities implemented
- curriculum materials developed and acquired
- pedagogical methodology used
- time-on-task studies
- educational and professional qualifications, including language competencies, of the staff responsible for planning and operating the project

Process evaluation information will be used to improve the program in the following ways during the first two years of implementation.

- Adjust implementation schedule to accommodate unanticipated events.
- Revise procedures for clarity and completeness.
- Revise materials for appropriateness to instructional task and ease of use for intended audience replicability.
- Focus project efforts on areas of student achievement/progress exhibiting the greatest need based on objective attainment.
- Change direction of, or emphasis on, development of project procedures and/or materials.
- Implement and/or change procedures related to staff/student/ community acceptance and support of the project as necessary.
- Adjust level of effort to insure rapid progress without alienation of project team members.

The dissemination manual will be evaluated by the teaching staff, guidance staff, administrative staff and expert consultants as to effectiveness and utility on the following criteria.

- clarity of text
- degree related to goals/objectives
- ease of implementation of community building activity
- unbiased as to ethnic background, sex and socioeconomic factors

The dissemination manual will be revised where appropriate. Content validity studies will be conducted to insure quality control of dissemination materials.

External Evaluator

The Sunshine School District will contract with Dr. William L. Callison, consultant, as external evaluator to evaluate our education plan and its relation to the scope and objectives of the project.

Dr. Callison has extensive experience in research and development, evaluation design and program management. He is on the faculty at California State University, Fullerton. He has provided evaluation services to numerous school districts in Los Angeles and Orange Counties. Dr. Callison has assisted in the development of the evaluation plan for this proposal.

It will be his responsibility to insure that the overall evaluation design is followed, and is kept consistent with the instructional and training objectives for this proposal.

The external evaluator will also advise the staff on data collection procedures and identify those which address evaluation questions, and which are appropriate for use with the project data. Dr. Callison has computer hardware and statistical software to carry out all necessary statistical analyses.

Both the external evaluator and the administrative staff will insure that the data obtained will contribute to improvements in the operation of the project, and meet all requirements of the grant.

PROJECT STAFFING, MANAGEMENT AND ORGANIZATION

Organizational Structure

This project will be sponsored by the Sunshine School District (see Figure B.3 for SAFE budget). As a local education agency (LEA), the Sunshine School District is governed by an elected board of trustees. The organizational chart reflects the organizational structure and management plan for local governance of the project, and follows the objectives, tasks and timeline charts.

Leadership Structure

The project director will be Mr. Jones, who is currently coordinating the dropout prevention and recovery program for the district. Mr. Jones reports to the assistant superintendent of instruction, Dr. Brown. Mr. Jones will be actively involved and devote at least half of his time to the project.

	U.S. DOE	Months	Time	District Contribution
A. Personnel				
One project director	28,325	12	50%	19,000
One resource teacher	19,000	10	100%	12,000
One project counselor	0	11	20%	
Two half-time school counselors	50,000	11	50%	
One clerical assistant	16,200	12	100%	5,400
Two after-school activities teachers at				
$14/hr. for eight hrs./wk.	8,064	10		
Staff Development	3,000			3,000
Seventy-five teachers—prevention				
Seventy-five staff—one-to-one partnership				
Active learning				
Total personnel	$124,589			$39,400
B. Fringe Benefits				
State teachers retirement	8,209			2,558
P.E.R.S.	1,239			413
O.A.S.D.I.	1,158			386
S.U.I.	71			22
W.C.	4,937			1,529
Medicare	1,705			528
RIP	1,293			400
Health and welfare	9,900			6,800
Total benefits	$ 28,512			$12,636

Figure B.3 SAFE *Budget.*

	U.S. DOE	Months	Time	District Contribution
C. Travel				
National and regional conferences				
Two people	5,000			3,000
Conferences	2,000			2,000
Total travel	$ 7,000			$ 5,000
D. Supplies				
Duplication	500			
Office supplies	200			500
Drug abuse prevention materials				15,000
Total supplies	$ 700			$15,500

Figure B.3 (continued) SAFE Budget.

(continued)

359

	U.S. DOE	Months	Time	District Contribution
E. Contractual				
Program evaluation				
.25% time	14,500			
Consultant/programmer				
three days at $1,000/day	3,000			
Consultant/minority				
Risk factors 350/day				
ten days	3,500			
Total contractual	$ 21,000			
F. Other				
Rent (store front)				7,000
Postage, xerox	779			
Total other	$ 779			$ 7,000
G. Total direct charges	$182,580			$79,536
H. Indirect costs (8.75%)	$ 15,976			
I. Total budget	$198,556			$79,536

Figure B.3 (continued) SAFE Budget.

360

Relationships between Organizations

As indicated in the "Approach" Section, the Sunshine School District will collaborate with local human services agencies as follows: city and county recreation departments to facilitate formal group membership; Los Angeles County Office of Education, Center for Health Education; County Mental Health; Los Angeles County Alcohol and Drug Abuse Prevention program and the YMCA.

Sunshine School District has been recognized for its efforts in meeting the needs of high-risk youth. For the last ten years they have operated a program of counseling and guidance for high-risk youth. Under the direction of a multidisciplinary team (principal, psychologist, resource teacher), a paraprofessional guidance assistant has provided individual and group counseling for high-risk youth.

With the addition of this grant, a resource teacher will assist in linking identified at-risk youth with interventions inside the school setting, after school and in the community. Home visits and parent education programs will provide follow-up activities at home. The project will use interventions based on the health promotion and social development models. Sunshine School District has an exemplary history of innovation to meet student needs. Over the past ten years, the district has received grants to provide bilingual education services as well as innovative at-risk programs. Currently, Sunshine has been selected to participate with the United Way Dropout Task Force to establish a model for at-risk youth in a minority community.

Organizational Capability

Sunshine School District has an exemplary record of working with special-needs youth. It is a recognized leader in servicing the needs of special education students. Their multidisciplinary team approach to diagnosis and program planning will be used as a component of the Sunshine School District's student and parent education programs.

Staffing

Key Personnel and Time Commitments to Project

The key personnel and the percentage of time that will be committed directly to the project are: project director, 50 percent; resource teacher, 100 percent; project counselor, 20 percent; school counselors, 50 percent; project evaluation consultant, 25 percent; computer programmer/analyst consultant, three days.

Project Director

The project director serves as educational leader and performs program planning, implementation and evaluation. Responsibilities include: providing leadership for all phases of project; coordination and articulation between schools; supporting principals with technical assistance; planning and implementing staff development program; coordinating with Sunshine School District business support staff to insure program's fiscal accountability; planning curriculum development component; dissemination of information to district personnel, community and other LEAs; preparation and submission of all reports required by state and federal agencies; performing other project duties as assigned; and liaison to state and federal departments of education.

Mr. Jones will serve as project director. He is presently an outreach consultant for Sunshine School District. He has twenty years of experience as a teacher and supervisor. He is recognized as a leading figure in guidance and high-risk youth programs. He has worked on numerous committees on drug prevention, at-risk students and community involvement. He has developed the district's Dropout Prevention Recovery program. He has managed grants and categorical programs. Mr. Jones is uniquely qualified to manage this project.

Resource Specialist

The resource specialist provides training to staff and parents on primary drug abuse prevention interventions. He or she assists local schools in developing community centers; assists the project director in collaboration with law enforcement, local government and other youth agencies; works with local guidance committees regarding student assessment in the development of dissemination of projects.

The resource teacher will have experience in drug prevention education, training staff and parents and developing curriculum. The individual will need at least five years of experience in education. The individual will need a graduate degree. The resource teacher will need to have excellent theoretical knowledge of substance abuse prevention and excellent interpersonal and presentation skills.

Project Counselor

The project counselor will be responsible for supervision of the school-based and family-based interventions, supervision of instrumentation and testing activities, supervision of school-based counseling activities and case consultation.

Ms. Maslow will serve as project counselor. She is a bilingual school counselor for Sunshine School District. She holds a masters degree in counseling and guidance and education psychology. She will complete her masters degree in marriage and family counseling in December. She is currently supervised by a licensed therapist. Previously she worked as a bilingual school psychologist. As project counselor, she will supervise instrumentation and testing activities. She will assist with coordination and development of projects and training materials. As a school counselor, Ms. Maslow provides direct drug/alcohol counseling and prevention activities to a sixth to eighth grade population, including LEP students. She is fluent in Spanish.

School Counselors

School counselors will present school-based and family-based interventions, survey teachers for referrals, interview students for risk factors, conduct group and individual counseling sessions, consult with teachers, work with target students' families and implement at-risk profile interventions.

The school counselor will have experience working with at-risk students. The school counselor will hold a school counseling credential, have at least three years classroom experience and have excellent interpersonal skills.

Computer Programmer/Analyst Consultant

Students-at-Risk, Inc. has created and implemented many expert systems and is an established software firm. Their previous experience with at-risk materials gives them the knowledge to design the intervention program for the computer.

Dr. Ochoa's experience as a sociologist, and his work toward meeting the needs of linguistically/ethnically divergent students, will add the depth needed to address the multicultural aspect of the proposal. He will work on the identification of ethnically-related risk factors.

Dr. William L. Callison is recommended as evaluation consultant. He has ten years of experience in evaluation. He has provided external evaluation services to numerous federal projects. He has conducted eight years of research on drug prevention programs. He has been on the faculty of California State University at Fullerton.

Recruitment and Selection

The Sunshine School District has a proven policy of affirmative action in its hiring practices. The district developed and implemented an Equal Employment Opportunity/Affirmative Action program (EEO/AA), and is committed to complying with the letter and spirit of state and federal laws prohibiting discrimination in employment. A copy of its EEO/AA is on file, and is available upon request. The district will seek employees for this high-risk youth project, as for all hiring, who have been traditionally underrepresented—that is, members of racial and ethnic minorities and handicapped persons.

Multidisciplinary Staffing

This project will use the expertise of several disciplines—education, psychology, sociology and health. Through the school guidance committees composed of psychologist, administrator and resource teacher, a multidisciplinary team will participate in the identification and program planning for high-risk youth.

RESOURCES

Facilities Are Adequate

The Sunshine School District has, and uses, schools, school buildings and classrooms that meet all the standards both within the state of California and with the U.S. Office of Civil Rights, Department of Education and other related and concerned offices and agencies.

The project will utilize, facilitate and develop classrooms that are located on regular elementary school campuses. The Sunshine School District is currently providing services to handicapped students on integrated sites.

The Sunshine School District provides adequate resources to operate classes and other educational opportunities, e.g., computer labs, cafeterias, gyms, locker areas, libraries. These facilities will be accessed by the high-risk youth to the maximum extent appropriate.

The Sunshine School District will provide an in-kind contribution of $79,036 to support this grant. This includes director's time, staff training, travel and supplies.

A STUDY OF THE OPPORTUNITY PROGRAM AT ROWLAND HIGH SCHOOL[30]

OVERVIEW

The school records from an identified population of at-risk ninth and tenth grade students, who were separated into an experimental group and a control group, were used to discover if a dropout prevention program was successful in helping at-risk students succeed. Using the data from the student's permanent records, significant differences were found on all measured items between the two groups. These items were the number of classes taken, grades, GPA, credits earned, number of absences and number of negative behavior referrals. The findings indicate that the dropout prevention program, Opportunity, is successful in helping at-risk students improve in the areas of attendance, grades, and behavior.

THE PROGRAM BEGINS

The Rowland Unified School District includes fifteen elementary schools, three junior high schools, two high schools and one continuation high school. The ethnic makeup of the district is: Caucasian, 19.9 percent; American Indian, 0.2 percent; Asian, 13.6 percent; African American, 8.0 percent; Filipino, 9.4 percent; Hispanic, 48.9 percent. The projected enrollment for 1991–1992 was 10,590 students for elementary, 2,823 students for junior high and 5,665 students for high school. The employee makeup for the district is 900 certificated and 965 classified. This is the setting for this study.

Eight years ago, several junior high school teachers of the Rowland District identified a population of students who were not achieving in their current

---

[30]The report presented in Appendix C was written by Lori Marie Wasson, of Rowland High School, Rowland, CA.

educational program. The district, being concerned about this population, allowed these teachers to develop a new educational program that would allow these students, identified as at risk, to succeed in school. The program the teachers developed was titled Opportunity. The name implied that at-risk students would be given an opportunity to get back on the educational track, and, by the end of the semester, progress to the current educational level of their classmates.

The program addressed several problem areas: length of the school day, student-teacher ratio, individualization of the education program and reduction of personal contact with other individuals during the school day.

Length of School Day

The first problem addressed by the teachers was the length of the school day. Since at-risk students tended to have a lower frustration level than students who were not at risk, it was thought that a shorter school day would benefit these students. With reduced class hours the students would not reach their top frustration level, thus allowing them to perform better in their schoolwork. The end result of their exploration and research was the formation of a three-hour school day for these students. The school day would consist of three straight hours of education and instruction with no breaks or interruptions, such as changing classes.

Student-Teacher Ratio

The second problem addressed by the teachers was the student-teacher ratio. In the regular classroom the ratio was thirty-five to one. At-risk students tended to need more individualized instruction and attention from the teacher in order to achieve. A reduced student-teacher ratio would allow the teacher to give more individual instruction, and allow more time for the teacher to deal with the educational and emotional problems of the students, while discovering ways to alleviate these problems so that the students could achieve educationally. The end result was a fifteen to one ratio at the junior high level. The use of a three-hour instruction aide was also implemented in the classroom to allow the teacher to be free from the paperwork of grading, thus increasing the amount of time the teacher had available to work with the students.

Individual Instruction

These teachers found a large portion of the at-risk students also have some type of learning problem. It was proposed that by providing individual instruction, the students could work at their own pace and have more success in their work without the pressure to keep up with their classmates. The students would work on a competency basis with individual instruction from the teacher, as compared to the regular program where the at-risk students would fail and continue on with the next lesson. In the Opportunity program the students would repeat the lesson if failed, until mastery was accomplished. This would allow the students more success, which would lead to greater self-esteem due to the mastery of a skill instead of repeated failures.

Personal Contact

The teachers recognized that at-risk students had trouble transferring from class period to class period. These students tended to interact with friends during these passing periods, and to forget that they had a class to attend. The teachers decided that the way to solve this problem was to form a self-contained classroom. The students would receive all of their required classes in one room. This would solve the problem of students transferring from class to class. A self-contained class would also limit the number of people the students had to interact with, such as teachers and other students. It would also minimize the time used in starting and ending class, thus allowing for more educational time which these at-risk students needed. Learning would also be interrupted less, and more would take place due to the fact that there would be no class changes.

The program worked so well at the junior high level, a version of it was implemented, with minor changes, at the high school level. These changes included the number of hours students attended, and the student-teacher ratio. The number of daily hours was increased to four hours a day, which translated into four class periods. The student-teacher ratio went from fifteen to one at the junior high level, to twenty to one at the high school level. Even with these changes, the high school program continued to do well with at-risk students.

The researcher was introduced to the program four years ago as a teacher. In the time that the program has been operating at the high school level, there have not been any studies to discover if the program is really making a difference. The researcher determined that a study was needed to discover if the program was really the contributing factor to the students' achievement, or if the achievement was due to some other factor, such as maturation. This question is the heart of the study.

WHAT THE STUDY SHOWED

A review of the literature on successful dropout prevention studies and programs shows that there are some interventions that do work. The first issue for a successful program is smaller class size. Students have a tendency to feel that teachers do not care about them. With a smaller class size, the teacher will have more time to spend with each student and to show that the teacher does care about the student. Another result of smaller class size is shown in a study by Glass and Smith (1978). Their results show that as class size increases, achievement decreases. This fact does not spell success for the at-risk student who is already receiving failing grades. In a recent study, Fidwell (1988) interviewed urban high school dropouts on their initial reason for dropping out. He found that the response given most often was poor grades. Glass and Smith also found that: in smaller classes each child received more individual attention from the teacher; the students paid more attention to their work; the curriculum took on greater depth, breadth and richness; discipline problems diminished. To reduce the number of dropouts, the students should be placed in small, highly structured groups that have explicit rules and are taught by teachers who work to elicit trust. Reducing class size should be a high priority item to help potential dropouts stay in school. With reduced class sizes, the students should perform better, keeping them from dropping out of school because of poor grades.

Structure is another consideration in assessing the success of a program. One researcher, Ernest Boyer, suggests that schools should organize alternative schools to give intensive, continuous help to some high-risk students. Other researchers, such as Callison and Richards-Colocino, state that successful dropout programs are often informal, small and accommodating to students who don't fit. Students who don't fit are students who, for one reason or another, do not perform well in, or fit the mold of, the regular classroom setting. They also state that one way to help the potential dropout is to put the dropout-prone students into specialized, individually focused programs, such as a school-within-a-school or an alternative school. Hamilton (1986) noted that successful dropout programs are characterized by curriculum diversity, particularly in the provision of nontraditional and vocationally oriented courses. Here again is the idea that at-risk students don't fit the regular program, and a nontraditional way needs to be implemented to keep these students in school and make them feel they fit.

How the dropout prevention programs are structured may be the deciding factor for a student thinking about dropping out of school. Research on this issue has come up with several theories as to what works with potential dropouts. The four researchers mentioned agree that small, individualized programs that give intensive help would be the way to structure a program which would help keep the potential dropout in school.

An important issue which goes along with class size and structure is the emotional tone of a school or program. As stated by Pittman and Haighwout (1987), the school social climate does have a considerable effect on the dropout rate. Potential dropouts need to feel they are a part of the school picture and that they belong. Callison and Richards-Colocino state that dropouts feel teachers have little interest in them and do not care about them. By reducing class size and developing individualized programs, it is projected that the tone of the school's socialization would increase in a positive direction for potential dropouts, making them less likely to drop out.

By combining the three issues of success for dropout prevention program – smaller class size, highly structured programs and a positive emotional tone – the model for a successful dropout prevention program has been developed. If the program is successful in dealing with this type of student, then the student will stay in school, which will solve the issue of parental pressure on the district. If a potential dropout stays in school and graduates, he or she is more likely to get a job, so that the community will not have to pay the way for the dropouts through such programs as welfare. Then the community pressure will decrease on the district. If the program is individualized, and mastery is a top priority, then the student will learn and graduate. The business community will be receiving educated employees, which again will take pressure off the district. In conclusion, a good dropout prevention program is valuable and important to everyone – business, the community, parents, students and the district. Everyone wins with a successful dropout prevention program.

The Rowland Unified dropout prevention program, Opportunity, encompasses all the components of a successful dropout prevention program. Its student-teacher ratio (twenty to one) goes along with the belief that smaller class sizes help the students achieve greater success in school by receiving more individualized attention. Opportunity has a highly structured program in which all the students receive intensive help. All expectations are spelled out at first so that there are no unexpected requirements placed on the students later. Standards are strict but fair to all. The emotional tone of Opportunity is one of caring and concern for the students. With all three of these items being part of the Opportunity program, there should be a significant difference between those students who participated in Opportunity and those who did not.

SELECTION OF SAMPLE

Treatment Group

The experimental group, which consisted of three tenth grade males, three tenth grade females, eleven ninth grade males and one ninth grade female, was selected by the at-risk counselor who had no knowledge of the study. There were only eighteen subjects in the experimental group instead of the twenty originally planned. One student did not return the permission slip, and one space was never filled by the counselor. The criterion for selection was the students' failure to succeed in the regular program during the current semester. Most students were failing all their classes and/or in danger of losing their classes due to absences numbering over fifteen. Rowland Unified has a policy of dropping high school students from a class once they have missed fifteen days in that class.

Control Group

The control group was comprised of eighteen at-risk students matched by sex and grade level to the experimental group. These subjects were selected from the school's identified at-risk population. These students were originally identified because Rowland High School is very concerned about their at-risk students and the school's dropout rate. The control group also consisted of three tenth grade males, three tenth grade females, eleven ninth grade males and one ninth grade female. These students were labeled at risk by the at-risk counselor because they were not on target for graduation. Being behind in credits was the most common reason. Several reasons for the missing credits were failed classes, dropped classes due to absences numbering over fifteen and/or nonattendance at any school.

PROCEDURE

The data gathered in this study included:

- number of credits earned (five credits per class passed with a D− or better)
- number of classes taken
- absences (excused and unexcused)
- semester grades
- number of negative behavior referrals
- grade point average (GPA)

The number of credits earned, and the number of classes taken, were used to derive the GPA. Since the students were identified as at risk by the lack of credits and lack of attendance, the data will show if the treatment was effective by exhibiting an increase in the number of credits earned, and a decrease in the number of absences of those students participating in the treatment group.

The treatment group was selected one by one, not as a group. As each student was placed in Opportunity, an entrance meeting was arranged between the parents, teacher and student. The meeting's purpose was to explain the program and the rules of the class. If the parents were still willing for their child to be placed in Opportunity, he or she was admitted. As each student entered Opportunity, he or she was assigned classes on an individual basis according to ability. Each student was to show mastery in each assignment before advancing to the next level. Mastery was shown by receiving a 70 percent or better on the assignment. If mastery was not achieved, the assignment was repeated. The students' papers were graded immediately to allow for positive feedback. This immediate feedback allowed the teacher to decide if the assignment was mastered or if intervention was necessary. Students were required as part of the program to stay after school to complete their assignments if necessary. If a student was not in attendance the teacher would telephone the home and/or workplace of the parents to locate the student. This was done to let the student know someone was interested in him or her so that the student would be less likely to be absent.

The control group received no treatment and had no contact with the researcher. The researcher came into contact only with the students' permanent records. At the end of the 1992 spring semester, a set of data was compiled for each student including number of credits earned, number of classes taken, semester grades, number of absences, number of negative behavior referrals and GPA. The averages for both groups in each of the five areas were compiled and recorded. *t*-Test scores were then compared for each category to see if the differences between the two groups were significant. The results were then written up.

RESULTS

In comparing the number of classes taken, the control group was enrolled in more classes (6.6) than the experimental group (5.1). The results of the *t*-test showed that there was a significant difference, at $p < .0001$ (the chances of this result occurring by chance are one in 10,000), between the two groups' means in the number of classes taken.

The control group took a significantly greater number of classes than the experimental group did, but the experimental group received more credits (23.0 to 20.6). The results of the *t*-test on the number of credits completed showed a difference at $p < .0375$ between the two groups.

When dealing with GPA, the experimental group received a mean of 2.5 (a letter grade of C), while the control group received a mean of 1.2 (a letter grade of D). A significant relationship was found between the two groups' GPAs at $p < .0001$.

In the number of negative referrals, the experimental group received a mean of 3.9 referrals for the spring semester, while the control group received a mean of 7.2 referrals. A *t*-test performed on these means showed that there was a significant difference at $p < 0.0571$ between the two groups.

When comparing the means on the number of days absent during the spring semester, the control group had a mean of 10.3 days absent, while the experimental group had a mean of 6.7 days absent. A significant relationship was found when a t-test was applied. The relationship was significant at $p <$ .0374.

CONCLUSION

The results show that although the control group was enrolled in significantly more classes than the experimental group, the control group earned less credit than the experimental group. This means that the experimental group passed more of their classes than the control group. The fact that there was a significant difference between the two groups in credits earned shows that the Opportunity program does make a significant difference in the students passing their classes and earning credits. So, even with the advantage of being able to enroll in more classes, the control group still earned fewer credits.

When the two items—credits earned and the number of classes taken—were divided to derive the GPA, the results showed a very significant difference between the two groups. This fact suggests that the program is very successful in increasing the GPA of the at-risk students who participate by at least one letter grade. In this study the improvement was from a letter grade of D to a letter grade of C.

The results on negative referrals show that the experimental group received fewer referrals than the control group (3.9 to 7.2). Since there was a significant difference found between the two groups, the study shows that Opportunity does decrease the number of negative referrals. There is less opportunity for the student to get into trouble while changing classes and interacting with friends. Also, the decrease in the number of referrals means the experimental group spent more time in the classroom than the control group did. Each referral means that a student was sent to the administrator in charge of discipline to be assigned such punishments as detention or writing paragraphs. Each referral had the possibility of an hour resolution or longer, if the administrator was busy. If the student was in the office, then he or she was not receiving the educational opportunity taking place in the classroom. If the students in Opportunity had fewer referrals than the control group, it means they received more class time, and this could be why they passed more classes with better grades.

In the area of attendance, a significant difference was found between the two groups. The control group was absent 10.3 days during the spring semester, while the experimental group was absent 6.7 days. This information shows that Opportunity's attendance policy of calling home each day, and the fact that the teacher shows concern about the students, is successful in decreasing the number of absences. The students know that someone is watching out for them and they therefore attend school.

In conclusion it seems that the Opportunity program is successful in all areas studied. It is most successful in raising the GPA of at-risk students. With the improvement in grades, GPA, attendance and behavior, the students feel better about themselves which raises their self-esteem. With better achievement and greater self-esteem, a student will stay in school longer and be more likely to graduate.

Overall, the study has produced some useful information. It shows that the teachers who developed the program were right in their assessments of at-risk students. These students do indeed achieve more educationally in smaller classes, with fewer class hours and more individual attention. The study also informs the present teacher that the program is accomplishing exactly what the program is supposed to accomplish. The Opportunity program is a success.

Now to answer the question at the heart of the study. Is the program the contributing factor in the students' achievement, or is it due to some other factor, such as maturation? The data shows that the program is indeed responsible for the changes which are observed in the students' achievement.

DEFINITIONS OF ABBREVIATIONS

ADA (Average Daily Attendance) Many states reimburse school districts based on the average daily attendance of students. Some states now require that attendance be taken every period of the day, and payment is based on period by period attendance.

BABES A social skills curriculum for the elementary grades, that is often used as a drug prevention curriculum.

DARE (Drug Abuse Resistance Education) A curriculum developed and taught by police officers, that is typically offered at grade six to supplement a drug prevention curriculum.

LEA (Local Education Agency) Typically this is the school district in many states.

OSS (Operation Safe Schools) The Orange County (California) Department of Education, with the assistance of the California Office of Criminal Justice Planning, created OSS in 1987. Its purpose is to offer participating school districts an "early intervention, prevention education program tailored to assist school districts in maintaining safe, secure and peaceful school environments" (Orange County Department of Education, 1987).

PAL (Peer Assistance Leadership) A program developed from the basic ideas of peer counseling, that trains talented young people to be careful listeners and to share concerns with students who are likely to use drugs.

PLATO A computer-managed instruction system of hardware and software that offers instruction in every content area from grade one to Ph.D. There are over 10,000 hours of instructional modules available in the program developed at the University of Illinois in the 1950s. The latest version of the program is called NOVANET.

QUEST A social skills curriculum that is widely used as a drug prevention curriculum.

SARB (School Attendance Review Board) A committee that brings together several professionals, such as teachers, administrators, counselors, psychol-

374

ogists and other community agency staff, to help improve the attitude and attendance of students who have not responded to school staff alone.

STAGES (Skills to Manage Stressful Changes) A coping skills curriculum that helps students deal with major changes in their lives, such as divorce, death or major moves. Written by Guidance Resources staff, Irvine USD. Order from Guidance Resources, Irvine Unified School District, 5050 Barranca Parkway, Irvine, CA 92714.

STAR (Social Thinking and Reasoning) A social skills curriculum based on assertion skills and understanding personality types. Written by Guidance Resources staff, Irvine USD. Order from Guidance Resources, Irvine Unified School District, 5050 Barranca Parkway, Irvine, CA 92714.

WICAT A computer hardware and software company based in Orem, Utah, that sells materials designed to offer basic skills preparation using a computer-managed instruction format.

DROPOUT PREVENTION AT SANTA ANA HIGH SCHOOL[31]

EXECUTIVE SUMMARY

This study showed that there is a strong relationship between at-risk students' poor behavior and academic performance, and the lack of self-esteem, self-worth and values.

The purpose of this study was to identify at-risk students through the Comprehensive Risk Assessment software, and provide intervention programs to develop the students' self-esteem, which is expected to provide the impetus that will improve their academic achievement and school attendance.

Thirty students (sixteen boys and fourteen girls), identified by Santa Ana High School (SAHS) administrators as having the characteristics of being potential school dropouts, were selected for participation in this study. They all completed the risk assessment questionnaire. The results of the questionnaire indicated that the majority of this group of students, who demonstrated a high level of absenteeism and low grades, came from families that were troubled due to drinking habits. Thirty-seven percent of the students answered that they knew five or more adults very well who were involved in the use of alcohol or drugs. Ninety percent of this group of students demonstrated anger frequently or sometimes.

In the program students were encouraged to verbally express their feelings to the rest of the group. This procedure proved to be highly successful. The students expressed feelings of being unwanted, not loved and not accepted by their families, teachers and friends. At the beginning of this study these students were very critical, and highly suspicious of authority and discipline. At the end

[31]The report in Appendix E was written by Eugenia Torres, of Santa Ana High School, Santa Ana, CA.

of the study students demonstrated a more positive attitude towards the school, teachers and their peers.

Half of the students were immigrants to this country. At the beginning they had no desire to continue into higher education because they felt like second-class members of the community.

The students were provided assistance through the Action and Commitment in Education (ACE) program, an intervention program that was designed as part of this study to assist students at risk with self-esteem building activities and peer tutoring. Ten participating students were assigned the task of being peer tutors in math, algebra, economics and English. This activity not only helped the students being tutored, but also helped the tutors, as indicated by improved grades in these subjects.

Findings indicated the interventions did result in a measurable improvement in attendance. The mean for days absent before the intervention indicates a score of 12.5, while the mean score for days absent in the postintervention period is 6.6, with a *t*-test significance at the .0001 level.

There was no significant improvement in grades. This indicates that students are not yet interested in improving their grade point average scores. The importance of achieving a high GPA will have to be stressed in the future. Teacher and student expectations need to be increased.

In final interviews all students said the program helped them. One female student left without notice to get married. Another student was forced to drop out to have a baby. However, it was later found out that both girls had transferred to a continuation school.

One member that showed considerable improvement in her behavior was a female gang member who decided to drop her gang friends and, instead, started associating with good students. As a result, she was beaten up for "saying no" to gangs. She asserted that without the training she received through participation in the ACE program she never would have reached the decision to quit being a gang member.

As part of the year ending ritual, and before saying goodbye to each other, the students promised to continue in this program next year.

Background

The study was conducted at Santa Ana High School, one of four high schools in the Santa Ana Unified School District, Santa Ana, California. The socioeconomic level of students at Santa Ana High is somewhere between low to middle income strata. The CBEDS (California Basic Educational Data System) information demonstrates the diversity of Santa Ana's student body as 94 percent Hispanic, 3 percent Caucasian, 2 percent Asian and Pacific Islander and 1 percent African American and others. Sixty-six percent of the student body is in the ESL (limited English proficiency) category. A pilot program has been set up at Santa Ana High School that identifies students at risk and develops a program that improves the students' school attendance habits through a process of getting the students involved in programs that will enhance their self-esteem.

The rapidly changing ethnic and economic diversity in the student population, as well as changing family traditions, has caught the educational system off guard. This country's educational system, particularly in the southwestern and western parts of the country where there is a high concentration of school-age immigrants, has failed to meet the needs of this new student population. Many serious problems among the student population have emerged. Students are dropping out of school due to low self-esteem, lack of motivation, peer pressure, poor academic performance and lack of positive support at home, primarily due to low moral values and low economic status among the adult immigrant population.

Without proper guidance and instruction, both at home and at school, these students find themselves lost in a new world, unable to find comfort or answers to their needs and desires. Feeling frustrated and, more often than not, rejected by those that are supposed to manage the development of their lives, the average student in this environment is soon pressured into substance abuse, promiscuity, dropping out of school or joining gangs.

Once these students decide to submit themselves to this low level of society, the problem takes on a new dimension. The problem is no longer confined to the development of the student's life. It is now a problem that affects American society as a whole.

Because the educational system found itself unprepared to handle the problem when it first manifested itself, that is, not having a structured system in place to detect signs of impending problems and the accompanying alternative courses of action to effectively stop the development of the problem, it has become everybody's problem. Research shows that there is a strong relationship between at-risk students' behavior and the lack of self-esteem, self-worth and values. This study intends to investigate the process of identifying students at risk (students who are potential school dropouts due to personal problems at home, poor school attendance, poor grades, classroom discipline problems, involvement in gangs, drug abuse, teenage pregnancies and involvement in crime and violence), and systematically provide them assistance through school intervention programs that will help them develop self-esteem and stay in school.

Understanding the nature of students at risk is key to determining the needed course of action for stopping the growth of the problem that touches everybody's lives. Helping the individual to find a way to become a good and productive citizen is believed to be the most cost-effective way to meet the problems faced by the students at risk.

The book titled *Students-at-Risk: Strategies for Schools,* authored by William L. Callison, Ph.D., and Nancy Richards-Colocino, Ph.D., was written to give school districts information about how to establish programs to prevent dropout and to recover students, who had dropped out, back into the school system. The strategies presented in this book are not yet widely used by schools faced by the aforementioned crises. The specific problem being addressed in this study is to define a process that links the problems faced by the students at risk with intervention programs such as those recommended by *Students-at-Risk: Strategies for Schools.* A pilot program has been set up at Santa Ana High School that identifies students at risk and develops a program that improves the students' school attendance habits through the process of getting the students involved in programs that will enhance their self-esteem.

The results from this study indicate that improved self-esteem can help serve as a cure for student dropout in our schools. Positive self-esteem can alleviate other problems dealing with crime, violence, substance abuse, teen pregnancy, child abuse and other reasons why students are not staying in school. Poor self-esteem is what triggered them to get involved in antisocial behavior in the first place and directed them out of school. The crisis intervention program that was introduced can be used as a model for other schools to follow. Preliminary indications show that such a program can be successful if the faculty and community members will stand behind it. Continued support for this pilot program has ensured its successful completion. The results can then be used to support the implementation of a permanent program.

METHOD OF RESEARCH

Data was collected for this study through personal observation, interviews, student questionnaires, tests and unobtrusive measures. The risk assessment questionnaire shown in Chapter 5 was used to collect data for evaluation using the Comprehensive Risk Assessment software.

The researcher received the assistant principal's approval to obtain school documents, student records and permission to conduct interviews with students, teachers and classified employees. The researcher also received the principal and assistant principal's support and approval in the implementation of this research. Interviews with the assistant principals in charge of discipline and attendance and office clerks were obtained to learn how to gain access to information required by the research study. The researcher requested access to attendance, discipline policy and the school safety plan, for evaluation. Access to CBEDS (California Basic Educational Data System) reports was required to evaluate the attrition rate. Different programs that have been successful in motivating students to stay in school were also carefully evaluated.

School Site

Santa Ana High School is a four-year comprehensive high school with a total enrollment exceeding 2,700 students and a teaching staff of 120, together with seventy classified employees. The curricular offerings of the school conform to state guidelines, model curriculum standards and University of California requirements. There is a large consolidated education program, consisting of ninth through twelfth grade counseling, SB65 (school-based program), Special Education Emergency Immigrant funds, VEA and migrant education. There are also large ROP (regional occupational program) components to the instructional program.

School Population

According to the CBEDS (California Basic Educational Data System) of 1992, 23 percent of the school enrollment at Santa Ana High School, drop out of high school every year. Students who drop out of school are identified as having the following characteristics: poor grades, poor attendance, poor reading achievement scores, retention during school history, mobility from school/home and maladjustment factors (juvenile delinquency record, citizenship record, special education record and physical disabilities).

Purpose of Research

The purpose of this research was to identify at-risk students through the Comprehensive Risk Assessment software, and to provide an intervention program to develop the student's self-esteem, which provides the impetus to improve his/her academic achievement.

Programs Being Offered at Santa Ana High

For the last five years the at-risk student at Santa Ana High has been one of the school's main concerns. A high percentage of at-risk students are dropping out of school. Through the many different programs that the school offers the dropout rate has improved somewhat but the job never ceases and with all the changes taking place in education, such as budget cuts, high enrollment of students and lack of school facilities, it is a battle that is hard to win. However, despite all the obstacles staff members have to overcome, hard work and determination are very evident. This year as part of the safety program the school conducted staff development programs dealing with crime, violence and gangs. For example, Project Pronto is a means by which administrators and support staff can assist teachers in:

(*1*) Reinforcing the expectation that students must be in class when the tardy bell rings

(*2*) Assisting teachers in dealing with habitual truants

It is the student's responsibility to be in class when the bell rings, every period. If the student is late, he/she must see a hall monitor, assistant principal or security person to receive a Project Pronto slip before entering class. The Student Relations Office also can issue pronto slips. The teacher must record tardy cases and not allow students to come into class without a pronto slip. The teacher must expect students to serve detention and must receive a verification from the Student Relations Office that detention has been served. The student has forty-eight hours to serve detention. If a student fails to serve detention, it is the teacher's responsibility to send him to the Student Relations Office on a Report of Incident.

After the third tardy a student will be assigned to the Saturday Day program, a four hour campus cleanup assignment or similar service. In the past there was no method to monitor students' tardiness. The researcher found that if a teacher was busy, or felt it was too much paperwork to take care of, he/she often ignored the Project Pronto procedure. Consequently, students became confused as to whether to follow the set rule or ignore it. They would follow it only when dealing with teachers who were known for doing their job, but not so with those teachers who were lenient on tardiness. To correct this problem the researcher developed a computerized accountability method that gave administrators, teachers and students information in the following manner.

(*1*) Every week pronto slips were counted. A pronto slip includes an original copy that goes to the teacher and a copy that stays with the staff member who issues the pronto slip. Students with more than one pronto slip were pulled out and alphabetized.

(*2*) A list with those names was issued to both assistant principals and to the school principal. Now students could no longer beat the system by ignoring the rules.

(*3*) Teachers were also made aware that they must be more responsible in following the rules in order for the system to work.

(*4*) After the researcher monitored tardies, the findings were recorded and a report was given to administrators, teachers and staff members in the Student Relations Office.

Project Pronto report for the month of October 1992

- total number of students observed—2,700
- total number of tardies recorded—2,033
- number of students tardy more than once—479

This project proved to be highly successful. In a matter of three months after implementation of the new monitoring system, student attendance to class on time improved over 50 percent. The team effort demonstrated by students, teachers and staff members was responsible for its success. Visitors to our campus were impressed to see how students seemed to be in a hurry to get to class.

Special Programs

To help the students develop self-esteem, Hispanic role models were invited to the school to lecture and share with students their experiences in achieving their goals.

Staff development programs are held to educate teachers on cultural values in the Hispanic family for better understanding of their students.

SB65 (state funded school-based program) is headed by an outreach consultant whose responsibility is to detect the at-risk student at an early stage and provide means to turn this student around and keep him/her in school.

PMU (Padres y Maestros Unidos) is a bilingual, bicultural parent organization along with the regular PTA (parents teachers association). These two groups have been highly successful in bringing parents into the school for the purpose of learning ways the parent can help and encourage their child to succeed in school.

Our athletic program has also been very instrumental in helping students develop self-esteem and stay in school. Every year hundreds of students participate in different sports teams. According to our physical education teachers, many students remain in school for the purpose of playing sports and enjoying the experiences involved. No matter how much sacrifice is required in staying long hours after school practicing, the benefits are worth it. For example, it is known that students who have gotten into trouble in school or in the community, who have also been discovered to have good athletic skills, often make a strong effort to maintain the required grade point average in order to maintain their athletic program eligibility. This year the Santa Ana High School Saints (football) demonstrated their loyalty to, and pride in, their school by being among the top high school teams in their own school district, as well as in their league.

Physical activity helps improve students' health and sense of well-being. Exercising has many positive effects on students' minds. When students are sick or cannot function normally in daily activities, their self-esteem suffers. One very important point to bring up is the development of working with others. When an athlete scores a point on the basketball court or hits a home run on the baseball field, he/she gains quite a bit of respect from his/her peers or teammates. Their self-esteem goes sky high for the moment, but a lot of it is retained, and as a result helps the student to better perform in the classroom. Also, vitality and ability to live well in the midst of stress depend on their physical and emotional health. Poor stress management contributes to problems such as heart disease, ulcers, mental breakdowns and emotional collapse. Under stress, students turn to stimulants or intoxicants.

When students are motivated to participate in sports the benefits gained include the development of a better self-concept. When students care for their themselves, they take care of their bodies, and are not likely to put any foreign matter in their mouths.

Another program that has been highly successful in developing student self-esteem is the school photography club. In this program students are encouraged to capture images with the camera that are meaningful to their lives and self-identity. Self-awareness through photography is the objective. Students become more aware of others after photographs are displayed in exhibits throughout the community for others to view. This year students exhibited at the Sanwa Bank and at the opening of the Bowers Museum.

Viva La Mujer (Hooray for Women) is another very successful program sponsored by the photography club. It originated when the photography teacher discovered that her female students lacked self-esteem when they had to get in front of a group to take photographs. Even though their photography technique was often better than that of the male students, they would panic when given an assignment to go out and interview and take photographs. Being a photographer or newspaper reporter was a career that few aspired to after graduation.

The photography teacher was sad to discover how difficult it is for Mexican-American women to learn to prepare themselves and compete for important and highly visible positions in our society, probably because of the nature of their upbringing. It is very sad to see that the Mexican culture is very slow in changing so as to allow la mujer (the woman) to develop her intellect, and to fully participate in the resolution of human issues.

However, despite the obstacles that have confronted the Mexican-American woman, there are some that have learned to overcome the obstacles that have confronted them and have managed to survive. And, some of these women have even managed to achieve high levels of success. The photography teacher went to work in finding these successful women and inviting them to come to school to speak to her female student photographers. After the speakers would speak to the students their portraits were taken by the student photographers. In 1989, the year this program originated, an exhibit of sixty-five women was held. Viva La Mujer, a photo exhibit of Hispanic women representing different fields, has been produced to develop the female students' self-esteem. Students interview these women from different walks of life, and invite them to come to the school as role model speakers.

The photography club offers numerous opportunities for self-expression. For example, this year as part of the school's international week celebrations the photography club sponsored the Cinco de Mayo presentation. The objective of the Cinco de Mayo presentation is to develop self-esteem in the students of Latin descent. Through the study of Mexican history, music, art and awareness of the positive contribution that the Mexican culture has made to this country, our students develop pride in their heritage. Over seventy-five student performers, such as singers, dancers and actors, participated in this project. The presentation was made to over 1,000 students, teachers, parents and members of the community. Tickets were sold and the money collected was used for scholarships. This event was a huge success and fulfilled the school's commitment to bring parents to the school when their children are being recognized for their accomplishments. A promotional letter was sent to parents and community leaders inviting them to attend this very important event.

The PASA program (Progress in Attendance and Student Achievement) targets the ninth and tenth grade at-risk students who demonstrate the following characteristics: absenteeism, truancy, poor grades, lack of graduation credits, boredom with school, disruptive behavior and rebellious attitudes toward authority. It provides additional counseling services, course work remediation, tutoring and guidance towards positive attendance patterns until they are able to function successfully in the regular high school program. This program has not been developed to its full potential. It is expected that when this program is integrated into the intervention program envisioned for Santa Ana High School the results will be greatly improved. Through the use of a computer data base the program can be better controlled and it can be easily monitored.

ANALYSIS OF FINDINGS

It is evident that Santa Ana High School is on track in providing a variety of programs to help students to develop self-esteem which helps them remain in school. However, the programs being offered remain separated from one another which makes it very difficult for students at risk to fully utilize the services being offered. There is not an organization structure under which all these programs can be systematically fitted. There is definitely a lot of room for improvement. These programs need to be systematically made available to every student through teachers, administrators, counselors and other staff members familiar with working directly with students at risk.

The present method used for placing students in these special programs is an assignment by the Student Relations Office, directed by two assistant principals in charge of discipline and student attendance. Students are referred to the assistant principal for reasons such as low grades, truancy, attendance, tardiness, disruptive behavior and vandalism. This method does not have criteria for determining corrective action. Nor does it have a way to systematically place a student in a program that meets his/her needs, or to keep records of the student's progress after the corrective action has been taken. The researcher found that improvements, involving modern methods and technology, were in order in SAHS.

Description of Program

In order to deal systematically with potential dropouts, it is necessary that each school implement some type of student information system that offers standard computer applications such as grade reporting, student scheduling, course progress history, period attendance and test scoring. Types of data that need to be processed include reasons for student referral, prereferral services, academic functioning in mathematics, reading and language arts, behavior in and out of the classroom, primary language, social agency background, previous special support at school, health background and period by period teacher evaluation. If possible, a current survey of faculty to identify causes of dropout would help. For students who have dropped out, the school needs a master file with leave-destination categories and leave-reasons categories.

The student information system should be developed to operate from a data base that stores all the pertinent data for each student that has been identified as a student at risk. A standard data format should be provided for student data entry and retrieval. This data base will be the cornerstone of the student information system. The student information system, or simply the system, will enable the analyst to conduct an interactive process that will involve entering data describing student behavior for the purpose of determining the best-fitted intervention for the student being served. The Comprehensive Risk Assessment computer software will associate the student data entered into the student information system with predetermined solutions provided by the staff and entered into the expert system of the software.

The system should provide a hard copy of the plan of action recommended for the student that includes a specific course of action, along with a schedule to be followed. This prescribed plan will be maintained in the computer system for tracking purposes. The program relative to this prescribed course of action can be tracked and recorded. These data can be analyzed to determine if adjustments need to be made, to see how the student is progressing relative to a defined standard or to compare similar cases that have been observed in the past. Clearly, a system such as this one will be able to not only save a great deal of time in determining what to do with a student at risk, but also allow staff to react at considerable speed. These features will be of great benefit to the students at risk, not to mention the money that will be saved by not having to staff a team of behavioral experts.

As the "Executive Summary" Section at the beginning indicated, this program reduced unexcused attendance from twelve to six days a semester. For a group of thirty students with an average improvement of six days we have 180 days. If the typical cost of supporting a high school student is $4,500 per year and there are 180 days of school, each student brings support of $25 per day. Twenty-five dollars times 180 days is $4,500, a nice addition to the school budget. This was achieved with the researcher receiving one free period per day in a difficult school situation where 66 percent of the students have limited English proficiency. Other schools utilizing the software have increased their attendance funds by over $100,000 by freeing up one full-time staff member to work with 100 students.

Comprehensive Risk Assessment Software

Students-At-Risk, Inc. (SAR) offers software using an expert system called Comprehensive Risk Assessment. It is available for both Macintosh and IBM-compatible computers. An expert system is a kind of artificial intelligence program that mimics human logic within a specific area of expertise, in this case, the characteristics of at-risk students. The SAR approach uses Scantron forms where students self-report the needed data, which is then put through the scanner, thus eliminating the time-consuming process of gathering data from each student's cumulative folder. The data is then automatically entered into the software, thus saving the time needed for data entry in an earlier system. The expert system further makes possible another big time saver, automatic scheduling of identified students into appropriate interventions. These recent developments save large amounts of time and expense, dramatically reducing the time required for a student study team, or the equivalent, to complete student placements.

The Comprehensive Risk Assessment software can be used at the school level and at the district level.

At the School Level

- Predict who will drop out.
- Predict who will be a substance abuser.
- Schedule them into needed activities.
- Track their progress.

At the District Level

- Identify schools with dropout/abuse problems.
- Identify students at lower levels who may drop out/abuse later.
- Identify interventions that fit identified needs.
- Evaluate interventions.
- Generate funds through improved attendance.

Developing a Prevention Plan and Recovery Plan for Students at Risk

Activities required by this program will include gaining staff and school board commitment to create a comprehensive program that includes preparing a prevention and recovery strategy and plan; creation of a dropout prevention and recovery delivery system; implementation of the system; and evaluation of system's effectiveness. The primary advantage of developing a comprehensive program for students at risk in the eyes of staff may be reduction of class disruptions and problem behavior. Many students at risk are seeking attention and want teachers to recognize their particular needs and situation. A plan that does allow for special relationships with teachers and, perhaps, a school-within-a-school or some other means for giving students and teachers a friendly, informal educational environment, may well reduce students' problematic behavior.

The school board may be most impressed by the significant improvement in attendance and the resultant increase in operating funds. This will be particularly true for students who are recovered dropouts who have not been attending. The board would thereby know that they have made an important effort to educate all the students in the district, even those who have difficulty fitting into the comprehensive school and standard curricula available. Researchers characterize dropouts with descriptors such as verbally deficient, overage in grade, lacking basic skills, exhibiting disruptive behavior and withdrawn. It is clear that any effort to deal with such a variety of concerns must include a variety of strategies and services.

Perhaps the place to begin in planning is to look carefully at what each school offers, in fact, not in intent, in the delivery of reading skills, mathematics skills, language skills, problem-solving skills, social skills, as well as the development of a positive self-image.

The program should be student centered so that the unique needs of each individual are considered. It should offer a variety of services in three areas: education, guidance and support services. Activities and services from both the school and the community should be included in the plan. The program should include both prevention and treatment efforts so that students who are predicted to drop out and those who already dropped out but have come back to school are also served well.

The ACE (Action and Commitment in Education) program is an intervention program that was developed to assist students at risk as part of the research study being conducted at Santa Ana High through the masters program at CSUF (California State University, Fullerton). Mackenzie has identified some characteristics of effective schools which were used as guidelines for designing this intervention program for students at risk at Santa Ana High School as part of this research study.

See Figure E.1 for a list of the characteristics of an effective school.

RESULTS OF THE PROGRAM

The intervention objectives of the project were to decrease antisocial, aggressive behaviors and develop prosocial behaviors; to decrease the tendency to associate with peers involved in gangs due to a poor self-image and lack of alternative activities; to improve attitudes and skills related to family management, value systems, modeling and communication; to increase student achievement and interest in school activities; to increase awareness of personality needs and develop healthy alternatives and resources for high-risk students who may be involved in crime and violence, and have a police record and/or have low self-esteem.

Sample and Procedures

Thirty students with characteristics of potential school dropouts were selected in the beginning of the school year. They were selected from the total population. The assistant principal recommended them to the researcher. Each student was given an assignment to attend the ACE program on two consecutive Fridays. He/she would be given a written description of the ACE program, the dates assigned and a parent permission form which the parent would sign for approval. At the first meeting the student was given the secondary risk assessment questionnaire and a self-report. The assessment software was used to identify causes of students' problems. The effect of the following variables on the student performance was evaluated.

(1) Significant variables from school records
  • gender
  • age
  • father/mother's occupation
  • cultural background
  • home environment

Core Elements	Facilitating Elements
Leadership	
Positive climate and overall atmosphere	Shared consensus on values and goals
Goal-focused activities toward clear, attainable and relevant objectives	Long-range planning and coordination
Teacher-directed classroom management and decision making	Stability and continuity of key staff
In-service staff training for effective teaching	District level support for school improvement
Efficacy	
High and positive achievement	Emphasis on homework and study
Expectations with a constant press for excellence	Positive accountability
Visible rewards for academic excellence and growth	Strategies to avoid nonpromotion of students
Cooperative activity and group interaction in the classroom	Deemphasis of strict ability grouping; interaction with more accomplished peers
Total staff involvement with school improvement	
Autonomy and flexibility to implement adaptive practices	
Appropriate levels of difficulty for learning tasks	
Teacher empathy, rapport and personal interaction with students	
Efficiency	
Effective use of instructional time; amount and intensity of engagement in school learning	Opportunities for individualized work
Orderly and disciplined school and classroom environments	Number and variety of opportunities to learn
Continuous diagnosis, evaluation and feedback	
Well-structured classroom activities	
Instruction guided by content coverage	
School-wide emphasis on basic and higher order skills	

Figure E.1 Characteristics of an Effective School.

- language spoken at home
- special education placement
- number of unacceptable grades
- reading achievement
- language achievement
- number of school suspensions
- number of teacher referrals to Student Relations Office

(2) Student self-report
- antisocial behaviors
- drug use and association
- involvement with the law
- family relations
- behavioral/emotional problems
- school achievement
- attitude towards school
- peer relationships

(3) Teacher referral form
- school grades
- attitude of student
- school attendance
- extracurricular activities
- disruptive behavior
- social behavior
- other comments

Hypothesis and Results

Students with poor school attendance, poor grades, discipline problems, personal problems and who come from poverty and a dysfunctional family, can be prevented from dropping out of school through the use of intervention programs.

ACE (Action and Commitment in Education), an intervention program, was designed to assist students at risk. Students participating in this program were engaged in self-esteem building activities. Emphasis was placed on learning personal and social responsibility skills. Participation in this program required parental approval. Students assigned to the ACE program met on a weekly basis, on Fridays from 3:00 P.M. to 4:30 P.M. For the first fifteen minutes the class would form a circle where everyone would face each other. At the beginning of the session they would introduce themselves, one by one, and would talk about something positive that happened during the week. They were also encouraged to talk about any subject or bring up a question they might want an answer to. In the beginning it was difficult to come up with something good that was happening in their lives. Most of the students were burdened with very serious problems, such as one student being caught, while ditching from school, in an empty house, stealing. In another case, two female students had recently been removed from their families because of physical abuse. Two students, a boyfriend/girlfriend, were very nice on the surface but it was later found that he was constantly beating her up because of quarrels over jealousy. The girl ended up getting pregnant and had to transfer to another school. Two female students ended up running away with their boyfriends, dropping out of school. These students were there for every meeting and were most eager to seek help. It was found that they would tell other students how much they looked forward to attending the ACE program every Friday. They made friends at these sessions, and appeared amazed at the friendly reception they got from their peers. It is assumed that it must have been very difficult for these troubled students to remain in the group since they left without any indication as to what the real reason was for their leaving.

The rest of the students stayed and finished the year. One very successful ending was that of a girl gang member who refused to join her gang buddies in anymore of their doings. She was beaten up but she stood her ground and bid them good-bye. The students praised her for her courage and she felt that what she did was heroic. The last meeting was a pizza party in celebration of a successful year. The final assignment was for the students to write an essay describing how the ACE program helped them. The following reports are indicative of the success that an intervention program such as ACE can bring to students at risk in Santa Ana High School.

Gilfrido's Report

El programa ACE me ha ayudado ha entenderme mejor a mi y a mis maestros. Cuando no pertenecia en este programa no sabia que pasaba conmigo, yo hacia cosas que no sabia como pero siempre me metiean en problemas. Luego cuando yo vine a este programa ya me calmando. Ya no me siento tan solo como antes. Ahora yo le agradesco a la maestra por lo que a hecho por mi. Como ha canbiado mi vida. Los problemas de la escuela se me han desaparecido. Ahora yo estoy tratando de agarrar mas creditos con la ayuda de este programa.

Translation: The ACE program has helped me to understand myself and my teachers better. Before I joined I did not know what was wrong with me, I used to cause a lot of trouble and had many problems. I didn't know why I was always getting into trouble. Since I've been in ACE I feel I've calmed down and I do not feel so alone. I appreciate what the teacher has done for me. I have changed a lot. My problems have disappeared. Now I am working towards achieving in earning more credits (Gilfrido Mendoza).

Victor's Report

ACE helped me realize what it is like to help others and be helped by others
as well. This program also helped me to think more about everything around
me and how to make the right decision as to choosing between bad and good
things. This was the first program I ever joined in all the years I've been in
school. I enjoyed it like anything else in school (Victor Perez).

Mario's Report

The ACE program really helped me because it was a place and time I could
talk about my problems and all the other members would listen. They would
then give me possible solutions. One thing I learned was that I was not the
only person with such problems. There is always a solution to a problem
regardless of how serious it is. I also felt I was finally a part of a group and
could participate in all the activities that were happening (Mario Bustos).

SUMMARY AND RECOMMENDATIONS

A comprehensive strategy for improving instruction and services for students at risk could include the following aspects. The first priority of this
dropout prevention effort is to help students stay in school, while recovery activities seek to get students to return to a structured program of education. The
student may need help in improving the basic areas mentioned, such as personal or family problems, understanding oneself or learning new job skills.
The main thing is to treat each student as an individual, and to provide remedial programs to dropout-prone students one by one.

Serves Each Student

Identification of each student's needs is key to getting the student on the
right track, and to the extent possible, fit him into intervention programs. At
the same time, some groups of students may need additional attention from
their teachers to bring them to a satisfactory level in reading or social skills,
for example.

Offers a Comprehensive Scope of Services

The range of services must be as broad as the varied problems students
have. Programs such as PASA, ACE, tutoring and studying period can provide
the needed services. These services might include instruction in basic and

social skills, tutoring in areas of individual need, counseling to help work on personal problems, testing to identify areas of competence and interest, as well as developing a safe and supportive learning environment.

Coordinates Resources and Personnel

The services that have been suggested may all be available through a school district but a potential dropout often does not know about them or how to go about getting help. Hence, there is need for a staff member or specialist to coordinate the efforts of teachers, librarians, counselors, health staff and contact persons in business who can provide training and employment opportunities. The role of this specialist is to quickly match the student with the service or program that will influence him/her to stay in school.

Incorporates Feedback and Evaluation into the System

The evaluation aspect of a dropout prevention plan is critical in that so much of the effort is one-on-one due to its nature. It is very difficult to keep staff informed about what is working and what isn't unless a formal effort to evaluate the program is implemented. A case system is one way to organize the effort. Each student with special needs is dealt with by the specialist using the proposed student information system which diagnoses needs and suggests intervention programs and/or remediation as appropriate. All of these efforts are recorded in permanent computer records.

With these characteristics of a comprehensive strategy in mind, and written up in a brief handout, an administrator can approach the school board for support to begin work on a specific district plan for dropout prevention and recovery. Once approval is gained, contacts with key staff can be initiated, and the elements of a strategy and implementation plan can be developed.

The proposed program was built on the ideas and strategies developed by Dr. William L. Callison and Dr. Nancy Richards-Colocino, authors of the book titled *Students-at-Risk: Strategies for Schools.* The program for dropouts is described earlier in that book. The program for substance abusers is described in this book by Dr. Callison, to be published by Technomic Publishing Company, Inc., titled *Dropout Prevention Handbook: Apprenticeships and Other Solutions.*

This dropout prevention program required the integration of ideas from multiple perspectives. Ideas for solutions to the problems faced by students at risk were sought from experienced teachers at Santa Ana High School and other schools with similar problems, as well as from community leaders who showed an interest in participating in the development of a better community from the bottom up. Special activities were designed for students who demonstrated an interest in the fine arts. Active student participation was encouraged, and flexibility in the use of resources was solicited from the school administration.

The criteria for implementation of this program included: full acceptance of the people being served, i.e., the student population; ideas that put into effect an organization that is flexible and forgiving; an approach that includes strategic planning techniques; and leadership that cultivates and monitors its organizational culture, develops and uses integrated organizational structures and empowers its people. Achievement of the goals of this program was confirmed by the positive response of the community at large.

The nature of the activities-making part of this program required special attention from all members taking part in its implementation. More quality time was required of the teachers and administration involved. Better coordinating and scheduling of the use of the facilities and resources was required. More active participation from the community will be sought in the future. Community members can help in many capacities, as teaching assistants, role models, money donors, tutors, safety monitors, team mothers and fathers and progress monitors, etc. The more community involvement in these different capacities, the greater the chances for success. And finally, modern computer technology will be effectively used, including Comprehensive Risk Assessment software.

In conclusion, it is recommended that an ACE-SAR program be established in Santa Ana Unified School District. It is also recommended that the position of ACE-SAR program director be created. The program director will be responsible for developing, directing, coordinating and controlling all activities related to this program.

References

Aiello, H. and T. Gatewood. 1989. "The Glasgow Mentor Model: A Program for At-Risk Middle Grades Students," *Mentoring International,* 3(3). Available from The International Centre for Mentoring, Suite 510, 1200 West Pender Street, Vancouver, British Columbia, Canada V6E 2S9.

Allen, S., M. E. Dougan and P. Marikian. "A Study of the Integral Role of a Change Agent in Facilitating Program Implementation," an unpublished masters project from the Educational Administration Program, California State University, Fullerton, California, describing strategies used under the leadership of Dr. Eileen Lilly in the Hacienda La Puente Unified School District (1987).

Ashton, P. and R. Webb. 1986. *Making a Difference.* New York, NY: Longman.

Battjes, R. J. and C. L. Jones. 1985. "Implications of Etiological Research for Preventive Interventions and Future Research," in *Etiology of Drug Abuse: Implications for Prevention,* C. L. Jones and R. J. Battjes, eds., NIDA Monograph Series 56, Washington, D.C.: U.S. Government Printing Office, pp. 269–276.

Baumarind, D. 1985. "Familial Antecedents of Adolescent Drug Use: A Developmental Perspective," in *Etiology of Drug Abuse: Implications for Prevention,* C. L. Jones and R. D. Battjes, eds., NIDA Monograph Series 56, Washington, D.C.: U.S. Government Printing Office.

Berman, P. and M. McLaughlin, et al. 1977. *Federal Programs Supporting Educational Change, Volume 7, Factors Affecting Implementation and Continuation.* Santa Monica, CA: The Rand Corporation.

Berrueta-Clement, J. R., L. J. Schweinhart, W. L. Barnett, A. S. Epstein and D. P. Weikart. 1984. *Changed Lives.* Ypsilanti, MI: High/Scope.

Berryman, S. E. 1992. "Apprenticeship as a Paradigm for Learning," in *Youth Apprenticeships in America: Guidelines for Building an Effective System.* Washington, D.C.: W. T. Grant Foundation.

Block, J., J. H. Block and S. Keyes. 1988. "Longitudinally Foretelling Drug Usage in Adolescence: Early Childhood Personality and Environmental Precursors," *Child Development,* 59:336–355.

Botvin, G. J. 1986. "Substance Abuse Prevention Research: Recent Developments and Future Directions," *Journal of School Health,* 56(9):369–374.

Bronfenbrenner, U. 1986. "Alienation and the Four Worlds of Childhood," *Phi Delta Kappan*, 67(6).

Burkle, F. 1986. ʰᵐ*Study Skills Program, Level B.* Alexandria, VA: National Association of Elementary Schools. This publication is for grades 3–4; there are materials in print form for all grade levels, and grades 8–12 have computer-assisted instruction as well.

Business Advisory Commission. 1985. *Reconnecting Youth: The Next Stage of Reform.* Denver, CO: Education Commission of the States, ECS Distribution Center.

Butler, K. and E. Gilmartin. 1986. *A Model Student Study Team.* Concord, CA: Mt. Diablo Unified School District.

Callison, W. "A Study of Reading Improvement in Grade 1," unpublished report to the Vermont State Department of Education (1973).

Callison, W. and N. Richards-Colocino. 1991. *Substance Abuse, Dropout and Gang Prevention Strategies.* Laguna Beach, CA: Students-at-Risk, Inc.

Callison, W., D. Crabtree, P. Ehlers, A. Evans, N. Richards, G. Sakanari and D. Youngblood. 1990. "Identifying Characteristics of Students at Risk of Substance Abuse," presentation of masters thesis and doctoral research to the Partnership Academy Committee Substance Abuse Project members, Orange Unified School District.

Carter, L. F. 1984. "The Sustaining Effects Study of Compensatory and Elementary Education," *Educational Researcher,* 13(7):4–13.

Conrad, D. and D. Hedin. 1991. "School-Based Community Service: What We Know from Research and Theory," *Phi Delta Kappan,* 72(10):743–749.

Cowen, E. L., M. Zax, L. D. Izzo and M. A. Trost. 1966. "Prevention of Emotional Disorders in the School Setting," *Journal of Consulting Psychology,* 30:381–387.

Duckenfield, M. and L. Swanson. 1992. *Service Learning: Meeting the Needs of Youth at Risk.* Clemson, SC: National Dropout Prevention Center.

Elliott, D. S., D. Haizinga and S. Ageton. 1982. *Explaining Delinquency and Drug Use.* Boulder, CO: Behavioral Research Institute, Report 21.

Fidwell, R. 1988. "Dropouts Speak Out: Qualitative Data on Early School Departures," *Adolescence,* 23(92):939–954.

Florida Center for Dropout Prevention. 1986. *Dropout Prevention: A Manual for Developing Comprehensive Plans.* Coral Gables, FL: Florida Department of Education and the University of Miami.

Friedman, A. S. 1985. "Does Drug and Alcohol Use Lead to Failure to Graduate from High School?" *Journal of Drug Education,* 15(4).

Gamoran, A. 1992. "Is Ability Grouping Equitable?" *Educational Leadership,* 50(2).

Gamson, W. 1968. *Power and Discontent.* Homewood, IL: Dorsey Press.

Glass, G. V. and M. L. Smith. 1978. *Meta-Analysis of Research on the Relationship of Class Size and Achievement.* San Francisco, CA: Far West Laboratory for Education Research and Development.

Goodlad, J. I. 1984. *A Place Called School.* New York, NY: McGraw Hill Book Company.

Goodstadt, M. S. and E. Mitchell. 1990. "Prevention Theory and Research Related to High Risk Youth," in *Breaking New Ground for Youth at Risk: Program Summaries,* E. N. Goplerud, ed., Washington, D.C.: U.S. Government Printing Office, DHHS publication no. ADM 89-1658.

Goplerud, E. N., ed. 1990. *Breaking New Ground for Youth at Risk: Program Summaries.* Washington, D.C.: U.S. Government Printing Office, DHHS publication no. ADM 89-1658.

Gottfredson, G. D. 1988. "You Get What You Measure—You Get What You Don't: Higher Test Scores, More Retention in Grade," paper presented at American Educational Research Association, New Orleans, April 1988.

Gray, K. 1991. "Vocational Education in High School: A Modern Phoenix?" *Phi Delta Kappan* (February).

Gray, W. A. 1989. "Advice on Planning Mentoring Programs for At-Risk Youth," *Mentoring International,* 3(3) see Aiello.

Haberman, M. 1991. "The Pedagogy of Good Teaching," *Phi Delta Kappan* (December):290-294.

Hamilton, S. 1986. "Raising Standards and Reducing Dropout Rates," *Teachers College Record,* New York, NY: Columbia University, 87:410-429.

Hammack, F. M. 1986. "Large School Systems' Dropout Reports: An Analysis of Definitions, Procedures, and Findings," *Teachers College Record* (Spring). New York, NY: Columbia University.

Hawkins, J. D. and R. F. Catalano. 1989. "Risk and Protective Factors for Alcohol and Other Drug Problems in Adolescence and Early Adulthood: Implications for Substance Abuse Prevention," revised paper presented October 1988 at the Symposium on the Prevention of Alcohol and Other Drug Problems, Center of Alcohol Studies, Rutgers University, NJ.

Hawkins, J. D. et al. 1985. "Childhood Predictors and the Prevention of Adolescent Substance Abuse," in *Etiology of Drug Abuse: Implications for Prevention,* C. L. Jones and R. J. Battjes, eds., NIDA Research Monograph 56, Washington, D.C.: U.S. Government Printing Office, pp. 75-126, DHHS publication no. ADM 85-1335.

Hyland, T. F. and R. J. Schrenker. 1982. "The Evolution of a Community Drug Abuse Program," *Research in Education* (February).

Irvine Unified School District. 1987. *GOAL (Guidance Opportunities for Affective Learning) Program; STAR (Social Thinking and Reasoning) Program; PLUS (Promoting Learning and Understanding Self) Program; and STAGES (Skills to Manage Stressful Changes) Program.* Irvine, CA: Irvine Unified School District.

Jessor, R. J. and S. L. Jessor. 1977. *Problem Behavior and Psychological Development: A Longitudinal Study of Youth.* New York, NY: Academic Press.

Jessor, R. J., J. E. Donovan and K. Windmer. "Psychosocial Factors in Adolescent Alcohol and Drug Use: The 1980 National Sample Study, and the 1974-1978 Panel Study," unpublished final report, Boulder, CO, University of Colorado, Institute of Behavioral Science (1980).

Johnson, L. D., P. M. O'Malley and J. G. Bachman. 1987. *National Trends in Drug Use and Related Factors among American High School Students and Young Adults.* Rockville, MD: National Institute of Drug Abuse.

Johnson, L. D., P. M. O'Malley and J. G. Bachman. 1989. *Drug Use, Drinking, and Smoking: National Survey Results from High School, College, and Young Adult Populations 1975-1988.* Washington, D.C.: U.S. Government Printing Office, DHHS publication no. ADM 89-1638.

Jones, C. L. and R. J. Battjes. 1985. "The Context and Caveats of Prevention Research on Drug Abuse," *Etiology of Drug Abuse: Implications for Prevention,* C. L. Jones and R. J. Battjes, eds., NIDA Monograph Series 56, Washington, D.C.: U.S. Government Printing Office, pp. 1–12.

Kandel, D. B. 1978. *Longitudinal Research on Drug Use: Empirical Findings and Methodological Issues.* New York, NY: John Wiley & Sons.

Kandel, D. B. 1982. "Epidemiological and Psychosocial Perspectives on Adolescent Drug Use," *Journal of American Academic Clinical Psychiatry,* 21(4):328–345.

Kaplan, H. B., S. S. Martin and C. Robins. 1982. "Applications of a General Theory of Deviant Behavior: Self-Degradation and Adolescent Drug Use," *Journal of Health and Social Behavior,* 23(4):274–294.

Kazdin, A. E. 1987. "Treatment of Antisocial Behavior in Children: Current Status and Future Directions," *Psychological Bulletin,* Vol. 102.

Kendrick, E. 1985. *Appalachia.* Washington D.C.: Appalachian Regional Commission.

Kierstead, J. 1986. "How Teachers Manage Individual and Small-Group Work in Active Classrooms," *Educational Leadership,* 44(October).

Kovach, J. A. and N. W. Glickman. 1986. "Levels and Psychosocial Correlates of Adolescent Drug Use," *Journal of Youth and Adolescence,* 15(1):61–77.

Levin, H. M. and W. Hopfenberg. 1991. "Don't Remediate: Accelerate!" *Principal,* 70(3).

Lewis, J., Jr. 1983. *Long-Range and Short-Range Planning for Educational Administrators.* Boston, MA: Allyn and Bacon, Inc.

Los Angeles Unified School District Dropout Prevention/Recovery Committee. "A Study of Student Dropout in the Los Angeles Unified School District" (1985).

Malizio, A. and D. Whitney. "Educational Credential in Employment: A Nationwide Survey," paper presented at Lifelong Learning Conference, College Park, Maryland, 1984.

Maspero, B. J. "Differences in the Characteristics of Dropouts and Graduates of a Continuation High School," unpublished doctoral dissertation, United States International University, San Diego, California (1989).

McPartland, J. and R. E. Slavin. 1990. *Policy Perspectives: Increasing Achievement of At-Risk Students at Each Grade Level.* Washington, D.C.: U.S. Government Printing Office, Superintendent of Documents.

Middle Grade Task Force. 1987. "Caught in the Middle, Educational Reform for Young Adolescents in California Public Schools," report of the Superintendent. Sacramento, CA: California State Department of Education, p. 29.

Moskowitz, J. M. 1989. "The Primary Prevention of Alcohol Problems: A Critical Review of the Research Literature," *Journal of Studies on Alcohol,* 50(1):54–88.

National Institute on Drug Abuse. 1988. *National Household Survey on Drug Abuse: Population Estimates 1988.* Washington, D.C.: U.S. Government Printing Office, DHHS publication no. ADM 89-1636.

Natriello, G. and S. Dornbusch. 1984. "Teacher Evaluative Standards and Student Effort," cited in McDill et al. 1984. *Raising Standards and Retaining Students.* Baltimore, MD: The VSP Industries.

Natriello, G., A. M. Pallas, E. L. McDill, J. M. McPartland and D. Royster. 1988. "An Examination of the Assumptions and Evidence for Alternative Dropout Prevention Programs in High School," Center for Social Organization of Schools, The Johns Hopkins University, Baltimore, MD, report no. 365.

Newcomb, M. D., E. Maddahian and P. M. Bentler. 1986. "Risk Factors for Drug Use among Adolescents: Concurrent and Longitudinal Analyses," *American Journal of Public Health*, 76:525–531.

Novak, J. and B. Dougherty. 1980. *Staying In . . . A Dropout Prevention Handbook K–12*. Madison, WI: University of Wisconsin.

Novak, J. and W. Hammerstrom. 1976. *Desk Reference: Facilitating Career Counseling and Placement*. Madison, WI: Wisconsin Vocational Studies Center, University of Wisconsin.

Oetting, E. R. and F. Beauvais. 1987. "Common Elements in Youth Drug Abuse: Peer Clusters and Other Psychosocial Factors," *Journal of Drug Issues*, 22(2):133–157.

Ogbu, J. 1983. "Minority Status and Schooling in Plural Societies," *Comparative Education Review*, 27(2).

Parker, J. G. and S. R. Asher. 1987. "Peer Relations and Later Personal Adjustment: Are Low-Accepted Children at Risk?" *Psychological Bulletin*, 102(3):357–398.

Patterson, G. R., B. D. DeBaryshe and E. Ramsey. 1989. "A Development Perspective on Antisocial Behavior," *American Psychologist*, 44(2):329–335.

Peng, S. S. and R. T. Takai. 1983. *High School Dropouts: Descriptive Information from High School and Beyond*. Washington, D.C.: National Center for Education Statistics.

Pentz, M. A. 1986. "Community Organization and School Liaisons: How to Get Programs Started," *Journal of School Health*, 56(9):382–388.

Peterson, J. 1987. "Service Jobs Dominate the Economy," *Los Angeles Times* (September 24).

Peterson, R. W. 1992. *A Taxonomy of Common Teaching Methods*. Laguna Beach, CA: Pelican Press.

Phillips, K. 1990. *The Politics of Rich and Poor*. New York, NY: Random House.

Pittman, R. B. and P. Haighwout. 1987. "Influence of High School Size on Dropout Rate," *Educational Evaluation and Policy Analysis*, 9(4):337–343.

Plakos, M. et al. 1978. *Workbook on Program Evaluation*. Princeton, NJ: Educational Testing Service.

Pogrow, S. 1989. *Higher Order Thinking Skills*. Tucson, AZ: University of Arizona.

Pritz, S. G. 1992. "Basics for Students at Risk: A Vocational-Academic Approach," *National Dropout Prevention Newsletter*, 5(4). Clemson, SC: National Dropout Prevention Center.

Rachal, J. V., L. L. Guess, R. L. Hubbard, S. A. Maisto, E. R. Cavanaugh, R. Waddell and C. H. Benrud. 1980. *Adolescent Drinking Behavior, 1: Sample Studies*. Chapel Hill, NC: Research Triangle Park, Research Triangle Institute.

Rachal, J. V., L. L. Guess, R. L. Hubbard, S. A. Maisto, E. R. Cavanaugh, R. Waddell and C. H. Benrud. 1982. "Alcohol Misuse by Adolescents," *Alcohol Health and Research World* (Spring).

Radius, M. and P. Lesniak. 1986. *Student Study Teams: A Resource Manual for Trainers*. Sacramento, CA: California State Department of Education, Special Education Division and the Special Education Resource Network.

Ravitch, D. et al. "Network Notes," Educational Excellence Network, Teachers College, Columbia University, New York, NY (1985).

Raywid, M. A. 1982. *The Current Status of Schools of Choice in Public Secondary Education.* Hempstead, NY: Hofstra University.

Reich, R. 1991. *The Work of Nations: Preparing Ourselves for 21st Century Capitalism.* New York, NY: Knopf.

Richards-Colocino, N. 1991. "School-Based Assessment of Students at Risk for Drug Abuse," dissertation, United States International University, San Diego, California.

Robins, L. N. 1980. "The Natural History of Drug Use. Evaluation of Treatment of Drug Abusers," *ACTA Psychiat. Scand.*, 62:284.

Robinson, T. N., J. D. Killen, C. B. Taylor, M. J. Telch, S. W. Bryson, K. E. Saylor, D. J. Maron, N. Maccoby and J. W. Farquhar. 1987. "Perspectives on Adolescent Substance Abuse: A Defined Population Study," *Journal of American Medical Association*, 258(15):2072–2076.

Rogus, J. F. and C. Wildenhaus. 1991. "Programming for At-Risk Learners: A Preventive Approach," *NASSP Bulletin* (November).

Rosenbaum, J. E. 1992. "Apprenticeship Learning: Principles for Connecting Schools and Workplaces," in *Youth Apprenticeships in America: Guidelines for Building an Effective System.* Washington, D.C.: W. T. Grant Foundation.

Rubin, R. A. and B. Balow. 1978. "Prevalence of Teacher-Identified Behavior Problems," *Exceptional Children*, 45:102–111.

Sappington, J. P. 1979. "The Predictive Strength of Nine School Related Indicators for Distinguishing Potential Dropouts," Ph.D. dissertation, United States International University, San Diego, CA.

Savage, D. 1992. *Los Angeles Times* (December 12).

Shepard, L. and M. Smith. 1989. *Flunking Grades: Research and Policies on Retention.* London: Falmer Press.

Simcha-Fagan, O., J. C. Gersten and T. S. Langner. 1986. "Early Precursors and Concurrent Correlates of Patterns of Illicit Drug Use in Adolescence," *Journal of Drug Issues*, 16(1):7–28.

Skager, R. and S. L. Frith. 1989. "Identifying High Risk Substance Users in Grades 9 and 11: A Report Based on the 1987/88 California Substance Use Survey," report to the Attorney General, John K. Van De Kamp, Sacramento, CA.

Slavin, R. E., N. L. Karweit and N. A. Madden, eds. 1989. *Effective Programs for Students At Risk.* Needham Heights, MA: Allyn and Bacon. Summarized in *Educational Leadership*, 46(5) (1989).

Smith, D. H. Testimony to the State of New York Legislative Hearing on Dropouts, New York State Legislature (1986).

Smith, G. A. 1989. "The Media Academy: Engaging Students in Meaningful Work," *Educational Leadership* (February).

Spivack, G. 1983. *High Risk Early Behaviors Indicating Vulnerability to Delinquency in the Community and School.* Washington, D.C.: National Institute of Juvenile Justice and Delinquency Prevention, Law Enforcement Assistance Administration.

Staff. 1983. *A Study of Children's Attitudes and Perceptions about Drugs and Alcohol.* Middletown, CT: Weekly Reader Publications.

Staff. 1985. "An Evaluation of the OMR Learning Center's CCC System," staff report, Office of Manpower Resources Learning Center, Baltimore, MD (April).

Staff. 1986a. "Dropout Prevention and Recovery," staff report, Hacienda La Puente Unified School District, La Puente, CA (May). All of the definitions are taken from this report.

Staff. 1986b. "Staff Prediction Study." Palo Alto, CA: Computer Curriculum Corporation.

Staff. 1992a. *Activ Courseware Catalog.* Herndon, VA: Industrial Training Corporation.

Staff. 1992b. *Fact Sheet.* New York, NY: Ventures in Education.

Stasz, C., D. McArthur, M. Lewis and K. Ramsey. 1990. "Teaching and Learning Generic Skills for the Workplace," R-4004-NCRVE/UCB. Berkeley, CA: University of California, National Center for Research in Vocational Education.

Stern, D. "Dropout Prevention and Recovery in California," paper written for the California State Department of Education, Sacramento, CA (1986).

Stern, D. 1992. "School-Based Work Experience," in *Youth Apprenticeships in America: Guidelines for Building an Effective System.* Washington, D.C.: W. T. Grant Foundation.

Swaim, R. C., E. R. Oetting, R. W. Edwards and F. Beauvais. 1989. "Links from Emotional Distress to Adolescent Drug Use: A Path Model," *Journal of Consulting and Clinical Psychology,* 57(2):227–231.

Towers, R. L. 1987. *Student Drug and Alcohol Abuse.* Washington, D.C.: National Education Association.

Treadway, P. G. 1985. *Beyond Statistics: Doing Something about Dropping Out of School.* Stanford, CA: Stanford University.

U.S. Congress. 1986a. *Drug Abuse and Dropouts.* A Report of the Select Committee on Narcotics Abuse and Control, Ninety-Ninth Congress, Second Session. Washington, D.C.: U.S. Government Printing Office.

U.S. Congress. 1986b. *Indian Juvenile Alcoholism and Eligibility of BIA Schools.* A hearing report before the Select Committee on Indian Affairs, United States Senate, Ninety-Ninth Congress, First Session.

U.S. Congress. The National Youth Apprenticeship Act of 1992, proposed legislation. Washington, D.C.: U.S. Government Printing Office.

Wehlage, G. G. "At-Risk Students and the Need for High School Reform," National Center on Effective Secondary Schools, University of Wisconsin, Madison, WI (May 1985).

Wehlage, G. G. and R. Rutter. "Evaluation of a Model Program for At-Risk Students," National Center on Effective Secondary Schools, University of Wisconsin, Madison, WI (1985).

Werner, E. E. and R. S. Smith. 1982. *Vulnerable but Invincible.* New York, NY: McGraw-Hill.

Wilson, T. "Students at Risk and Educational Technology," unpublished evaluation report, Corona-Norco Unified School District, Corona, CA (March 1989).

Wirt, J. G. 1991. "A New Federal Law on Vocational Education: Will Reform Follow?" *Phi Delta Kappan* (February).

Zuboff, S. 1988. *In the Age of the Smart Machine: The Future of Work and Power.* New York, NY: Basic Books.

AUTHOR'S NOTE:

Two types of software mentioned in this book have been designed specifically to assist school staff in implementing the strategies suggested. They are:

Comprehensive Risk Assessment

Comprehensive Risk Assessment is available in a manual-entry version for $49.95. It allows a staff member to enter student data into the program, which then predicts each student's risk for substance abuse and dropout, and schedules individuals into interventions.

If you are working with 100–200 students we recommend that you purchase scanner forms from us for $1.00 per student for each administration. We then furnish the forms and send you a report for each student after you mail us the completed forms.

The scanner version, which is needed when you are working with 200 or more students, costs $495.00.

Peer Assistant

Peer Assistant is filled out by each student manually on Apple or IBM compatible computers. It costs $49.95 and is designed to help students become aware of the possible consequences of dropping out of school, or using drugs and alcohol. A manual comes with the software to guide teachers as they set up peer assistant/peer counseling programs.

Both programs can be ordered from:

Students-at-Risk, Inc.
1260 Brangwyn Way
Laguna Beach, CA 92651